a curriculum of difficulty

omPLiCATED

A Book Series of Curriculum Studies

William F. Pinar
General Editor

VOLUME 17

PETER LANG
New York • Washington, D.C./Baltimore • Bern
Frankfurt am Main • Berlin • Brussels • Vienna • Oxford

Leah C. Fowler

a curriculum of difficulty

narrative research in education
and the practice of teaching

PETER LANG
New York • Washington, D.C./Baltimore • Bern
Frankfurt am Main • Berlin • Brussels • Vienna • Oxford

Library of Congress Cataloging-in-Publication Data

Fowler, Leah C.
A curriculum of difficulty: narrative research in education
and the practice of teaching / Leah C. Fowler.
p. cm. — (Complicated conversation; v. 17)
Includes bibliographical references and index.
1. Teaching. 2. Discourse analysis, Narrative—Research.
3. Curriculum planning. I. Title. II. Series.
LB1775.F67   370.11'5   2005035619
ISBN 0-8204-8150-5
ISSN 1534-2816

Bibliographic information published by **Die Deutsche Bibliothek**.
Die Deutsche Bibliothek lists this publication in the "Deutsche
Nationalbibliografie"; detailed bibliographic data is available
on the Internet at http://dnb.ddb.de/.

Cover art by W. Donawa and L. Fowler
Cover design by Joni Holst

The paper in this book meets the guidelines for permanence and durability
of the Committee on Production Guidelines for Book Longevity
of the Council of Library Resources.

© 2006 Peter Lang Publishing, Inc., New York
29 Broadway, New York, NY 10006
www.peterlang.com

Printed in the United States of America

Contents

Preface

This book charts fifteen years of narrative research on difficulty at the site of the teaching self. Woven between the chapters on narrative research are stories I wrote about difficulty in teaching; I call them internarratives. Those narratives alone (the text and the telling of them) do not constitute full research. However, those I have written (mainly fictional for ethical purposes) have served me as a *temenos* of narrative "data" for multiple orbitals of mindful attention and analytical thought. Although I value many kinds of authentic research, this work particularly has contributed qualitatively to my understanding and knowledge about difficulty in education, narrative research, the practice of teaching, and the curriculum of being.

I do not presume to write a narrative "methods" textbook prescribing how others might conduct inquiries around their own compelling questions, although it may be useful to those who are working methodologically with narrative in their research and teaching. Instead, I offer an honest phenomenological description, a hermeneutic inquiry into difficulties arising at the site of the teaching self, as a way of learning to be present in the generative space of educational work. Narrative understanding is a large part of that ability to connect with, understand, and have compassion for all of us engaged in learning more about being human. During narrative and after narrative research I speak to my own education, which has evolved into a quality of *educaritas* in my teaching, my research, and my life. Narrative is a fertile ground for listening and witnessing all lives in a world where all beings matter. This book is a study of that human adventure toward a more professional, personal, relational, social, cultural, and political wholeness.

Acknowledgments

Thank you, dear Reader, for picking up this book amid so many others.

The writing of acknowledgments is itself a curriculum of difficulty. What resides under the desire to recognize, thank, and appreciate the influences, presences, shapers, helpers, editors, assistants, teachers, mentors, colleagues, students, companions, family, critics, worthy opponents, loving intimates, nurturing co-travelers, unexpected light bearers, and sustaining soul-mates?

The richness of my inner life and outer dwelling has evolved in relationship, always, no matter how romantic the notion of the solitary heart-ful creative intellect. So I do thank all my families—biological, social, cultural, educational, epistemological, ontological, theoretical, narrative, poetic, musical, aesthetic, reluctant, littoral, geographic, spiritual, transcendent.

And some naming of the names: Thank you, William Pinar, for belief, invitation, generous guidance, sentient reading, curriculum theory mentoring, hospitality, readings in common, laughter, linguistic play, responsiveness, and enduring innovative, humane and ethical thought and work in the local and global field of curriculum studies in these rough times.

In the doctoral gaze at difficulty, thank you, Antoinette Oberg, for provocative questions and steadfast watching for signs of living well. Gratitude continues for you, Laurie Rae Baxter, for multiple lessons in laughter, difficulty, and mindfulness. In memoriam, thanks to Terry Johnston and Sheilah Allen. Teacher Tetsuo Aoki: You had a permanent and great effect on my life. Thank you to all my teachers and all my students: Each has taught me.

The Universities of Victoria and Lethbridge must also be thanked for remarkable administration, faculty, and staff. I especially want to say thank you Cynthia Chambers for your curriculum theory, studies, and visionary wisdom about curricula of difficulty. Thanks to all of you in the Faculty of Education in Lethbridge.

Melinda Maunsell, thank you for superb editing, disciplined proofreading, and careful indexing.

Paul Dawson, thank you for your remarkable text/tech wizardry and steadfast technical help.

Thanks to my curriculum studies family from local to national to global work over time and geography and culture for the benefit of all citizens.

To everyone at Peter Lang, especially Chris Myer, Sid Sokol, and Bernadette Shade, thank you for apprenticeship and belief in the text and me.

Thanks to Mom, Dad, Timothy, Peter, and Neva: How far we have come. Neva, soul-sister: your witnessing and care of my life and your way of being have taught me so much; you should be the big sister.

Claire, Robbie, Aritha, Thomas, Marsha, Avis, Jane: thank you, my heart teachers, through the making of this. Thank you, Lous, for reading, deep thought, conversations, and new friendship.

Michelle H-duke: thank you for your running through all the difficulty, for the periodic table, and for your steadfast standing still without judgment. There will never be enough words for all your lessons, care, and loving mindfulness through the labyrinths both dark and beautiful toward wholeness of Being and freedom.

Wendy Donawa: Your design of the representation of the narrative orbitals of analysis was brilliant, and shows the intent and process of narrative research as I conceive it. There is more to be said of course: you have been with me through such a difficult period of my life. You have read, encouraged, invited, loved, trusted, shared, given, offered beauty, truth, justice, help, literary play, art, meditation, care, advice, compassion, and endured with grace and dignity. I thank you with such deep gratitude.

In life, as in education and research, with an extensive curriculum of difficulty, I must continue to believe that Love endureth all things.

Namaste.

And now, begin again. Let us tell a different story of the curriculum of Being and learning and teaching.

Part 1: Introduction—Narrative Research in Education

Internarrative: Home Run

But I don't know how to fight. All I know how to do is stay alive.

–Walker, 1982, Letter 11

In my thirteenth year of teaching, a young man named Khalid was entrusted to me in three of my classes: Social Studies 13, English 13, and Reading 10. He arrived mid-September, as had I, hired late after enrolment numbers exceeded expectation. Khalid had come straight from the Middle East, and the only other classes he had were ESL, or English as a Second Language.

Only his smile saved Khalid that year. He was bullied and shoved and pro-pelled along the burgeoning corridors at class-change, enduring with a shy, patient, perpetually confused grin, white teeth bared, in hope of another day's reprieve on the planet without being killed.

He sat alone. He arrived first, every class. He always had his books, pencils, papers, and work attempts. He had no idea how to write, how to speak English, how to understand what was going on around him. After multiple inquiries on my part to the administration, I was, in the end (September 30), simply to allow him to "be a warm body in class" and heard, "He'll pick up what he can; no one expects him to do anything this year anyway." No knowledge of family or friends was available. A social worker had registered him.

So every day he sat, and we grinned at each other for at least three weeks and mumbled, "Hi." The first English I heard him try to say to me was my name. He asked me how to say Miss Maple and practised forty or fifty times that day until he was satisfied that he could call me by name and get my atten-tion if he needed to. I, in turn, practised and practised his name—"Khalid"— until he grinned widely and nodded his head. From our mutual naming, we began to develop a relationship.

That year was also the first time I had ever taught Social Studies, and I had to learn along with the students. Of course, I did a better job because I had a better sense of the time that is needed in learning. Together we studied gov-ernment, maps, Canada's history and economic systems, human rights, and immigration policies. Most of the students could name only five or six of the provinces, and most could not even accurately place their own city on a map of their province, let alone construct convincing, supported arguments for persuasive essay writing.

One day I got a huge, old globe from an abandoned resource room (the globe was about five feet in diameter), set it in the middle of the room, and asked, "Where in the world are we?" The students were fascinated with the relic.

I asked each one to go to the globe and locate herself or himself on the earth's referent. When Khalid took his turn, his face lit up as his fingers floated over the surface of the world and came to rest with his index finger firmly pressed on Iraq. And then the smile began to fade into a weak grimace as he located our city.

"Khalid, we are very glad you are here with us, but do you wish to go back to Iraq?"

He sadly shook his head and watched his feet: "No. Too vi-o-lent!" and returned to his seat. That was December.

Not once in any of the three classes during the year would this disparate bunch of kids at risk interact with Khalid; they all had their own difficulties. In spite of a lot of group work, contrived assignments, and "cooperative" curriculum, he would anticipate their reluctance and always say, "I work alone, okay Miss Maple?" twirling his pen deftly over his fingers and putting down his head to work close by the paper. When pressed to join others, he would whisper, "No, please," and I respected his request, while trying again to plan some other way to involve him.

Khalid may not have been "expected to do anything," but he did begin to learn English and began to get 20–30 percent on his assignments. He was enormously pleased with himself because he could see that he was making progress.

By June of that year, the students and I had exhausted more than was prescribed in the syllabus, viewed all the "classics" on film from the school library, and certainly exhausted many more activities with possibilities for development of cohesive group process. I tried to think up interesting reviews and games on content to fill up those last two long, hot weeks and to increase the students' chances at success (50 percent magic of a passing grade) on their final exams so they could get on with their lives. But we were all getting impatient and crabby with one another and I needed to think of something else for us to explore together. I wasn't used to negative culminations with year-long classes.

One lazy, hot June morning, I phoned the principal from the classroom and said, "I know this contravenes 'previous permission policy' for field trips, but forgiveness is easier to get than permission, so I am taking my double-period Social 13s to the park by the river. If you have to report the pedagogical value, we will be playing parliamentary baseball," and hung up.

I phoned the cafeteria and then sent two students to get three dozen doughnuts for us, charged to Maple who would pay at noon. Another two students were dispatched to bring back bats, balls, and gloves. Off we went. The students hooted and shouted and whistled and raced each other to the park. Except Khalid. He watched everybody very closely, walked right next to me, his shoulder gently bumping into mine, and asked worriedly, "Miss Maple, why we are not in classroom? What we do now?"

"Baseball, Khalid. We are going to play baseball at the park. For a little break. We need to get out of the classroom and just have fun together for a while. That will relax us so we can work better tomorrow. If not, well, we will at least have fun now. Have you played baseball before?"

Appearing puzzled, Khalid responded, "No."

Bette, a "gutsy tough street chick" as she called herself, overheard our conversation and Khalid's quiet "no." "What!" she yelled, "Ya never played baseball? Jeez . . . whatta you guys do over there in Iraq?"

"They fight and kill my family, so I go away to here," said Khalid.

"Jee-sus. Is that true, Miss Maple? ... Khalid, I'm real sorry. Wow! You're a real gentle dude and kind too—I seen ya. Who'da figured you had all that terrible stuff happen to ya. C'mon, I'll show ya how ta play. No problem."

And she began to teach him. And one by one each of the other students added baseball advice and tips and explanations and rules to the bewildered but happy Khalid. We ran and skipped and nudged each other the rest of the way to the ball diamond.

Sides were chosen (PCs and Liberals), umpire named (speaker of the house), and suddenly they invented parliamentary baseball and used all the right terms. I was benched (back "bencher" from a small riding they said).

When it was Khalid's turn to bat, having watched a few batters ahead of him, he stood in the batting position, getting advice on how to "choke up on the bat" and where to place the ball past the centre fielder, and was promised by the pitcher (leader of the opposition) that he'd get a gentle pitch on the first throw. Khalid nodded and smiled throughout and pointed several times to the outfield—"Over there? Hit this ball, that place, very far?"

"Yes, yes," he was assured by twenty-two other voices. I sat on the bench cheering, providing the senate function and periodic "stadium waves."

Khalid connected with the "sweet spot" on that first throw and the ball hurtled like an Exocet missile over the pitcher, over the centre fielder, out of the diamond, out of the park, and deep into the bush near the river, never to be found again.

Khalid stood beaming on home plate. "Like that?" he asked. And twenty-two students yelled, "Home run, Khalid, home run. Run. Run! Holy crap, did ja see that?" and "Jeez, Khalid, try out for the Jays. No, run . . . run . . . run!"

"Run where?" he asked.

His whole team took him by the hand in turn and ran him around all the bases back to home plate. The whole class stood there cheering and yelling. "Welcome to Canada, Khalid," said Bette. The group sighed "Yeah, Khalid, Welcome to Canada, sorry we didn't try harder to get to ya before. But now we can."

The next day when I entered class, Khalid was there on time as usual with his books waiting, but this time he was listening intently as Bette talked her usual non-stop monologues, listening because she was talking to him. On my desk was a note:

Dear Miss Maple,
Thank you that we left the classroom. I never forget yesterday.
Your student,
Khalid

He looked over Bette's talking head and we grinned at each other. I was sorry it was June; I wanted to begin again with him.

Chapter 1: A Curriculum of Difficulty

"A Carbon-Based Life Form"
A person tired from happiness grows sober.
Another, worn through
by sadness, stumbles into a kind of joy.
It is like a dog alone in a house, barking to hear its own kind.
Nothing needs to be added yet we do.

–Hirshfield, 2001, *Given Sugar, Given Salt*, p. 44

An Honourable Profession: Difficult Intentions

We do add: meaning, interpretation, importance, intention, desire, communication, teaching, narrating. Because we human beings become attached to storied lives, the increased use of narrative in education research has me worried. Narrative research can be an authentic, autobiographical project (see the work of curriculum reconceptualists such as Greene, Grumet, J. L. Miller, Pinar), which requires ethical stewardship, literary skill, intelligent attention, erudite writing craft, and a persistent, sentient, honest hermeneutic vision on the part of such a researcher. Narrative research also can be too narcissistic, a banal project that involves mostly self-interest, lack of scholarly discipline, misappropriation of the experiences of one's "research subjects," and simplistic, weak, reflective interpretation and facile judgment. Insight that informs positive change in education seems often absent. In such attractive narrative research, if theory is derived, it sometimes is fitted into popularized advice to teachers or recipes for teaching success, which serve to trivialize real difficulty in teaching. Rather than moving to new reflective practice of understanding and responsible participation in the educational enterprise, we inadvertently reinscribe poor practice but feel better about it.

Integrated throughout this book are stories of teaching I wrote (over several years) as a creative writer to deal with difficulty I encountered. Those resulting narratives subsequently "troubled" my practice, my identity, my thinking, and my being. Through the narrative research that attended those stories, I have reconstituted my own teaching, understanding, learning, and professional growth as an educator. More important, I continue to learn that narratives themselves are a curriculum of difficulty. In this book I want to explore that curriculum as a curriculum. Narratives provide a site to study the intentions and goals and learning outcomes ("objectives") of narrative research, the resources and material and display of it, the activities of the narrative project, and, finally, the evaluation that can be made about stories and the kind of narrative knowledge that research can construct and deconstruct. The goal is always to understand more and increase meaning about teaching.

The reasons and intentions for narrative have proliferated in research in education. In the past six years I have had graduate students unknown to me come to my university office door to say: "I want to do narrative research and I heard you do that—will you work with me?" We often have a brief conversation about their intentions for choosing a narrative method. Sometimes they come with a story they have written about a difficulty with a student, a parent, a co-worker, or an administrator. They have become attached to their story of difficulty and want to use it because of the power narrating it has for them.

Narratives do signify a knot, a matrix of issues, a professional development challenge. Narrative is a starting point for authentic research, although obviously just telling or writing stories is not narrative research. Particularly if those who want to do narrative research are neither readers nor writers themselves, I do rigorously question the choice of narrative research and frequently find myself suggesting other methods of research that more usefully open knowledge about the identified research question, even though the story itself may have been a genesis.

My research interest lies in the curricular spaces between stillness of narrated difficulties of teaching and intentional pedagogical movement made possible by narrating such difficulty located at the site of the teacher. Questions persist: What might be asked and learned in the spaces between narrative theory and the practice of teaching? What is the curriculum of a lost teacher, one in difficulty? What it is we need to learn/to study/to know/to ask/to say when we locate ourselves in language-scapes of difficulty? How can narrative research lead to an aesthetic and ethical inner government of a teaching self? Partial answers to these questions emerge for me during narrative research and analysis.

Teachers, like all practitioners, must be careful with the stories they tell, both about themselves and their work, because stories can be dangerous as well as inspiring in their teachings. Simple little stories are not. Stories seduce: they build desire—to know *what* happened, to watch *who*, to visualize *where* and *when*, to make meaning about how, and to more deeply understand *why*. There is a loss of innocence each time the teller tells, the listener hears, the reader reads. Stories educate because they lead us to see, know, become, want, construct something else as the heart matures or withers, as the mind connects or disengages. Stories have power but I want to make a distinction between a story and a narrative. A narrative includes not only the story, but also the teller, the told, the context and conditions of the story telling, and the reasons and intentions for narrating (Carr, Genette, for example).

As a feminist narrative researcher, I want to locate myself before I get to the theoretical frames of my proposed narrative method so you know *who* is writing about this narrative method. The rest of this chapter explicates who holds this pen, before I describe seven orbitals of narrative analysis that emerge from my research around issues of difficulty in teaching.

Beginning Narratively: Once upon My Time

Before I could speak, I heard stories of Christian grand narratives of creation, of the fall from grace, of wrath, prophecy, despair, redemption, love, cruelty, forgiveness, and revelation.[1] Worship twice a day in our Western Canadian Anglo-Saxon household consisted of reading Bible stories before prayer on bended knee. I learned to read during my fourth year, using the Bible as my main text. Long before I went to elementary school, I had heard most of the nursery rhymes, myths, and fairy tales written or translated in English. Narrative knowing (Polkinghorne, 1988) became a central part of my early childhood (and consequently, lifelong) environment.

My narratives (both official and unofficial stories) were pieced together from excerpts of our extended family's conversations, which sometimes switched topic if I entered the room. I knew who had the best stories to tell over tea or after the evening meal while I listened for tidbits through partially closed doors or eavesdropped through hot-air registers. Repeatedly I heard distant, generational, Irish-American stories of my paternal grandfather, and English United Empire Loyalist kinfolk stories of my grandmother. These preceded my grandparents' own growing-up narratives and personal recollections of terrible poverty, dis/ease,[2] and suffering on the Canadian prairies during the Depression years. I learned my genealogy, history, culture, and religion in narrative form. I had yet to learn about significant "Other/s." I was still extrapolating and normalizing my own experience as the only human truths of being. I will admit that reading the stories of others in those days served to sandpaper away most of those illusions, egocentrisms, and contrived innocences of protected middle-class-White childhoods.

Like many in our culture, I had an abusive and strange childhood but thought it was normal at the time . . . just life. As I read throughout my life, I find other authors who speak of similar circumstances. Not to succumb to the popular culture fixation on "woundology" but to understand developmental experiences and critical life incidents, I continue to discover important writers who contribute to my human knowledge.

Anne-Marie MacDonald's *Fall on Your Knees* and *The Way the Crow Flies* and Margaret Atwood's *Cat's Eye* are three worthwhile Canadian novels that closely resonate with, even mirror, many of my inner landscapes and experiences as a growing child. I read those writers, remember, and think to myself, "Yes, that is exactly how it was." I have gratitude for such courageous writers to reveal particular truths through literary means: New modes of being are made possible because of their narrative work and study of ancient, no-longer-needed stories. It also allowed Sisyphus-me to put down boulders and get on with generative work in the world community. I can lose the personal pronouns.

Narrative Was the Only Power I Had as a Child

My stories in childhood served as my only true possessions, my only place of dignity and privacy, my sole place of power where I could write myself into the world as a significant character whose life had some meaning. I wrote my childish self into the adult worlds of work and romance and purpose. As an inveterate meaning maker, I had to believe my living had some meaning—the alternative was, and still is, unthinkable.[3]

The blue spruce in grandmother's yard served as my first writing studio. I had adventures under that tree. People never knew that under the lovely tree on Reverend Fowler's corner lot, there was a scrawny, blond, blue-eyed girl-assassin armed with semi-automatic coat hangers and pine-cone hand grenades. Under that tree, possibilities of being good vied with possibilities of being evil. Mondays I kidnapped, and Tuesdays I rescued brave and beautiful young women and men. I performed imaginative surgeries on Nobel prize-winning scientists. I flew planes in war and banners in peace, climbed mountains, won Olympic medals, fell in love in the Swiss Alps. I starred with Ingrid Bergman and Katharine Hepburn in famous movies, magically learned seven languages, and astonishingly performed all of Beethoven's works for piano and violin—before I was ten years old! Now it seems embarrassing how I lived in my stories, understood and engaged with the world through them. Still, I see how early experiences of personal agency as an acting, selfable being were possible through my narrative constructions.

Developing a Writer's Memory and Perception

Growing up on central Alberta's prairies, I learned a vast range of plot lines; I studied the patterns, connections, historical detail, cultural niches and social relations of people's real and possible lives, mine among them (Kerby, 1991; Polkinghorne, 1988). Under that blue spruce, I developed a writer's memory and perception, began to cultivate a writer's memory to pay attention to detail, attuned to the smallest particle of soil or tiniest insect, to notice infinitesimal changes in light waves of the late evening prairie summer sun on tree sap. A five-degree drop in temperature or a fifteen-degree shift in wind direction could foreshadow so much. A baby's bonnet colour being pink or blue; a chickadee with its neck broken, splayed below delphiniums under the dining room window; only the mouth of a face smiling while the eyes remained cold; a phone call hung up too quickly; a restrained outflow of breath: as a child I noticed how any of these had the power to alter story plots and change everything in a twinkling of an eye. As a child I needed to pay attention to clues. Everything depended upon what one was able to notice. Very early—intuitively one might say—I developed the eye of a researcher and the ear and the voice of a storyteller.

An Affair with Text

By the time I was twelve I had read all the books in our local town library in the children's and youth sections, so I had a formal interview with the head librarian, Mrs. Russell, for special permission to sign out books from the adult section. I needed those books because, as I struggled through reading, often at the edge of my ability, I began to uncover and understand my being with its experienced problems and emergent knowing. Reading made life more bearable somehow. By reading, I seemed to unlearn loneliness and to learn myself as a self, long before I considered realms of inner dialectics and ethics of inner government. (Pablo Neruda imagines that heaven is a kind of library, and judging from the inordinate amount of time I still spend in libraries, perhaps I have already had the privilege of tasting the textual afterlife of eternity.)

At fifteen I began to work in the school library. I learned cataloguing systems as textual nomenclature. I was apprentice to the care, repair, and binding of broken books. (Even now, to open a new book, press it wide, smell the new ink, and anticipate the pleasure of reading therein is to maintain an enduring physical bond I have developed with text.) Also, I began to work as a cleaning woman on Saturdays for the head school librarian. Using some of that money, I bought flowers for her main assistant, on whom I developed an adolescent crush because we could laugh while we worked, playing literary jokes and giving clues to each other for passages in books to be read. All history's weighty tomes served as currency in our restrained, platonic, *heady* affair of text. My entire world opened, because I understood how story worked, had done a sturdy journeyman program as both reader and writer of fiction. Sometimes I even thought confidently of myself as an author of fiction, and I did not always agree with my English teachers about their imposed meanings of stories. Although I learned and understood their interpretations, even as a public school student I resisted the notion of a "right answer" to literary analysis, always wishing for more time to think, interpret, and open meaning. Hermes whispered in my ears even then.

Most of my adolescent reading was fiction, which I then naively understood as neither *real* nor *factual*, yet in which I recognized the human truths of relationship, understanding, affect, pattern, motivation, and power. Most importantly for this work, I developed a strong ability to pay attention to story. Narrative truth became a kind of measuring stick for me about what really was going on in the world, in my own life, in the lives of those I knew, and in the lives of more public figures. As Weil writes:

> There is something else which has the power to awaken us to the truth. It is the works of writers of genius. . . . They give us, in the guise of fiction, something equivalent to the actual density of the real, that density which life offers us every day but which we are unable to grasp because we are amusing ourselves with lies.
>
> –Simone Weil, in Zwicky, 1992, p. 79

Whenever I heard, read, or wrote narratives, meaning began to take shape. I could understand why people did what they did, that what happened to people made them the way they were. I could see the relational networks over time and space that shaped each self. I learned that narratives were a place where people had freedom and responsibility to tell truth, however difficult. The power of good narrative, then, lends itself particularly well to the chaotic, contextual, and complex matrices of educational research.

Resisting Coming to Teaching

Before coming to teaching I performed many jobs, all of them roads less-taken than those of my peers. I worked as a book clerk, a Canada Post mail sorter, a waitress, a driving instructor, a house-painter, a gardener. At the same time, at university, I studied literature, drama, linguistics, languages, organic and inorganic sciences, and physical education. After obtaining my degree in biology, I studied radiation genetics research on resistant strains of bacteria and super-antibiotics. All of these separate lives, deep with multiple narratives of self, subject disciplines, and other(s), are enfolded beneath the narratives I bring to my teaching work.

At the age of twenty-six after a tragicomedy of errors in applying to medical school, I found myself catapulted into teaching and into learning more about myself, my assumptions, my commitments, my direction, my very existence. It became important to me to be conscious of what I was bringing to the classroom, which was useful because it drew my attention to the need also to be present in teaching, a lifelong enterprise of both self-understanding and self-forgetting, while attending seriously to my students.

My first teaching post was at a new high school in a small, rural, prairie town a forty-minute drive each morning. To my surprise, I discovered I was good at teaching science and English and began to invest my whole being into educational work. After four years of high school teaching and eight at a community college, I returned to the public school system. My first year there, and twelfth year of my teaching career, the students were all "non-academic" (such labels we assign), and the courses were all new to me. Both the students and I learned a great deal and we did well together. The second year there, I became an English department head of sixteen teachers, and the third year I served as curriculum coordinator where I developed programs for *kids at risk* and began Advanced Placement and Staying in School programs.

My students thrived in those programs. Although by most standards this was success, I noticed that difficulties began to be glossed over in the rhetoric we fashioned, in the stories and presentations we were encouraged to submit, as the school basked in its ameliorating work. I was in the classroom less and less. Gaps in practice and theory began to widen and I began to feel like a guest speaker in my own classroom. I was no longer present in my teaching, so the learning attenuated. Things began to fall apart.

I noticed I was becoming like teachers I used to criticize. Lessons in compassion.

Experienced Teachers and Difficulty

My own life-stopping difficulty came one icy January morning. As my woollen mitten stuck to the metal handle on the front door of the school, my teaching suddenly became "unready to hand" (as Heidegger might say); I quietly decided that that would be my last winter with the school board. Ironically, that very week I was told I was being nominated for a provincial excellence-in-teaching award. The following year, after exiling myself to a West Coast Gulf Island where I worked as gardener and firewood provider, I formally resigned, and used my accrued teachers' retirement money toward more education in curriculum studies at the University of Victoria.

Perhaps the main reason for my resigning was the widening chasm between what I physically and emotionally experienced in the daily broken world of a large inner-city school and the public rhetoric about our amazing successes. We used language to construct the reality of what we were doing so that it was tolerable, but I kept falling through the linguistic cracks into the abyss below where other falling souls seemed to dwell. The possibility of meaningful existence, truth, ethics, and beauty trickled away from my work and life into a life-threatening, fissured slippage between my outer, successful, public educator role and my inner, distressed, private mortal human being role. The inconsistencies and paradoxes began to tear at my (teaching) self. For the good of my students and my own being, I withdrew from teaching because I was in extreme difficulty, having lost an understanding of how to work generatively amid chaos, and not knowing how to go on living and teaching. I succumbed to *Erleichterung*—a desire to make things easier—and I tried to escape.

Instead, I found a teacher-professor who asked me hard questions arising out of my own life and work, returned to school, began to write again, to read extensively, and to think deeply more than ever before. Stories began to tumble out of my pen before I was aware of what was happening and what might lie beneath the surface of those storied texts. To discover what I think, know, and understand about difficulty in teaching, I began at the beginning again, thrown back to first experiences and naive, inchoate writings. What I learned through those five years of intensive narrative research is embedded in my method of narrative analysis that follows.

In/visible work: Dis/playing Generative Pedagogy

All the invisible work performed in the years of teaching and then of studying quietly for hours a day has changed me and changed my work in teaching.

Because of the research I do on difficulty, I have been able to re-enter practice with a much more generative and mindful pedagogy now.

In my life work of teaching where sempiternal difficulty abounds, where all the subtextual underpinnings and hidden curricula dwell underneath teaching and learning relationships, a rigorous narrative method enables me to better understand questions of difficulty in education and what it means to teach. Wherever difficulty exists, there is a story behind it, often "whole, bright, and deep with understanding" (Pinar, 1981, p. 173). While we must remember that "stories are *constructions* that give a meaning to events and convey a particular sense of experience" (Carter, 1993, p. 5), often it is the story that explains reasons enough to go on in life, however uncertainly, to keep dwelling in difficulty without giving up, and to give a semblance of significance to actions and people (Kerby, 1991).

As a result of the "regressive, progressive, analytical, synthetical" narrative work I do ("The Method of *Currere*," Pinar, 1994), I continue to revolutionize my own teaching practices, experience a "coming home" to myself that allows me a sense of entitlement to all that any human may claim: a quiet celebration of living an extraordinary ordinary life with loving relationships, hard work, social and ethical responsibility, and creative problem-solving amid the difficulties a (teaching) life presents in the dismaying dregs by which we begin the twenty-first century.

Some of my stories included that form an integral part of my narrative research, explore the underside of teaching. Some are "counternarratives" (Giroux, Lankshear, McLaren, & Peters, 1996), which the teaching community of readers may find difficult to accept or know, and which they may prefer to leave untold. Still others of my stories are memories of originary, often preconceptual, difficulty as I try (regressively) to retrace and understand my own epistemologies. Some are deliberate (progressive, synthetical) products of literary fictive craft meant to create openings for more study, for multiple tellings, and for diverse interpretations—as with any piece of good literature.[4] All have their roots in some form of autobiography, although they may blossom into fiction. Through my "working from within" (Pinar, 1994), the truths that continue to be uncovered in these narratives are something much more than factual reports. All of them have served as force-field containers (in the Greek sense of *temenos*, or crucible, a container of hot and dangerous materials) that textually hold still the shards and images of difficulty long enough to examine, through those seven intensive orbitals, the site of self, especially in teaching.

Inner Government: Legislative, Executive, and Judicial
Branches of the Professional, Researching Self

The result of that thorough research using narrative method has changed my thought and action around my own inner government and, in turn, has given me a lighter and freer sense of myself as an educator and human being. What is important in this self-work of researching difficulty through narrative is that the narratives constitute a kind of daily, practical, if lyric (Zwicky, 1992), philosophy. These serve to ground a reflective practitioner, who is able to call her *shadow* (Jungian interpretations of that term) to "heel," to leave practices of unhealthy transference outside the door[5] and to dwell in embodied action with her students. With more inner work done on the professional, researching self, it is possible to form a new sense of internal government of the self—to establish a safe country of educative being in teaching. I am able to practice my profession with an internalized set of principles, policies, and personal regulations that makes me a better educator, less unpredictably taken from my ground in teaching. Instead I govern myself from a quantum inner constitution that at the same time provides professional freedoms alongside an educator's rights and responsibilities. I strive to be a collective of democratic selves making good and thoughtful choices, working at being executively ethical in my daily work, and willing aside judgment in a mindful attempt to be *just* in my pedagogical decisions.

Evaluating Difficulty: Revaluing the Teaching Self in the 21st Century

Schools have never been more dangerous than they are now. As I write, more than 200 school souls have died in Russia from terrorists who took over the school to use as currency in furthering their agendas. Beslan, Taber, Montreal, Columbine: Schools around the world practice drills for lockdown procedures. Child poverty, hunger, and abuse rates continue to increase in spite of all our knowing "better." Regard for teachers and the importance of education and governmental spending on schools is at an all-time low, because budgets have to balance. Line items of despair, suicide, alcoholism, drug abuse, illness do not appear on the other side of formal ledgers, so little changes. And as always, the young continue to serve as our fields of dreams, whether to colonize to desired religion, politics, commodity, or consumerism, because children do invariably learn what they are taught, whether in explicit extant curricula or implicit hidden lived curricula. Teachers, regardless of social or political climate, above all need to be mindful of what is being learned and how they themselves are texts that students read and learn as integral parts of the syllabus. Authentic narrative research is one way of making life texts visible for study. Such study opens questions about the qualities of a teaching text and being.

I do not want to live my life as a teacher "without qualities,"[6] risking a blank pedagogic form to be filled with whatever political trend or curricular flavour of the month is being administered. Our entire global education systems are in deep curricular, institutional, economic, and evaluative difficulty, but I only have the right and responsibility to govern *myself*. I must build a constitution of teaching and regularly reconstitute and update my own theory of practice. This is how I am able to work with others at the center of those difficulties, becoming a durable, intelligent, wise, humble, generative, compassionate self.

Narrative research has opened a praxical answer to the questions I raised at the beginning of this chapter. Along with a description of seven spheres of narrative analysis, I make a passionate plea to move beyond naive storying. I engage stories as the narrative plains on which we construct deeper knowledge and understanding about narrative, education, and research in curriculum studies. There is much we must learn as human beings if we are to continue to survive and thrive. The physics of narrative research is one good place to do this work.

Reinvention of a Quantum Teaching Role in the Public School

The common questions asked by experienced teachers straddling fault lines at the borders of self and system in their professional lives also call for a radical hermeneutics along with honest narration. Knowledge and experience need to be integrated like a wave and particle theory of the sciences, so that a quantum, durable self, subject to and freed by all the best laws of physics, chemistry, and biology, is brought to the participatory democracy of public education. Embodied, physical and psychological teaching beings ask: *Who* in the world am I by now? *Where* am I and how did I get here? How do I go on from here? What interpretations can I make of my professional being and practice? How can I move into a mature, meaningful, aware, compassionate, knowledgeable, effective teaching being? How do I remain present amid difficulty?

How do my relational work, researched understanding, and professional skills and resources contribute to a much larger human enterprise of learning, living, and being well? What ways and means of teaching are appropriate for whatever emerges?

I Teach; Therefore, There Will Be Difficulty:
The Need for Relational Education

My best answers to those issues still lie, in part, with strong and valid narrative research, which concerns itself with stories and narrative analysis in educational research. Narrative, at some primal level, always concerns itself structurally with issues of setting, character, plot, point of view, symbolism. Multiple resonances occur in narrative because we understand the concept of story at a fundamental, epistemological level. Although narrative appears to be the DNA, the genetic code of human consciousness, I want to problematize a traditional certainty of definition and assumption about narrative understanding and narrative research work, especially in the domain of education and curriculum theory. I do this by developing a method of narrative analysis as a mode of engagement with elemental, sometimes naive, stories of teaching that are sometimes presented as narrative research, even though they appear without analysis.[7]

Although people usually find meaning and can develop insight through the process of narratizing life, a caveat should come with storying experience in education research. The narrative knot for researchers does not constitute the whole of the research. Stories as data are sufficient as stories, but they are not sufficient as research and are not inherent analyses of a compelling research question such as one of the nature of difficulty in teaching at the site of the teaching/learning self.

From the narrative craft (theory and writing) of my prairied lifetime, I call into question naive, "cheerful," unproblematized frames for narrative research. I suggest instead, the use of at least seven interpretive spheres in narrative research of difficulty, which may lead to *educaritas* and new ways of being generative amid difficulty.

Educaritas: An Invitation Arising out of Story

In the old Greek lexicon there were four classical kinds of love explicated. I wish to invoke the notion of another (fifth) kind of appropriate love in teaching: *educaritas*. The film *Etre et Avoir* is worth seeing as an example: its story is a phenomenological study of *educaritas* and slow schooling. Likewise, such a love involves the pedagogic tact of van Manen. The "engaged pedagogy" (cf. bell hooks) is revealed throughout the film.

The complicated conversations Pinar describes of a reconceptualized understanding of curriculum have *educaritas* at the centre. The constructivist attitude of Vygotsky, the Buber "I-Thou," *Namaste* regard for other, ethical will toward greater good evinced by Plato hold the same kind of *educaritas*. The quiet enduring witnessing gaze of a mentoring, Noddings-care educator that fosters individuation in community, healthy steady growth in new knowledge and being is a living *educaritas*. A Huebnerian stance of stewardship of life and being in teaching embodies a relational *educaritas* to which I suspect all true educators aspire. This book is part of the exploration toward re-understanding a curriculum of difficulty using narrative research. Especially in education and practices of teaching in this new century of sophisticated violence, thoughtful malice, and too many citizens without heart, spirit, and basic life resources, *educaritas* may be essential. Narrative research can inform as insight and practice coalesce.

Internarrative: Discovering the Shadow

> It is quite within the bounds of possibility for [one] to recognize the relative evil of [one's] nature, but it is a rare and shattering experience . . . to gaze into the face of absolute evil.
>
> —Jung, 1971, p. 148

The age of seven is often touted as a critical age for religious awareness, but I remember first becoming aware of my own shadow and its potential at age four-and-a-half.

It was Friday, a late summer evening in the mid-1950s, and my parents were to go to a "young adult" social in the basement of the church. It was that evening I became aware that something in me might be dangerous, might require self-knowledge, self-control, and conscious awareness. There might be something in me in need of forgiveness, about which I had heard so much— probably since before my birth.

That particular evening, babysitting arrangements had been made for the parents attending church: some teenage girls, with one "old maid" supervisor, would mind the children in nearby Sunday school rooms, while the adults had their fun in the large community room. We, the charges, were sorted according to ages that night, so I was led to the room for three-to-five-year-olds. I was delighted to find myself in the room with the sandbox table, a large rectangular box three-quarters filled with fine, clean sand. There was a heavy plywood lid so it could double as a worktable. The whole sandbox was set on sturdy oak legs about two feet off the ground so that all the little girls bedecked in fancy ruffled pants and little organza dresses of pink, white, and yellow wouldn't get dirty on the floor or in the sand. On the prairies that sandbox was about as close to dreaming-of-distant-shores as possible.

I joined the others standing around politely shovelling sand from one container to the other. From time to time, one of us would grab a container from the little girl or boy next to us, in surly assertion of more prestigious ownership, while the "old maid" talked to us about "God is Love" and "Jesus Bids Us Shine," or sang "This Little Light of Mine" in her watery voice that made me think of spiders.

That night one little boy was a particularly aggressive offender. He was whisked away from the conference sandbox while the rest of us looked on with disinterested amusement and puzzlement. We never ceased our shovelling and pouring, although most of us missed our buckets while watching him leave the room, presumably to be reattached to his parents who would do something with him.

Depending on the adult present, all the little boys were on one side and all the little girls on the other, or else were arranged studiously in a boy-girl-boy-girl pattern. If one made the mistake, as I did that night, of expressing a preference about who stood next to me, one was admonished severely and told that we must get along with everybody and love everybody, even the little bugger who stood on my brand new white shoes when I wouldn't give up my blue pail for his red one.

While I was being chastised, another little girl threw up, probably because of fear of conflict and separation anxiety. Immediately all the adults went to her aid. In the flurry of activity I took the opportunity to escape and crept up the stairs into the huge dark sanctuary where formal Sunday services were held. I closed the door behind me in the tomb-like space and waited in the silence.

Then I hissed, loudly, and noticed the marvellous acoustic amplification.

I wondered if God was hard of hearing. I hissed again and whispered loudly, "Hey God, if this is your house, how come you are never home?" I waited, knowing even then I would not get a direct answer. As my eyes grew more accustomed to the dim light from the red exit signs, between the pews I could see the hymnals, visitor cards, and tithe envelopes resting on the specially designed ledges. I drew out one of the stubby red pencils for writing in the amount of tithe, pulled out a hymnbook, and printed the word fuck in the back of the devotional section. I waited in the darkness for a response. Gently I slipped the pencil back in its holder and returned the hymnal to its proper place. Noises of people approaching! I lay down on the tiled floor with my cheek against the cold, hard surface and looked under the pews all the way to the altar in front. The sound of footsteps out in the foyer advanced toward me. I slid forward on my belly like they did in the war movies I saw on our neighbour's television, pulling myself along on my elbows. I hopped over the altar and lay down flat on the carpet, waiting, holding my breath intermittently. I got into my own movie in a deliberate bid for marginalization: *Them Against Me*. Adrenaline surged to prepare me for anything. Just before the sanctuary door opened, I dashed behind the choir seats and edged toward the door at the back, hidden from view.

I took the back stairs down, returning to the basement room, and was playing sweetly in the sand when the adults returned. When asked where I had been, I smiled, gave my pail to the little boy beside me, brushed some "dirt" from my white knee socks and retired from sand play. I chose a book from the shelf about Jesus at the temple when he was twelve, sat on one of the small chairs like a "little lady," and opened the book. The "old maid" patted my hair gently and said matronizingly, "My goodness, can you read already?"

"Yes—and spell, too."

Internarrative: Power Can Be Sweet

To get power over is to defile.

–Simone Weil, as cited in Zwicky, 1992

Every teacher has the responsibility to get in touch with her inner fascist.

–Leah Fowler, while teaching a university curriculum class, 1997

Perhaps my shadow first consciously went to work the first day of Grade 1 in public elementary school when I caught the Dutch baker's son stealing a bicycle and discovered he was terrified I would tell. He didn't think to return the bicycle or confess, but my knowing gave me a surprisingly strong and immediate power over him, unlike any I had ever experienced in my strictly disciplined upbringing.

Even though school didn't start until 9:00 a.m., I left at 8:15 every morning after my parents went to work and headed for the bakery beside the corner store, halfway between home and school. Each day I stood outside the large steamy picture windows waiting for the doors to open at 8:30. Inside I could see the Dutch baker's matronly wife (and bike-stealer's mother) setting out trays of sugared doughnuts, chocolate-covered long johns, raspberry jam-filled bismarcks, cake doughnuts, and cinnamon twists with sticky thick glaze oozing down and settling into dark, syrupy pools on the trays.

After the doughnuts, the baker's wife would set out crusty loaves of Boston round bread, long torpedoes of French and Italian loaves, ordinary white loaves (the kind we always had, sliced), brown loaves, cracked wheat, whole wheat, bran, rye, oat, and barley flour loaves—placed side-by-side in neat rows on tall metal shelves.

After the breads—of no abiding interest to me—cakes were set out: mocha tortes, black forest cakes, hazelnut tortes with heavy butter-cream icings swirled into intricate little baroque designs to tempt the middle-aged whose only joy in life had become eating fresh cakes from the Dutch bakery.

This bakery had not yet heard of the advertising and marketing techniques that placed merchandise within the customer's pudgy little reach. Probably it had something to do with health regulations, but all goodies were in trays inside glass cases, so there was absolutely no way a kid or anybody could steal a maple long john or fluffy white meringue or milk chocolate-chip cookie: You had to have legal tender.

I used to get my legal tender in those days from found or taken pop bottles—two cents for the little glass ones and five cents for the big ones. I would trade them in at the corner store, then head next door to order six long johns for twenty-five cents. After the Dutch boy's theft, I extorted money from him by threatening to tell. He became a constant source of "liquid assets." Sometimes I accepted bottles directly and sometimes I required cash of him. Only once or twice a month would I give him one of the doughnuts. The rest of the time I was careful to convey that I held him in utmost scorn.

His mother was another matter altogether: She had beautiful rosy cheeks and flawless skin and mammoth breasts that were at least as attractive as the doughnuts. Her beautiful smile and warm, husky voice told me the same price every morning with her enigmatic Dutch accent. That was where I learned any art of small talk I possess, because I would think up comments to entice her to answer so I could hear her voice as much as possible.

Her mysterious European background provided child-me with weeks and possibly months of stories. I imagined them coming over the Atlantic huddled together in a wind-tossed tiny skiff, untold tragedy in her lovely lined face. I imagined that the bakery was just a front; they were really European aristocrats, but with the death of many of their loved ones they fled the country, leaving everything behind, never to return. I tried to let her know that at least I loved her, by my coming every day to the bakery to help their business.

She never learned my name nor I hers, but I just knew our relationship was special. After all, once every three or four weeks she would slip me an extra doughnut, or ask me to try a new kind of baked goodie and ask me if I liked it. Always I replied that it was delicious, even if it had coconut or walnuts in it. The light in her face was worth the slight prevarication.

Her son received none of the same kind of interest or benevolence. He had stolen a bicycle after all and was beneath my six-year-old contempt. I convinced myself my Dutch lady had only adopted him out of altruistic compassion as a child-victim of the war, because his real parents had died. In that way I could separate him from his mother in my mind and keep him anonymous—which somehow helped to justify my blackmail.

He was terrified of my telling, still imbued with that immigrant sense that if you aren't good, they might send you back. I did everything I could to perpetuate that fear in him. As a result, for several months he collected pop bottles and money for me, at least fifty cents a day until the summer. For that price I agreed to keep from "spilling" my knowledge to his parents, his principal, and my principal. What he didn't seem to know is that I never would have tattled. He missed some mornings of course, and I would threaten him anew. It is not that difficult for a kid to find ten large pop bottles a day. He made it possible for me to visit his "surrogate" mother each day and talk with her, while he stood outside, horrified that at any moment I might TELL.

Such power was sweet—then.

Chapter 2: Narrative Analysis Model for Education Research

Studying Dangerously: Stories as Temenos for Difficulty

Canadian novelist Carol Shields (2002) speaks in her novel *Unless* of formative difficulties of ignorance that threaten the development of each of us:

> Most of what I remember from the early years is my own appalling ignorance. A partial view of the world was handed to me…and the rest I had to pretend to know. Like all children, I was obliged to stagger from one faulty recognition to the next, always about to stumble into shame. It isn't what we know but what we don't know that does us in. Blushing and fumbling, shuffling and stuttering—these are surface expression of a deeper pain. The shame of ignorance is killing. [The] questions, more like miracles in their phenomenological shapes, gathered around me and formed the oxygen I breathed and what they whispered to me was: You will very possibly be killed because of your ignorance. It could happen at any moment.
>
> –pp. 142-143

As a teacher educator, I am in the business of anti-ignorance curriculum, but it is still so humbling to look at the epistemological roots of unknowing. It is still, even as a professor, painful to examine sites of difficulty, particularly within the teaching self. I perpetually ask as a part of reflection and research, what is difficult about teaching? Who is the self that teaches? What are the original and archetypal difficulties in teaching? What work is called for on/in me as a teacher who stands as part of the curriculum? Struggle and difficulty in teaching are NOT a sign of incompetence: they are a sign that research must be done to ask "What is going on? So what? Now what?" Then some construction of knowledge can evolve into theory, which really can inform our practices.

Happy Stories; Harried Research; Harassed Researchers

In childhood, I used to listen on the radio and later watch *Our Miss Brooks*. I played "school," because even in my preschool day, I realized power was connected to controlling learning. (Interesting study is being done with the phenomenon of students' power through their controlling learning because of their Internet knowledge, which exceeds that of their teachers: see McClay

2003, for example.) On the Olympic end of teaching I saw *The Miracle Worker*, then I saw myself as the marvellous and inspired teacher. In my professional fifties, I think I identify more with the Helen Keller figure, painfully coming to know the extent of my blindness and deafness in the world. Of course I read and watch the happy stories of inspired teaching: *Dead Poets Society* often shown to inspire young teachers (but the main character was fired after all); *Mr. Holland's Opus; Stand and Deliver,* even *The Karate Kid.* Books like *Chicken Soup for the Teaching Soul, Children of My Heart, Everything I Need to Know I Learned in Kindergarten,* and even Parker Palmer's books are important, happy popularized stories of the essential teacher. We admire the turning-point pedagogue as a happy story we like and need to tell often to valorize our own profession, to recognize the worth and importance of our work. There is a place for those stories, even as part of research. But there are some untold and darker stories that need to emerge and be examined as well.

When teachers become harried, lose their confidence, begin to question life in teaching, lose patience with students, colleagues, administrators, parents, and politicians, they often construct stories of their increasing difficulty. They may tell them to themselves, or even to each other, but when all their stories do not change and the endings become less good, teachers can become silent, withdraw, or choose to go back to graduate studies, perhaps even with the vague hope of getting out of the classroom, without losing their status, knowledge, and expertise. Possibility reawakens as they see that their professional difficulties have been experienced and researched by others. They try their stories and experiences out in classes anew. There is often a polite acknowledgment in graduate classes, but as experienced educators they often are told by professors that their stories may well be true, and too bad about all that, but of course that will not form part of their real graduate research. Besides, the ethical standards hoops would be too daunting.

In this way, inner stories of difficulty are re-called by the narrators themselves, often in quiet embarrassment. For their tuition fees they do not receive educative guidance, professional development, or scholarly advice about how to work with those difficult storied experiences, so they are devalued again as professionals at an even deeper level. There is a kind of post-secondary institutional harassment that still abides, this time because they may be drawn to qualitative, interpretive inquiry. Because teachers and school administrators themselves are so well institutionalized, most conform and follow widely accepted forms of research, usually in the quantitative, scientific traditions. They may get grants, have more power and are listened to as having more validity and reliability because they have controlled their variables well and can speak with authority about the number or degree or coefficient of a certain question. Beneficial funding may even result from such studies, but there is still a rich field of non-included data left on the research clipping and editing floors that hold shards and artifacts and genetic-consciousness material that ought not to be ignored: the stories and narratives that get deleted by harassed researchers on timelines and budgetary restraints, sometimes supported and put in conflicting positions by other vested interests. The educational equivalent of drug research funded by pharmaceutical companies where only the benefits are measured, are those would-be administrators caught in districts who may provide subtle pressure to research a board's implementation and report its good effects while getting a master's or doctorate in education. In that kind of research, stories of difficulty are not welcomed or given authentic attention as a source of important knowledge. Precisely what is not to be included is a very rich site of research, a mindful place, where many fear to look. And researchers do have a right, freedom, and responsibility to study what calls them. Narratives in teaching call me.

Stories as Data for Educational Research:
Qualitative Interpretive Research

For my work, data consist of stories of difficulty in teaching. Often people stop at the first telling of the story (albeit compelling) and say that that is their research. But for me, it is just the starting point. As a result of looking at narrative research in education over the past decade, I have developed a method of narrative analysis that is proving useful to teachers, administrators, and other practitioners who work with narrative data, which can then inform the practices of the professional (teaching) self and development.

> Self-reflexiveness becomes not just possible but necessary, since one of the central implications of post-structuralist perspectives is that there is no privileged position from which one can speak without one's own discourse being itself put into question.
> —Elbaz & Elbaz, 1988, pp. 127-128

Once we put ourselves, and especially our professional selves into question, movement and professional growth become possible. Fortunately, other researchers have gone before us, to guide us:

> Research methodology has evolved to enable students to study their biographies and practices. If we can extend this idea to the murky world of identity, and provide spaces for student teachers to rethink how their constructions of the teacher make for lived experiences, then I think students . . . will be better able to politically theorize about the terrible problem of knowing thyself. . . . Students may come to understand knowing thyself as a construction and eventually, as socially empowering.
>
> –Britzman, 1992, p. 43

The "terrible problem of knowing thyself" clearly does need to be an essential part of the work of student teachers (indeed, of all teachers). As a professor of student teachers and graduate educators, I also have the terrible problem of teaching my self what it needs to know and be able to do at multiple teaching levels. The narratives I have written in this book represent a sample of some of the ways I have studied the difficulty of self-knowledge and will continue throughout my life as long as I am able to write. But the work does not end with the telling of the narrative, if one is to approach wisdom, judicial practice, and conscious understanding in teaching.

Self-knowledge and understanding have emerged through my hermeneutic, reflexive struggles in writing and interpreting these narratives (fiction and autobiography always blur). My thinking and speaking about self and narrative have shifted in the crucibular labyrinths of storied "I" where my fiercest minotaurs seemed to lie in wait. I have shifted to a place where I construct a vision of the self with its own flexible, nuclear, electromagnetic field, which allows me to stay with any difficulty. It is a post-structural understanding of self which is narratively/linguistically constructed, but which also has a claim to authenticity of self as a coherent, nuclear, integrated, individuated, situated, historical Being. The process of coming to this reconceptualized understanding of self is a central subject of this book.

A Modest Proposal for a Narrative Analysis Model: Seven Orbitals to Narrative Knowledge of Difficulty in Teaching

Narrative analysis is not for the faint of heart, certainly not for those seeking escape from quantitative research. Horizons unfamiliar will emerge, some daunting, some redemptive. A choice to engage in narrative research should arise out of authentic research questions. It is the very difficulty itself revealed in emerging narrative that draws deeper study, luring the teacherly and writerly mind to more benthic zones of the self and profession. From my fictional, autobiographical, and educational writing, I recognize at least seven significant, interconnected, recursive, interpretive *orbitals*, of narrative analysis that could be useful to researchers in education using stories, counternarratives, narrative interviews or critical incidents in qualitative interpretive inquiry:

1. *Naive storying,* which requires breaking silence, finding language and voice to (pre)consciously tell an experience, image, event, conflict, or puzzlement about a difficulty that exists either in the common world or the private world. Something happened; what is being told at the elemental story level?

2. *Psychological re/construction,* which includes *affect* and cognition, about the knot in the narrative at hand. Feeling is inextricably linked (superimposed) with the cognitive process of making sense. At this second analytical orbital, the narrative researcher asks about the emotions in the story, in the narrator, and in the reader. Here a researcher asks: how one can think about the story, what emotions are evinced, what cognitive work of understanding more fully is called for?

3. *Psychotherapeutic ethics,* which asks the researcher/author/reader (all problematic roles) to engage in issues surrounding (professional) ethics and morality, as each of us confronts our own potential for harm in teaching and research. In this third orbital of narrative method, researchers attend to how to recall our shadows, own our capacity for projection and transference, and do honest work on our own psyche (spirit/soul/self). This third orbital is concerned with inter- and intra-relational literacy.

4. *Narrative craft,* which refocuses on elements of convention, structure, and craft that constitute the safe zone, precinct, or container (*temenos*) of story. This fourth orbital focuses on how the narrative construction safely holds everything in one place—people, events, relationships, settings, and difficulty or conflict—long enough to study it.

5. *Hermeneutic philosophy,* which requires careful interpretive exploration of what is "uncovering" and "revealing." This fifth orbital concerns itself with what messages might lie beneath the surface text as one moves toward opening deeper meaning. Archetypal research questions persist in this phase of narrative analysis, returning to original difficulties of Being and self. The perennial question is always: What other interpretations can be made about the story in

question? While any of the formulated answers must arise out of the story at hand, multiple lenses must be applied for thinking about what is both embedded and contextual, as well as the many layers of interpretation present in the narratized difficulty being studied.

6. *Curriculum pedagogy*, which raises questions about what the story text offers in terms of insightful implications for teachers. This sixth orbital of analysis focuses on pedagogy and what can be learned and known about teaching from the narrative data.

7. *Poetics of teaching*, which are not just artistic gestures to the final draft of a story let out into the public domain but conscious reconstitution of our selves toward beauty, truth, justice, wisdom, art, and meaning while we mindfully dwell in the present moment on this planet. This seventh analytical orbital (and for my current research purposes, the last) is where I think clarity of insight and essence can develop. Sometimes in a simple clarity of pure learning, a happiness of discovery startles us, which is an unencumbered authenticity that unveils truth and beauty in education. It is a feeling of knowing something worthwhile and mattering in the world. It is the experience of pure value in being. It can encompass forgiveness and a letting go of all excess. It is the moment when Sisyphus sets down his rock, the moment when the child's machete in *The Mission* releases Robert de Niro's burlap bundle with a slice of the rope, the moment of a quiet place where we really know we are mortal and we freely set down all our narrative bundles and simply breathe in the miracle of existence as human beings.

Narrative research can serve as entry points or gates to understanding across differences, borders, and ruptures. Studying narratives of difficulty especially can provide exploration of the qualities of auto-historical and allo-historical curricula that makes possible understanding. It offers a bridge to generative co-dwelling on our shared lands and languages of being. Analysis of those stories begins to construct narrative research as an authentic mode of educational inquiry. Perhaps we also need to reconsider Hayakawa's legendary claim that the map is not the territory. What if the map is part of the territory? What curriculum studies research and theoretical maps do we draw from the narrative research we construct, and into which new territories and plains must we journey and dwell? Through narrative research, how can we reconstitute understanding of self and not self, in community, especially in uncomfortable places?

Within each of these seven interpretive orbitals, I am drawn toward six significant clusters of (academic research) engagement in the lesson-revealing narratives I write:

1. Mode of narrative engagement,
2. Persistent questions and openings,
3. Difficulty revealed,
4. Ongoing self-work (teacher as learner),
5. Ongoing relational work with other (learner as teacher) and,
6. Creative possibilities for pleasures and play.

In these textual orbitals of darkness and light, my stories assist research into auto-historical understanding of what is being narratively revealed. I strive toward a wisdom and poetics of an educated (imaginative) self. I teach myself by writing and researching stories of difficulty. I learn by being startled by my own text as I think analytically through seven orbitals to construct knowledge about difficulty. As a result, I have learned how to stay with difficulty in teaching. I have revolutionized my understanding of the (teaching) self. I have created openings to think about and work as a teacher (of teachers). Most of all, I have reconstituted my understanding of narrative, that double helix of human consciousness, to better my life personally and professionally. In chapter 3 I begin with the first narrative analytical orbital of naive storying.

Part II: Fowler's Seven Orbital Spheres of Narrative Research

Diagram: Seven Orbitals of
Narrative Analysis

Figure 1. Fowler's seven orbitals of narrative analysis.
(Courtesy of Peter Lang, L. Fowler, and W. Donawa)

Chapter 3: First Orbital—Naive Storying

Much is made of an ethical ability that I call "perception," after both Aristotle and James. By this I mean the ability to discern, acutely and responsively, the salient features of one's particular situation.

–Nussbaum, 1990, p. 27

Startling the Confessional Pedagogue

Narrative expression and discernment involve a complex form of meaning-making that

recognizes the meaningfulness of individual experiences by noting how they function as parts of a whole. . . . One's own actions, the actions of others, and chance natural happenings will appear as meaningful contributions, positive as well as negative, toward the fulfillment of a personal or social aim.

–Polkinghorne, 1988, p. 35

One of my central assumptions in my educational work is that stories do indeed contribute to our personal and social construction of knowledge. As a conscious professional pedagogue, I find the need to tell my stories, mostly to myself but sometimes to others, to make meaning of my existence. Often these stories begin as a kind of confession that I am "not as good" as I would like to be in my profession. I encounter difficulty, make mistakes, and often feel in need of forgiveness or self-encouragement so that I can go on again the next day. I strive for an emptying of the pain and shortcomings of my own performance within a compassionate and mindful frame. Like Coleridge's ancient mariner, teachers frequently confess tales of difficulty in staff rooms or to loved ones to be understood and forgiven.

If one of my human intentions is to be a reflective practitioner engaged in the lived poetics of teaching and learning, then analysis of stories about teaching and learning can enhance self-understanding as both teacher and learner. The danger and terror in this research is the startlement in what is revealed, which asks me to change and grow as a professional educator.

Ricoeur (as cited in Polkinghorne, 1988) provides some support for these assumptions when—interested in the kind of light that narrative throws on the nature of human existence through hermeneutical-interpretive readings—he links narrative in its elementary, storytelling sense with three features of current historical inquiry:

1. Although history makes claims to objectivity, it studies singular events and sequences instead of seeking general laws;
2. Although current history concerns itself with societies, communities, and states, these entities are composed of individuals and exist by virtue of an individual's sense of belonging to and participating in them;
3. Although historians differentiate between long time spans as unchanging, and short time spans as changing, all like events in a story derive their significance from their place in the whole. (pp. 62-69)

The stories I wrote include some of the singular events and sequences of the history underneath my present teaching self. The nature of teaching as Being seeks to organize itself into a meaningful unity. The question of my own mortality also is made explicit along with my life stories. We know the ending of a life, but if "what happened" in between matters at all, then we know *more* contextually through narrative. The self in a "characterized, storied" life becomes a dynamic, constructed, and constructing narrative essence within the total field-of-self, which seeks not to be lost but rather continually to reconstitute itself. In order to reconstitute self, one might begin, as I did, with a careful inquiry into the already constituted.

> I am lost in a world not of my making, in a personality not of my making. How to constitute the already constituted?
> –Pinar, 1978, as cited in Pinar, Reynolds, Slattery, & Taubman, 1995, p. 520

My initial effort at answering the important question about the reconstituted self arises in the very process of naive storying where I come to a different way of seeing, knowing, and understanding. That, in turn, leads to rewriting the texts of the self toward (re)constitution of being. Just by writing out the difficulty as a story for the first time, I am changed. I am affected by the stories I tell, and I notice others are too. But how?

In the beginning of life and the beginning of (student) teaching, things happen to us. We are often passive beings within an educational hierarchy, with choice only about our attitude toward the events that occur from day to day. We plan classes but rarely, if ever, are they lived as planned. We encounter students, curriculum, the business of the school. More things happen. We perceive, take in, and (re)member incidents.

How can I say *we*? *I* perceive, take in, (re)member incidents. I become an explorer, am startled by my own text, which is an inchoate mapping of self. Abed and not sleeping, I take up my pen (the comfortable pen with the correct weight and flow and inkiness). I scribble a word or phrase, two or three lines on a bookmark, perhaps wedged into page 83 in Stegner's (1971) *Angle of Repose*; I will remember tomorrow evening where I was in that text. It is my own life-text I am unsure of, and I lay my head on the coolness of the fine cotton pillow slip, slipping below the gauze of consciousness to swim in mental waters unavailable to me awake in the common world.

The next day in front of the computer keyboard, I give myself permission to write badly. I threaten unspeakable things to my negative *animus* censor whispering maliciously in my ear, "not good enough, trivial, whining, stop writing this crap." It laughs quietly under its jealous breath in an attempt to steal my possibility for meaning. "Shut up," I tell it, "I am writing now. Shut up. I have been quiet for more than forty years. It is my turn to tell my story, if only to myself. I already know the stories of the censors. I do not know yet the story of myself." And then I laugh at myself, for it will always be like this, always knowing only in part. This life has its perpetual "yet-ness" quality.

Fictional Autobiography: Storying the
Embodied, Socio-Historical Teaching Self

And so the beginning of narrative research of the self begins alone, in naive storying of something from an image, a word, a phrase, a still inner "photograph" constructed in my (embodied) mind. Perhaps I remember through perception but memory is always constructed. I look at the interior photograph until it begins to move again, as an inner *film* across the inner eye, and the sound comes up into my inner ear. Then I watch that inner story as a child sees a movie for the first time. From that, I (re)port, freewrite, draft, note what and whom I see, trying to pay attention to everything I notice and write it down in the nearest language possible. At this first stage of narrative engagement, I interrupt myself often, have to get up and move around, go for *café au lait*, walk, see an unrelated video, listen to opera, watch baseball, garden—all part of incubation so often described in the creative process.[1] This naive storying unfolds as the first place of *situating* the self, the first place of *finding* persistent questions and openings.

Who? When? How? Where? What? I find these early questions do not appear at first with any conscious thought of being creative. They sit behind my *pre-understanding* and incite journalistic tendencies to satisfy a particular kind of curiosity in the life of a temporal mind. There is puzzlement about what *was* and how it differs from what *is*, a Doppler effect between knowing then and knowing now—the education that living gives us. Answering those "simple" questions seems to be a common human enterprise in an attempt to integrate it into a denser, richer state than when first experienced. There is both pre-understanding (naive knowledge) and understanding (emerging knowledge) once experience is "languaged" in early drafts of story, before I know why I am writing and what I mean.

Even before storying begins, I am prepared to work narratively: on a regular basis, I carry pocketable, little brown journal books of natural fibre paper. When puzzled about life and being I write to *apprehend* (in advance of comprehending) and record snippets of image, thought, and emotion. I dwell on the phenomenological edge as I begin to pay focused attention in my naive storying to persistent questions and openings into the lived world I struggle to tell and describe. I become concerned with questions of what precisely (while only half believing in pre/cision) happened in a particular moment, which (auto)biographical contexts were at work in a specific event, or where and how a certain conflict or conversation vividly took place. Syn/chronicity of events that rupture the course (*currere*) of things, and sometimes even cleave the past from the present—often one key event, but also the thousands of remarkable, unplanned encounters in ordinary life—fascinates me in the same way that historians are interested in the factors and conditions that led to a particular battle or coup or invention. *Chance* meetings occur and it seems to be my writerly penchant to unravel backward (and forward) from the event in all coalescing directions.[2]

> Once in the south of Germany, I was walking with a friend in the rain. We found ourselves in a narrow street of local shops for fruit, meat, threads, and all manner of domestic sundries. Half a block away, we noticed a bakery and headed toward it in search of good dark rye bread. When we were within about fifty feet of the bakery, an old woman in a brown dress, brown sweater, brown scarf, and brown shoes came out of the shop, slipped her homemade—yes, brown—shopping bag over the handlebars of an ancient brown bicycle, and set off away from us, pedaling slowly. I began to run after her and called back over my shoulder to my friend, "I will be back in a minute." Running "flat out" toward the cycling woman, I was in place beside her when her front

wheel wobbled, skidded on the rainy cobblestone lane, and veered off balance. I caught the woman and her bicycle and held them upright so that neither fell. She looked up at me like she'd known me all her life and grunted, "Scheise Wetter."[3] I laughed and agreed and as she disappeared into the rain, I thought of the bakery of my childhood. Rain pouring over me outside the German bakery, I thought of the ancient bakery shop owner in my birth town, mother of the boy I blackmailed (see "Power Can Be Sweet"). Later that night in Germany, joining present with past in my journal, I first felt conscious shame about blackmailing that boy from my childhood. I wished I could remember his name so I could write an apology to him.

Language of shame, confession, and possibility of redemption—only half a scribbled page in a 1988 travel diary, naively storying a remarkable meeting with the woman in brown, sparked memories—those long narrative ripple-effects like flat, smooth stones skipped across still waters until at the last unexpected contact, each drops through the surface into a deep Neptunean world where things are experienced differently.

In these preliminary acts of narrative engagement, I scrawl out roughly hewn word sketches of the story's "what-happenedness" (not yet *plot*) including setting (place, time, tone), characters (suspending judgment if possible and concentrating on "writing" the persons as fully as possible), and conflict, if one occurs to me at that point.

Of course as a socio-historically located storyteller, I worry about how to say everything about the story that is necessary yet cannot know what is necessary until I try it on paper. Especially in stories of difficulty, which break personal silences, like early drafts of "Learning to Lie" or the swarming incident in Augie Bricoleur's story, just making the letters form words that form meaning is a struggle. My hand resists, and my mind resists knowing what my hand is doing. I become unsure of what did happen, as memory and imagination cloud my phenomenological perception from the original event. What *was* It like? What *is* It like? Auto(biographical) storying breathes and bleeds into fictive narrative. I lose my certainty about my self as difficulty is revealed, but I know I can stay with difficulty through writing language from my inner (un)common reality. I can write and read my own stories first, with some ethical agency of selfhood.

Writing Counternarratives and Petit-Récits:
Colonizing Institutions and Subjects

My original naive story (the blackmail tale "Power Can Be Sweet") later became a site for confronting my own potential for corruption through relations of power. It may be a simple story, but it asks about what teacherly extortions I might be complicit in, where questions suddenly open about my own praxis and self-reflexive work. I was a subject, used to being colonized by parents, by adults in the community, by school teachers, by institutions, but suddenly found myself (through the lens of the story) in the "awful" role of colonizer. As I begin to uncover a story and construct a force field of language around the briefest image, phrase, or feeling, a narrative discovery becomes a flutter of butterfly wing across my experiential globe, which causes a *tsunami* on the other side of my subconscious. Many assumptions lost their lives in that cognitive tidal wave. Persistent questions develop curiosities that are abated only by further writing and deeper reading. Through those disciplined activities, I find more openings for possible meanings and sense enough to stay with the difficulty of narrative research of the (teaching) self.

Difficulties are continually revealed in this naive storying sphere of self-research. Long after originary, lived experiences, from the safety and distance of years, ink spills unbidden in a slopping-down freewriting laid in the muddy foundational wor(l)ds of teaching praxis. Something troubles me, presents itself as deeply problematic, and will not go away. This is evident in the examples of such stories as "The Anger in Our Miss Maple," "The (Un) Becoming Teaching Self," "The Abysmal Performance of Miss Tofelize," or "Dr. Mercanfract." I cast my net of language toward the difficulty and wait. Ruptures, discomforts, and difficulties emerge, even through the most naive of tellings; so again I lay the censor aside, refusing concern for consequences or judgments.

Again, like the ancient mariner, I need to tell the story. Not knowing who the guest/reader is, I tell it to myself first because I need to hear this narrative and that narrative and consider the intertextual[4] results of them both. But when I finish telling the whole story for the first time, I plunge into deeper constructions that I have made in my narrative exploration. I am surprised, moved, bothered, a little anxious.

I try to reassure myself—it is just a little story, after all, about a fictional teacher, but what about the anger or cruelty that I may hide, hold, mete out, or that could explode? I re-enter the narrative as controlling author, more to comfort myself than to learn or to improve the text. Not really having learned Holden Caulfield's lesson, I try to control my fall from innocence. I attempt clumsy manipulation of structures of craft to transmute experience to knowledge as I first notice things, think about them. The long task of exploring self in difficulty has begun. Resisting the desire to make clearer, to see better, I think more deeply, begin to construct other less-comforting meaning. This may be a point of "separation from the text" (an "out-of-textual-body-experience") that makes it possible to look *underneath*, however difficult. This physical/metaphysical work in narrative remains a puzzlement but does allow one to persist beyond com/fort as a researcher. I can still engage with the topic of difficulty in authentic ways.

In first readings of a story, during first losses of innocence, unlighted places emerge, danger points un-hide, signposts are constructed. I am propelled into more intense confrontations with subconscious intentions, needs, and motives that begin to reveal themselves. Both in the text written and in writing the text, I question my own ethics as the storyteller and the storied. Because there is more visible in the text than I wanted to say, deeper spheres of research reveal themselves. My critical censor begins to whisper again, this time from behind the textual mirrorings I have produced. I am afraid of the narrative for the truths it bears and forces me to behold. The story has startled me, provoked me, frightened me, niggled at me in unguarded moments. Risk explodes[5] as I come to recognize that there is far more in the story than I could see at first, worry about what I cannot see yet. Each time I hear the story, read it, tell it, rewrite, something else in the text is illuminated, something underneath reveals itself, adding to the wholeness of the narrative (self) palimpsest. My former teacherly self becomes fisher-queen.[6] Every story in this collection is a difficulty story that would not go away. Each story points to places for in/tensive work on the self.

The very difficulty itself revealed in emerging narrative draws deeper study, lures the teacherly and writerly mind to more benthic zones of the self. "It is a fault to wish to be understood before we have made ourselves clear to ourselves" (Simone Weil, as cited in Zwicky, 1992, p. 114). So I continue with my narrative-making pen.

As I write out stories of individual moments from my own life frame, I notice a need to make myself "clear," to locate myself biologically, historically, sociologically, culturally, and politically, as I do with such narratives as "Discovering the Shadow," "Power Can Be Sweet," and "The Power of Naming: A Sixteen-Year-Old with a Dodge Ball in a Large Dayroom." Noticing occurs in ever-increasing depth with each writing and each reading of the stories. The difficulties of biology and gender, subsumed in many stories, are further uncovered in studying the stories from a writerly and teacherly distance. Under the ever-present autobiographical, storied blue spruce at my grandmother's during my first score of years, I discover I am "girl," diminutive noun of the (once?)

diminutive nouns of *wo/man* and *fe/male* and expected-to-be nouns *wife* and *mother*. I learn I am white, part of the bourgeoisie, Anglo-Saxon, born a Canadian in the middle of Albertan prairies on a snowy March 17, 1951, eldest child of a traditionally patriarchal family, with two brothers ten and twelve years younger and one sister thirteen years younger than I.

Almost always I have had a bed to sleep in, clothes to wear, and food to eat. I began to find out those are not a *given* in the lives of so many others. I am thankful that I have not known physical hunger, nor been exposed to the horrors of armed conflicts. The raw hungers I knew were not from too little food or bad politics, but from too little safety, too little kindness and beauty, from secret cruelties. The wars I witnessed or participated in were not between snipers and bombers over grassy terrains, ports, and cities, but between wills over territories of the psyche. I did not learn the word *privilege* until postsecondary education, when I began to encounter feminist and Marxist critical theories. Individual narrative (however disturbing those narratives may be) provides the bridge to integrate theory and practice.

Such uncomfortable knowledge of the self seems remote from pedagogy and poetics in the early stages of narrative research. Raw material of a naive story raises relational questions calling for attention and understanding. I notice that my life narrative is not front-and-center; the ego sits down and takes its turn as I find my place in community.

Dialogue, action, and description from a variety of literary points of views reveal the structures and qualities of relationship between and among people. Listening to how people talk, in their preferred or necessary discourses about what they say to themselves and to one another, is an essential part of what needs to be written into the first research sphere of naive storying. Stories, like "Getting Clearer Vision," "The Power of Naming," and "Home Run," for example, are occasions to be better witnesses to the lives of (student) others, to hear stories of those who dwell with us in this community of mortals (Caputo, 1987, final chapter).

Invoking the Professional Self

As a teacher among teachers—both *in loco parentis* in public schools and in the role of professor—I suggest that narratively seeing and understanding the lives of others make it possible to abide with difficulty in education. Anger, impatience, and judgments about the lives of others stem largely from unmindful ignorance about their lived and spoken narratives. Becoming a teacher and maintaining a healthy teaching self requires as much self-knowledge as possible, but it also requires heeding and respecting the complex narratives of others. This naive storying orbital is one of the first places within the force field of narrative to see what others say and do in relation to the self, to notice the other characters in our lived narratives, and to negotiate life in community in a humane way.

By storying the self in difficulty, the underlying truth emerges that the individual, specific Being is a mattering subject of value. Confronting those things in our lives that have presented us with the most difficulty can be enormously rewarding. Illness, death, loss of love, loss of meaningful work have the power to stop us in our life tracks and force us to pay attention to living, at breath level. I do believe (like Viktor Frankl, 1963) that meaning in life comes from exploring, understanding, and accepting meaningful suffering, creating meaningful work, and being capable of meaningful love. Teaching and learning are inextricably linked with those difficulties in meaning. Rather than "smooth over," deny, and even lie about difficulty, we need to pay attention to its lessons.

Pages roll out of the printer with "data" about our attention to things that matter: stories—however awkward or erudite—represent authentic engagement toward understanding. Several of the stories I have written do not make "good literature," but they are rich spheres in which to dwell and (re)search. I play/work with meanings as I read, muttering to myself, "Oh. Ah. Hmm. I hadn't realized until now that . . ." The realizations, even in this first naive storying orbital of self-exploration, open and yield pleasure of discovering meaning, even in the stiff breeze of harsh past realities. The honest awarenesses that emerge or crash down are like a cleansing astringent to the consciousness. Understanding (wisdom about being) is its own reward and allows a larger perspective that increases our capacity to live, be, and play. Often, in play, unexpected, revealing (hermeneutic) turns occur and skip into a second, deeper sphere of psychological construction in the field-of-self. New and different questions of existential and relational difficulty in affect and cognition become the focus of the second orbital of my narrative research method: psychological de/re/construction.

Internarrative: Learning to Lie

Is it necessary for me to write obliquely
about the situation? Is that what
you would have me do?

–Rich, 1995, p. 25

Chalk poised on the blackboard in mid-sentence about plot structure in narratives, I glimpse a Grade 10 girl as she tries to slip quietly into my English literature classroom, ten minutes after the bell has gone. We have a late policy in our school, so I stop her before she gets through the door.

"Where were you?" I demand, elbows jutting akimbo . . . and notice the twig and dried leaf in her left running shoe and notice her eyes. The blank mirror of my five-year-old self is returned to me.

. . .

"Where were you?" she demands, elbows jutting akimbo from glove-size-six hands on shapely hips, thumb adjusting the twist on her ruby engagement ring that has been soldered to her wedding band.

I stand just a little more than arm's length from her and notice the dark purple teardrops in my new lavender paisley cotton dress and smooth them twice with both hands, from the waist to below my knees. And wait.

"Well?"

I notice there is a piece of twig, with one dried, dark brown leaf, wedged in the tiny buckle of my new black patent leather shoes, and I slide that shoe behind the other one so she can't see it. I clear my throat and look at her shoes so much bigger and wider than mine. Red, they are, with tall spiked heels. I wonder how she walks in them without breaking her ankles or falling. I suppose the time will come when I am required to get shoes like that. She may even buy a pair for me, before I am ready. I imagine her catching a heel in one of the grates in the sidewalk on Main Street beside the new Eaton's store where she got my dress. In my mind I see her fall, hit her head, and bleed to match her shoes. Still imagining, in my mind I calmly call out for an ambulance, collect her purse and gloves, and ride with them, to wait in the waiting room of the emergency ward of the hospital on the north hill, for the news of her demise.

"I'm only going to ask you one more time. Where were you?"

I know she will ask more than once and I stop myself from sighing. For a moment I consider telling her, but see something in the pressure in the line between her lips, see that dangerous darkness behind the narrowed pale blue eyes. Possible answers begin to type themselves across the back of my vision, like telegrams of newspaper headlines:

"Local child playing with her dog called Shadow in the garden,"

"Little girl looking at books on the front porch,"

"Small child upstairs visiting the Grandmother,"

"Girl playing hide and seek in the yard."

No, not that one: too close. The telegrams begin to come in blank, out of ink. I worry about the twig stuck in my shoe and tip the other heel up and press it so the leaf and twig are completely hidden. I will have to wait, later, for the few seconds she isn't looking to change my shoes and flush the twig and leaf down the toilet.

"How many times have I told you never to go out of the yard? I called and called you but no little girl appeared. So where were you?"

The spring on the back porch door squeaks open, then slams shut.

We both glance upstairs. It might be my father, so now there will be two sets of questioners and they will talk between themselves about what should be done with me. But it's not my father; it's "him," and I hear him talking in the kitchen above us. I know I must never tell.

"If you can't learn to answer me, maybe you will have to go to bed without any supper and think about being bad. Good little girls answer their mothers nicely. Jesus doesn't like bad little girls. Well?"

No, not well. I think about the picture of Jesus on our church sanctuary wall behind where the preacher talks—the one where the face is looking sky-ward, with a soft brown beard, long flowing hair, brown robe. In fact the whole picture is in shades of brown. The colors in my aunt's paint box appear in my mind: sepia, ochre, burnt sienna, burnt umber. I am pretty sure the picture in the church doesn't have anything to do with me, although what if my mother is right and the man in the picture doesn't like me and will punish me for being bad. I close my left fist more tightly around the peppermint in my hand not wanting to be asked about that either. I bend over to pull up my white knee socks and slip the peppermint inside the elastic at the top behind my left knee and think about peppermint as food.

"Answer me. What were you doing when I called you?"

I wonder how long we will stand here together before she sends me to my bed in the corner of the kitchen to turn my face to the wall. I can lift the little brass door on the water meter there and see the numbers tick by. I wonder how they know to measure the water and if you could trick the meter by running the water very fast or would you have to run it really slowly so the little mechanism they put inside wouldn't notice much. I can't see the seams at the back of my mother's nylons so I am pretty sure she can't see the peppermint lump in the back of my sock. I will have to wait until she is busy to get ready for bed, carefully timing when I put my panties into the laundry. I think about flushing them instead, like the leaf and twig, but I am afraid that they will not go down and when my father uses the big, red plunger they would come floating up to the surface again and that would be worse. I don't think I can get away with throwing them out. I wait, hands clasped together in front of my dress. I wish I were wearing my navy-blue jodhpurs. I don't like how dresses make me feel.

"If you can't learn to tell the truth, they won't take you at the kindergarten next year and you know you want to go there like Margaret did, to colour and read books and learn your numbers. Where were you? I want you to TELL ME RIGHT NOW!"

I already know my letters and numbers, and I can read a little, but they don't know that yet. Instead I concentrate on remembering that her voice doesn't always sound like this to me. She has a beautiful singing voice. She often takes off her muskrat stole and lays it on my lap so I can pinch its plastic clothespin mouth on my fingers, before she slips out of the fifth pew and crickets her stockings up to the pulpit to move people with her rendition of "God Hath Not Promised" or "O Holy Night" or "It Is Well with My Soul" or "Great Is Thy Faithfulness." But there is no music in her voice now. And her singing never has had anything to do with me.

"I want you to talk to me, but you must have been doing something you shouldn't have. 'Be sure your sins will find you out.' Remember that. God sees everything you do even when I am not there. It's not just me you are disappointing. You better go to your bed, but first kneel down and ask Jesus for forgiveness. Have you ANYTHING to say?"

Yes. I have lots I could say, but my throat constricts and I find it hard to breathe. I certainly cannot talk. I feel sick to my stomach but ignore it. This time has been too close. Maybe I could get a really bad cold in my lungs again and go to the hospital, again. I like it there, especially inside the clear plastic tent. I can really breathe in there, and they pass little cups full of apple juice with straws with crinkly bends in them to drink when you are lying down. It's a skill to do that without choking but I can do it. I have practised, lots. And the nurses are clean and white and cool. At bedtime they rub my back with lotion and then sprinkle baby powder on and tuck me in with an extra pillow to hug. They don't ask me questions all the time. And I get to read little Golden Books or sometimes they read to me from the big storybook in the dayroom. Even the nurses with blue shirts and white aprons who bring my food on a tray will read to me. I can sit in the sunroom and listen to records too. I can play Fish with the little girl who broke her leg, but I know to put away the cards when I hear their footsteps on the brown linoleum. They say we don't play cards; they are bad. And they don't say why, and I know not to ask them again.

. . .

Thirty-five years later, chalk poised on the blackboard in mid-sentence about plot structure, I glimpse a Grade 10 girl as she tries to slip quietly into my English literature classroom, ten minutes after the bell has gone. We have a late policy in our school, so I stop her before she gets through the door.

"Where were you?" I demand, elbows jutting akimbo . . . and notice the twig and leaf in her left running shoe and notice her eyes. The blank mirror of my five-year-old self is returned to me. I set the chalk gently on the ledge and ask the class to begin reading. I whisper quietly to her, "I was worried about you. Are you all right?"

"No," comes the answer, and we go together to get her the help she needs.

Chapter 4: Second Orbital—
Psychological De/Re-construction

Narrative . . . like rhetoric, pulls us in through the cognitive mind as much as through the emotions. It answers both our curiosity and our longing for shapely forms: our profound desire to know what happens, and our persistent hope that what happens will somehow make sense. Narrative instructs us in both these hungers and their satisfaction, teaching us to perceive and to relish the arc of moments and the arc of lives. If shapeliness is illusion, it is one we require—it shields against arbitrariness and against chaos's companion, despair.

—Hirshfield, 1997, *Nine Gates,* p. 26

Mind, Cognition, and Thought: Thinking About the Self in Teaching

In the quest of constructing meaning for ourselves, making sense of lived ambiguity and experienced difficulty, narratives offer important temporary cognitive *scaffolding*.[1] A learner can go beyond existing prior knowledge with the help of experts and peers, toward building more extensive inner meaning systems. Without assistance, such a process of growth and learning is slowed, even arrested. Narratives temporarily slow life down in a different, opening way (perhaps the closest way of having a "time-out" from physical existence). In a world where global information doubles every eighteen months, researching narratives can focus attention cognitively and affectively so that exploring life-meaning and the (teaching) self becomes possible and *do-able*. Cognition (thinking) and affect (feeling) are two ways of learning the self as a teaching text within this second orbital of narrative interpretation.

Constructing meaning from narrative is psychologically engaged in at least three main ways, which parallel Jerome Bruner's (1986) famous terms of *enactive, iconic,* and *symbolic* learning: *doing* by the hand (enactive learning), *seeing* by the (mind's) eye as descriptive writer and Being reader (iconic learning), *restating in words* by the mind (symbolic learning). Writing and reading narratives change the way I think, learn, and reconceptualize teaching difficulty. I notice a field-of-self included in the nexus of curriculum theory and practice. In that way, autobiographical/fictive narratives become what I choose to call "teacherly" texts, more thoroughly discussed in the curriculum pedagogy section.

The well-known American drama educator Betty Jane Wagner (1997) reminded me that we can educate our feelings as well as our mind—that reason and emotion ought not to be split. Writers such as Jonathan Swift and Bertolt Brecht certainly made that knowledge about the danger of separating reason and emotion an integral part of their work. History is full of tragic events that show the horrific casualties of such divisions of the psyche. Narratives provide that (re)integration because they embody places of emotional and rational work. As a teacher and a professor, I need to remember to be conscious of the need for integration of knowledge and emotion when I am working with the curricula of self and student and the knowledge we produce and negotiate together.

Engaging narrative knowledge, the rawest emotions can surface, once events and characters intentionally have been recorded during the naive storying phase. Even the setting of the story (for example, the overwhelming, large, inner-city high school in "The (Un)Becoming Teaching Self") in its tone, style, and diction as well as place and time, supports and ex/poses both original, known but unexpressed feelings and repressed, unexplored affective truths. Thought can be blocked at the level of emotions until feelings are expressed, but as hidden feelings reveal themselves behind the text, catharsis can allow a new psychological balance in the field-of-self and heightened ability to focus on the present more accurately. Rather than carrying old emotions from the past that come to play in moments of difficulty, the stuff of dangerous projection and unhealthy transference can be navigated with conscious awareness and professional mindfulness.[2] Narrative landscapes are one place to do this kind of "scouting" of the self before going further into unknown territories. More authentic pedagogic spaces can open as a result of this responsible research and professional development in our practices.

In laying out the narratives and going back as reader/researcher, I also begin to see the existing/ existential structures of our languaged way of being in the world—our living, our actions, and interactions—before they characterize our knowledge and our sciences: "Our existence is such that we are history. We live toward a future whose possibilities are both created and limited by the present and the past" (Packer & Addison, 1990, p. 34).

In narrative we see those patterns of possibilities and limitations and can confront the mirrored projections of our Being. As affect and cognition are narratively revealed and explored, openings for connections, shifts in patterns, and rewritings of relationships occur. Moving easily between storied reason and emotion heightens our awareness, calls to consciousness that which has been hidden, and illuminates more inner territory, drawing us ever to the edge of self-knowing. In the very act of writing and reading a full-story draft about difficulty in teaching, paying focused attention to questions of psychological construc-tions shifts understanding about the cognitive and affective teaching psyche. The result is often therapeutic, even cathartic. The temptation can be to stop working at this point in narrative research because of learning something new or feeling better. I would argue this is just good preparatory work that clears (machetes?) the way through inner forests and allows one to stay with a deeper study of difficulty in successive orbitals.

Working in the psychological construction orbital, examining how we think and feel about ourselves in teaching, we work in the research of the psyche, so progress and synthesis of a healthy teaching self are not arrested. This is one of the research orbitals most likely to close down one's sense of being able to stay with difficulty. Uncovering authentic personal feeling and deep thought can cause a temporary dissolving into weeping despair and assuming fetal positions under literal quilts. Sleep does knit up the ravelled sleeve of care, so upon waking again, breathing and narrating again, even in the midst of difficulty I can make sense. Writing narratively keeps me connected, engaged, continually at work in the struggle of meaning-making with the perpetual hope that meanings can be rewritten by breaking the repetitions of the past and inventing new narrative lines that will change the way I think and feel about being (a teacher).

In paying writerly attention to psychological expression in narrative in this second orbital, adjectives and adverbs with precise power and meaning are studied. This flies in the face of some writing pedagogy, where language arts teachers *correct* students' writing processes, telling the writing hand to ignore the pictorial mind, saying "no purple prose," no overwriting, no bleeding of sloppy emotion all over the page. (Why do many of us constrain such expression of all school children in the firm conviction of our rightness? Writing and editing are such separate and different functions, and I am speaking of writing here.) Not to express old injustices, passions, and heightened responses of an earlier, more immature stage of being is to stay arrested at that level of cognition and feeling. The sooner the overwriting can fully vent its spleen, perhaps the sooner reflec-tive thought is possible, which opens more important levels of understanding for teachers and narrative researchers alike.

This second orbital of narrative research is precisely the place to overwrite, put in too many words, be overly dramatic and exaggerative in ex/pressed language, and give full voice to emotion. Such a reading is the very place and time to be sentient, even sentimental toward the story. When I was writing/reading at this level, especially with "Black Oxfords" and "Learning to Lie," I felt the grief and the anxiety, the fear or revulsion, all over again and thought and thought for days about all that I wrote (and did not write) into each narrative. There is an ameliorative, therapeutic effect in the very struggle to write as a way of staying with (psychological) difficulty, although that is not the goal of narrative research. Remnant sensibilities and psychic ores and dross are excavated and recycled through the voice and experienced once more, but with greater understanding in this second orbital, well past naive storying of original events.

This kind of careful, psychological exploration of self in difficulty brings much to consciousness that accounts for present feelings in certain circumstances. A certain kind of puzzlement subsides as we come to awareness about the ways in which old emotions influence and constitute current feelings as life unfolds. If we are to learn to stay *present* cognitively and affectively in (teaching) life, we must continually weed predispositions of thought and emotion. If we cannot, we miss our own lives by dwelling only in the past or the future. Narrative work has a way of keeping us in the eternal present and providing "privileged access that narrative provides for understanding the way we articulate our experience of time" (Polkinghorne, 1988, pp. 128-129)—both our inner-time consciousness and our lived Being in the world.

This second writing, reading, and research in the sphere of psychological construction constitutes a way of preparing oneself, almost like a scuba diver, for deeper pelagic and benthic zones[3] of difficulty where illumination of the self is more difficult. Questions recurring about "What and how am I thinking?" and "What and how am I feeling?" (associated with Ricoeur's (term of *intentional understanding*) are two perpetual ones that reside with the writer and the reader as narratives are encountered. They are substrate questions to the larger ones of "What does this mean now and what else might it mean?" Louise Rosenblatt called for praxical work in literature and language arts as early as 1938 in her concept of "literature as exploration," and her pioneering work in reader-response theory certainly extends to auto-narratives of professional practice.

Heart in a Storying Teacher:
E/Motions and Feeling in Teaching Narratives

How the characters feel, what emotions are at play, how the author feels, how the reader might feel, who the narrator is, become critical questions at this stage in narrative research. As writer and teller I begin to use language to express feeling more strongly, matching explicit verbs to fit the affect of the character. For example, in "Our Miss Maple," original verbs, adjectives, and adverbs from the first naive storying were replaced with ones that were connected to anger. The tension of rage needs to be held and contained and also built throughout the story until it escalates to the breaking point. I use the Jungian alchemical dream imagery of the *rubedo* (red, gold) world of power and fire. Images are embedded within the language, behind the obvious events, to increase the simmering quality as one reads or hears the story.

In the narrative about the institutional dayrooms of my first teaching experience, the *nigredo* world called to my dreaming, and those memories were full of scatological, dark, underworld imagery (still not written to my satisfaction) that influence the style and diction and figurative speech in the narratives.

Each story (fiction or literal) opens questions about how I have been living my life, how what has happened to me affects the direction of my self-development, why I am as I am. It revisits the possibility of rewriting my teaching life in advance of living so that I reconstitute myself differently in my educational work, using understanding from narratives to abide well with difficulties of a (teaching) life.

As I persist with research in this second orbital of psychological construction where I notice my discomforts—guilt, shame, fear, regret, loneliness, longing, pride—I am required to begin to take responsibility for my feelings, learning those simple lessons of counselling. I cannot make another person feel a certain way, just as my feelings are my own difficulty and not for another to placate, amend, control, or claim. Remembering this responsibility can be a challenge in the messy, demanding, and heated daily work in schools and teacher education faculties.

Ruptures in my thinking and ruptures in emotion are both implicit and explicit in narratives as I engage both the writer and the reader in my researching self. Again and again, recursively, I go back into the narrative text and pay conscious, deliberate attention to the desires, psychic pain, grief of lost possibility in teaching moments, noticing both familiar and unfamiliar emotions as I read and rewrite each story. "Learning to Lie" is a conscious attempt to convert difficult feelings to usefulness in my teaching work. It reveals how transference and projection manifest with students and how to work more generatively in compassionate ways. My narrative work helps me pay sensitive attention to subtext in classrooms, in faculty meetings, in everyday exchanges. Awareness of how transference and projection work invites mindfulness about susceptibility to reading too much or incorrectly in situations requiring personal tact and withdrawal from transgressing boundaries of others in over-eager pedagogy. I learn not to *matronize*, to respect the capability of students and colleagues without jumping to rescue and fixing, which robs them of their own agency. I learn what is my appropriate responsibility.

Places of extreme emotion, of rage or fear, are made visible in the text, sometimes in a startling, unexpected way—in a line I give a character to say, out of my pen, before thinking—that reveals my pre-understanding. Characters' plotted actions show difficulty in context, and when I see more than I intended to write, I am invited once more by text to engage in work on my own psyche. The difficulty for me as a teacher is of being psychologically present, sentient, alert, and authentically engaged while attempting to be less encumbered by satchels of excess feeling.

Particularly as a researcher involved in studying difficulty in the teaching self, I find that narratives have a discomforting but productive way of forcing my attention to cognitive and affective *stuff*. Judgment of others is set aside as I notice places of difficulty in emotion in my quantum field-of-self. It is easier to judge or criticize other teachers or students for their attitudes and affect. Initially I can say, yeah, that Miss Maple, well, she had a real problem with anger, but wait a minute: if Miss Maple is a character in a fictional story, why is the emotional power of her anger so bothersome? Because it points directly back at me! I told that story, enjoyed getting the right cranky adjectives, the viciousness in her spelling list, and her invocation to a student to draw blood for ink because she didn't bring a pen. I progenitively (the sex of the text capable of infinite recombination is dealt with in the narrative craft phase) quilled her the will to burn up student work, put her students at risk, and be quite prepared to immolate her teaching self. The story of Miss Maple reveals, even uncomfortably forces me through its very language to confront hard questions about the way in which our (potential and kinetic) anger might leak, cut, or wound in the daily-ness of our professional practices.

I am not the only teacher in the world bearing possibilities of "Miss Maplean" anger, but that story calls us to think more deeply about the difficulty of escalating rage in teaching—in both the teacher and the students. How can I recognize my own anger in the moment and convert it to more generative work with others?

In the naive storying orbital I attend to the words and deeds of the other characters in my life narrative. This second orbital focussed on thinking and feeling provides opportunities to stop seeing myself as the conquering heroine or main character and begin noticing and constructing my understanding of the language and spaces between self and other in a more complex, professional way.

Learning my own emotional and cognitive relationships with the world is an essential and ongoing part of teaching myself meaning, being, and relational health. This may not seem an earth-shaking revelation to many, but as a child and young person, I spent most of my consciousness in my own head, feeling as though a large glass cylinder had somehow been placed down around me. I watched and acted and heard, but I always felt at least once removed and separate from the primary, common world. Instead I took my psychological home in the secondary world of text, not unlike Jung's description of his patients as being individuals who have been separated from their own stories. We need to return to our own narratives and share them with others.

Relational Integration of the Mind and Heart in the Teaching Self

Through writing my narratives, I have begun to learn I also need to place myself actively in the company of other teachers who value their work with students and are committed to authentic, ethical, and meaningful practice. As teachers, we are rarely trained to deal with the underside of the teaching profession, and we need to open up those difficulties and collectively work in generative ways together. Often difficulty in teaching is viewed as a sign of incompetence, of something wrong and best ignored, rather than experiencing those moments as opportunities to reconceptualize teaching and self. Teaching IS difficult. Mostly I (we) try to forget difficult days and instead report with pride about five or six best classes of a year or a career and remain remarkably and strangely silent about the rest.

Breaking those silences narratively and reading them aloud at conferences and in small informal gatherings, has resulted in teachers whom I have never met coming to talk with me after hearing my stories, sometimes weeping about their untold pain in teaching, and beginning to tell their own narratives. Openings like that, perhaps especially with strangers, lead me to think that as a profession, we might study difficulties as possible sites for re-understanding and reconstituting feeling and thinking. Within the safety of narrative, I want to reach behind the loneliness of the long-suffering Maple or Bricoleur or Gray as a character in a story, to find the purpose and meaning in my own isolating days within institutions that conspire toward the sensation of *anomie*. I inquire about how we, as educators, talk to one another and how we might rewrite the scripts of relational networks in education without repeating the ignorance and broken learning of the past.

Narratives offer a "real," specific, and "safe" space in which to linger with this discomfort in emotions of teaching, while we attempt to regard, study deeply, and construct (embodied, praxical) knowledge around those experiences. All of the narratives about teaching here are intended to serve as narrative data in order to provoke and invite conversation about the epistemology and ontology of psychological teaching ground. Those readings and conversations invoke further inquiry into the teaching psyche.

Such inquiry looks at ruptures for the psyche in teaching. Laughter and weeping, silence, and deep thinking are not often visible in teaching, and yet at critical moments of difficulty, extreme feelings and resonances give us a richness, depth, and connection that are essential in learning. Such moments break repeated patterns in teaching, force attention to what the original difficulties are, and open different spaces for learning. When my grandmother died in my arms, everything shifted (see "Black Oxfords"). *Everything* shifted, including my teaching. The week following her death and burial, my lesson plans had construed that that date in the agenda called me to teach Margaret Laurence's (1964) novel, *The Stone Angel*, in conjunction with the film, *Trip to Bountiful*, both about old women past 80 years of age attempting to sort out their own life narratives in order to finish their lives well by learning what meaning they need. Both tell their life stories to obtain a sense of inner peace and significant understanding about being. The synchronicity was astonishing: At that point of my life as a teacher, I brought my immediate understanding and life experience to the classroom as we explored the literature at hand.

Several of the students muttered half-heartedly that they were enjoying the first few chapters of the novel, *The Stone Angel*, but several students asked why we were reading a novel and seeing a film about a couple of old ladies who were "past it all now anyway." I set aside my comprehension questions for the day and told them the story of my grandmother's life and of her so-recent and amazing death. That story, which visibly moved them, made it possible for them to see the crones in the stories differently. They could see the dangers of withdrawing affect and care in relationships and the dangers of living an unexamined life that could lead one to become a "stone angel." We talked of the importance of story in curriculum and of integrating the narrating selves both students and teachers bring to learning that takes place in the relational spaces among them.

Ten years later two different students from that class met me independently by chance and spoke about the impact of Laurence's novel and the concomitant story of my grandmother that was so intimately connected. They each explained that that one class was most important. Since then from that grounded place, I have been able to be with grieving students in any classroom. We can articulate the emotions of grief as we also move toward thinking well about loss, pain, and despair and learn the meanings we can from suffering, to ultimately enrich our capacity to live well in the present. We learn how to stay with psychic existential difficulty.

In this psychological orbital of exploration, the value of each individual is strengthened as the story progresses by the writerly and readerly attention to passages that are moving to the spirit or surprising to the psyche of a teaching self. Narratives can teach us how to honour these feelings of ourselves and of others, asking how emotions influence learning and curriculum in the generative curiosity of lifelong learning. A purity of emotion is illuminated, as each character becomes an individual who matters and belongs fully to the sentient human species. The potential arises for mental health, for sanity in an insane world, with an enduring presence of hopefulness and interest in understanding what it means to live.

Internarrative: The Anger in Our Miss Maple

"Matthew."

"Here."

"Mary."

"Present, Miss Maple."

"Mark."

"Present."

"Luke?"

"Yuh . . . here."

"Miriam?"

"Uh-huh."

"Miriam, what was that?"

"Here, Mzzzzzz Maple."

"That's better. John. John?"

" . . . "

"Ruth?"

"Ya. Here . . . Missssss Maple."

"John! You ARE here. I called your name. Are you with us or against us? It is common courtesy to speak when spoken to, people."

"How come ya always call us 'people' when you only mean one of us?" sneered Luke, who was the brightest in this class of English 17, and whom Miss Maple privately scorned because she knew he wanted to get into medicine but felt certain he would be lucky if he could pass a first aid course.

"Luke, I wasn't speaking to you. John, answer me."

"What? Okay, okay, so I'm here. Ya can see that. Don't get yer . . . uh self in a twist."

"Peter?"

"Yes."

"Esther."

"Yeah, whatever."

"'Present, Miss Maple' would be nice. Timothy?"

"Present, Miss Maple, sir."

"Okay, okay. David, Sarah, Joshua . . . you are all here too. All right, class, I want to begin a new section of study. We just finished the novel *Hunter in the Dark* and now . . . "

"That guy was a faggot." John took a long "drag" on his slurpee and looked over the edge of the huge, waxed-cardboard rim at Miss Maple.

"John, that'll be enough. Every time you see a male character deal with hard human problems and show a little tenderness of feeling in friendship, it doesn't mean he is a homosexual. Although there are plenty of wonderful people who do happen to prefer their own sex. It is time you opened your horizons a bit, my boy. How do you think you would react if you were told that you were dying?"

"I ain't dying. I use safe sex, eh," and he enjoyed the raucous, if nervous, laughter of the class.

"Good one, John. Hey! Yeah. 'Rad' point is, how come we do always read this candy shit in school? It's such 'Little-House-on-the-Prairie-Walton's-Brady-Bunch-homey do-do.' I mean take a look around . . . life ain't like that . . . it just ain't." Mary snapped her gum, bathed her teeth in fresh air, and blew John a kiss.

"Well, we have finished the book now anyway, and we are going to start a new section today, as I said, and I think you will like what I have planned. Usually I have taught poetry using the textbook but this time . . . "

Matthew wadded a blank piece of loose-leaf paper and "made a basket" into the garbage tin at the front of the room. "Two points. D'jou guys see that? Poetry—like it? Poetry? NOT! Nah, I don't think so, Teach."

"Let me finish, peop—class. What I would like you to do is each choose a group or musician whom you like and pick three or four of their songs to bring to class. You write out the lyrics, the words to the song, and I'll make copies for us to study. We will use the poetry that is being listened to and written now as our texts to study together."

"Yeah, that's 'rad.' Maryanne Faithful . . . I am bringing Maryanne Faithful, a little 'snatch' of music," Peter chuckled lewdly.

"Nah, Corrosion of Conformity's better," Esther whined.

"We have twelve people left in the class. I want four songs from each of you with no overlap."

"Where's the sign-up sheet; I'm doing Eminem everybody, so butt out." Mark got up and seized a piece of foolscap from the teacher's desk. He wrote his name at the top in capital letters and then slouched over to John. "Your 'quick-pik-double-dip,' man, winner takes all."

Miss Maple strode over to John and reached for the paper, but he whisked it neatly out of her grasp. She glared at him and backed up to the front of the room. "It is fitting that you should have the 'fool's cap,' John. Keep it then."

Ruth tilted backward on the two back legs of her chair and leered, "Oooooh Schweeeeet, Studley-you-da-man, you have just been insulted."

"Shut it, bitch."

"All right; that will be ENOUGH! Spelling test. Get some paper. There will be words from the novel we just finished. It's worth fifty marks. Your report cards are in a week. If you cannot conduct yourselves like Grade 10 human beings, then we will conduct it like an elementary class until you can begin to behave like adults."

"I don't have any paper."

"Then borrow some, Esther."

"I don't have a pen."

"Then cut yourself and use blood. First word: *leukemia*. Second word: *melancholia*. Third word: *disciple*. Fourth word: *labour*."

"Could d'ja slow down, jeez."

"No. I can speed up: *anachronism-tedious-Neanderthal-irritable-stupidity-prejudice-dyslexic-neurasthenia-wrath* . . . "

"Miss Maple . . . Miss Maple. We never took these words."

"Yes, well. You are taking them now; you will need to know what they mean in your little lives, that's for sure."

"Hey, Miss Maple. Hey. . .what is this. . .you on the 'rag'?"

"Fifty marks: *violence, bile, venom, slaughter, volatile*," and so she dictated and so they wrote, or tried to, in a frightened and eerie new silence until the bell rang for a ten-minute break before next class.

. . . .

The warning bell signalling five minutes to the start of the next, the third, class of the morning sounded through the halls of Isis Banes Composite High School, but our Miss Maple would be late again. Since September first, eight months ago, at 10:38 every weekday morning, our Miss Maple had been vomiting her diligently prepared breakfast. Then she'd brush her teeth, gargle, compose herself, and march back to class with new confidence.

She had not been vomiting from early pregnancy as Linda Knight did before the first class, or from alcoholism as Dylis Framley did before second class. As nearly as she could tell, our Miss Maple had been vomiting from rage—that kind that erupts from lack of control and lack of hope.

Until this morning though, provoked beyond her usual mask of professional decorum, it had not really occurred to her that she could actually change things, and she had even resigned herself to the fact that matinal purging was simply to be one of her personal aspects in the job of teaching English to a new species of adolescent cretins.

This morning as she lifted the lid on the toilet to be sick, she read scribbled in permanent-black-felt pen "Fuk You, Mis Mapel." The entire contents of her stomach projected themselves unbidden into the porcelain bowl. Those words scrawled in learning-disabled graffiti unleashed something in her that had been building over twenty years of marking illiterate papers and lesson planning, cafeteria supervision, and PTA meetings, teaching remedial reading and interminable English classes half-full of students on the ten-year plan for high school.

So when our Miss Maple returned, albeit just a little late, to the third class of English 17 on that Wednesday morning after the bathroom episode, she was a changed woman and well armed. She had lesson-planned her next class over the recess, but it was planned as none ever had been planned before in her teaching career.

They were crowded out in the hall around her locked classroom door and began the harassment the minute she came into view.

"Yo! Teach! You're a little late for class. Thirty-five push-ups and go to the office for a late slip, and you're suspended for the day and don't you ever come back to this class late again, young lady. Huh? Huh? Isn't that what you'd say, Teach? Huh? Am I right? Take your own, Teach."

Miss Maple smiled and shifted the bundle in her arm and slowly unlocked the door. The disciple-dozen of her *in loco parentis* charges, for the second of their double period with her that day, ambled and scurried, shoved and slouched their way toward disabled desks. Miss Maple watched their faces carefully, one by one, one arm on the bundle and not moving away from her desk.

"What's doin', Teach?"

With a few efficient brush strokes, Miss Maple erased the neatly printed agenda and the entire set of notes from the board, leaving a chalky green open wall space below artists' renditions of the classical authors.

"Nothin', pupes." She liked that. It made her think of the metamorphosis pupa stage of caterpillars unfinished in their development, only to become moths. She'd be the first in line to light the candle for them, because clearly, cursing the darkness hadn't worked. She smiled again, and closed the classroom door and locked it with her key.

The twelve students shifted nervously and improved their posture as Miss Maple shoved the teacher's large desk up against the only door to the room and placed the large metal garbage can on top of the desk, right in the middle.

"Oh, I get it," Joshua said, "We done so terrible on our assignments you're gonna throw 'em in the garbage, right?"

"NOT! Wrong as usual, Joshua."

The lad was hurt because he was sure Miss Maple had liked him and he was confused by her strange tone and words. He glanced out the window and was temporarily comforted by the warm yellow glow of the early morning spring sunshine.

Miss Maple, still smiling serenely, dumped all the papers, file folders, memo, letters, journals, and handouts into the huge gunmetal-gray can.

"We are going to have Spring today, a new beginning and a little poetic mythology lesson that you will always remember."

For the first time during the whole school year, that April morning she had the attention of every student in the class. She opened the side drawer of the desk and emptied the contents of seven butane lighter tins (confiscated over the course of the years from her students with pyromaniacal tendencies) over the papers, into the garbage can. She wrote the single word "Phoenix" on the front board, began to hum melodiously, sat on the desk with her left arm around the garbage bin, and lit a match to the paper nest.

Internarrative: The (Un)Becoming Teaching Self—Ms Bricoleur Requests a Sabbatical

> I think of what it is like to write stories. It is a completion. It is discovering something you didn't know you'd lost. It is finding an answer to a question you didn't ask.
>
> –Doerr, 1995, p. 30

Ms Augusta Bricoleur saw them coming. For seven days she had watched from all the windows in the southeast corner of the school. For seven days, whenever she was not in her classroom teaching, and sometimes even when she should have been, she paced the hallway territory on the second floor of the south and east corridors, watching, watching for them. She fingered chalk in her pockets like worry beads.

She remembered finding the memo in her mailbox seven days ago, labelled "SPECIAL SCHOOL MEASURES IN EXTRAORDINARY CIRCUMSTANCES"—a fearsome document in block capital letters, not a memo to toss casually into recycling. The procedures were clear:

> Notify the office IMMEDIATELY. Notify Bruce [the school police-man] IMMEDIATELY. Notify all TEACHERS in your area to close and lock all classroom, laboratory, lunchroom, office, hallway, and washroom doors. CLEAR ALL CORRIDORS. KEEP ALL STUDENTS LOCKED IN CLASSROOMS UNTIL THE ALL-CLEAR SIGN IS GIVEN. DO NOT, under any circumstances, confront THEM directly. DO NOT try to stop them YOURSELF. DO NOT get in their way. Please do not alarm the students or discuss this memo with them.

For seven days she had cajoled and joked and admonished and talked with students in those hallways as though everything was fine, while maintaining the constant vigilance of a mother robin searching the skies for the steady circling of hungry hawks. Each day she had nodded to the other two administrators as they met and turned back at the corners of their watches. Somehow she knew it would be she who would discover them. Every morning she read over the memo, trying to keep the instructions clear in her mind as though she had trouble with learning what was written there, as though something in her could not learn this information.

Of course the students knew, in spite of the memo. There are no secrets from a high school student body two-thousand strong. They even knew that Augusta and the other administrators weren't allowed to speak about it. They knew the teachers were nervous, watching, waiting for directions. The students themselves were nervous, and they had put an unspoken hold on the usual shenanigans and fighting with each other. The whole school was uncannily quiet. People scurried along corridors. Class changes were strangely silent. There was something larger, beyond their control, and, they knew, beyond their teachers' control. That was what frightened them most—the tacit fear of those in command. There was to be a code—the students "osmosed"—that would come over the public address system, sounding like any other: "Would 'so-and-so' please report to the main office immediately." But one of those messages would be the sign to bunker in together and hope reinforcements would take care of what might follow. They were, as usual, quite correct.

. . .

For several weeks in the local papers there had been reported incidents of a phenomenon called *swarming*, allegedly retaliatory responses to acts of racial discrimination. Some rumours had it that a group calling themselves the Brown Nation was responsible, a kind of terrorist antidote to Neo-Aryan-Nation attacks. There had been three or four violent incidents, all at local high schools, and these reports made it to the newspaper. The most recent event of swarming had occurred at an academic high school nearby. There, one of the football-player-sized English teachers who had tried to intervene ended up being badly beaten, with over a hundred stitches "from the nave to the chops." He was still in hospital. The report went on to say that *swarming* was a term to describe a phenomenon in which anywhere from fifty to two hundred masked young men armed with hammers and baseball bats (which had been drilled out and filled with lead) agreed to converge on a particular spot of an agreed radius (for example, twenty–fifty feet) at an exact, planned time. For two minutes the "swarm" of angry people would smash everything and anybody in that spot, doing maximum destruction. Nothing was to be spared. The attacks worked because no one knew where or when they were to occur, and after exactly two minutes by the watch, the demolitionists stopped abruptly and left, quickly bleeding unnoticed into the arteries of the city.

Augusta responded to that article with rage. She too was deeply preju-diced—not about anybody's skin colour, but prejudiced against the wilfully violent and the persistently mean. She was also shocked by her own feelings and reactions of dreamed retaliation. Her limited karate knowledge, gained long ago for personal safety, welled up into clenched fists, legs ready to kick out in defence of her students' safety. Something really was wrong with a society where young people could not even be safe in their own classrooms. She even found herself reviewing the best lethal blow points on the human body should such attackers enter her classroom this very afternoon. She wondered where the loving pacifist persona was that she had carefully constructed. Where was the unconditionally accepting, patient teacher she'd been told she was, the wise, fair-minded, educating soul she claimed to possess? She noticed all these signs in herself, and they shook her too near a new abyss of which she had been unaware. Outwardly she spoke calmly and clearly to her staff and students, showing good leadership, listening while some confessed how relieved they were not to be administrators that week.

Such comments provoked Augusta to wrath and made her wild. It was an instance of opening a fusty door into a black hole instead of a safe living room where teachers and administrators worked together generatively. In times of extreme trouble like these, what was occurring ought to belong to everyone. Instead it belonged to administrators, and this very fragmentation of informa-tion and responsibility probably did more to perpetuate than to prevent such violence and power-mongering enterprises. She herself got most of the "infor-mation" from brief news articles and one ominous central office directive. The rest was left to fester in imaginations and the rumour mill.

And then early this morning, seven days after that first memo, just after 7:00, the school received an anonymous telephone call that "they" would be coming today to Isis Banes Composite High. Her special supervision team was to be on hyper-alert; the RCMP had been notified and unmarked cars were waiting within a five-block radius.

All morning Augusta watched from the second floor windows, opera glasses concealed in the generous folds of her skirt pockets.

At noon someone relieved her so she could do her lunch supervision and get something to eat. On her way, striving for some semblance of normalcy, she stopped into the staff room to call Calvin Doolittle's mother to inform her he was skipping, again, that he was in danger of failing, and to ask what was she prepared to do about it. As Augusta listened to Calvin's mother on the phone, her face flushed to ever brighter shades of high choler. She snapped into the mouthpiece, "I suggest you do that. We don't need or want him at this school, or your nonsense for that matter." She slammed the receiver down and swore, "That's the ninety-third asshole this week, and I've had it."

"You seem pretty riled lately. Maybe you should take a break, or maybe you should see someone," Rhoda suggested, green pen hovering over the history essay she was marking. She lowered her half-glasses further, warm, chocolate-coloured eyes gazing in steady concern at her colleague and department head—Augusta Bricoleur, affectionately known by a favoured few as Augie.

"Don't be bloody silly. I'm fine, just tired. I just need to get through two classes this afternoon. Maybe I'll leave lesson plans and take a mental-health day tomorrow, catch up on my marking, and come back fresh on Monday. Don't need a written medical excuse for one day away, right? Just a statistic in the teacher absenteeism reports that school administrators get every five years or so. They just chalk it up to illness, or medical appointment, or funeral attendance, or jury duty, right? They wouldn't dare write the real stories behind teacher absences—nobody would ever become a teacher again. There's a rich source for the fiction muse, to begin new directions in literature. Even better, they'd be great fodder for opera plots! Ah, it's probably just all this extra supervision."

Augie laughed, but Rhoda Thixotrope's comments rattled her. She didn't like to think that how she'd been feeling lately was obvious to her staff or worse, that it might interfere with her work as English department head and superb high school teacher. And she certainly should never have spoken to that parent that way and would need to phone and make another apology. It wouldn't be the first time this week.

Ms Bricoleur quietly herded together a paper stack of raggedy paragraph assignments, memos, left-over photocopies of class handouts, attendance sheets, a serviette, and two overhead transparencies into a dog-eared file folder. She mumbled something about this being her week for cafeteria supervision for the second half of the lunch hour and slammed the staff room door on her way out. She opened it again, hollered, "Sorry!" back through the space and let it slam a second time.

Gerhardt Lebenkrafft pressed the locks closed on his Gucci briefcase, folded his linen luncheon napkin, brushed away imaginary flucklings on his navy lapel and checked the crease on his Armani grey flannels. "Mid-life crises are so unbecoming. People should go to New York in October, Vienna for Christmas, Paris for Easter, and Stratford for the summer like I do. Then one has a cultural life outside the ludicrous and primitive demands of having to make a living by teaching public high school Neanderthals. Augie needs to have an adventure, travel, do something about her wardrobe, hire a valet or personal secretary to keep her tidy and organized. It's so disgusting to see teachers' lives unravel in public like that."

But privately he respected Augusta's mind and work and was deeply concerned about her. His supercilious sarcasm was possible because he had only two more years to work before "Freedom 55" retirement. Those two years would feed his ego very nicely too, since a local academic magnet school had recently wooed and won him. He was moving in two months time to new students, ones who wanted to learn—a feeder school to the medical, legal, business, and political science departments at universities across the country. While he would be extolling the virtues of critical thought, designing fabulous real projects for students' portfolios that they could proudly carry over the threshold of graduation, and having fierce lunch-time debates and chess matches during the first week of January, Augie would be struggling for her second wind to give her enough strength and courage to survive the usual school year's round of rallies and riots until the end of June.

Gerhardt remained one of the most highly sought-after teachers by students and principals alike because of his engaging classes, his high student examination results, and his outrageous entertainment value in brilliantly witty and wise lectures. For years he had taught all senior-level academic courses in social studies and English, because he kept the school at the top of provincial performance ratings. But even he had to admit he was no longer interested in dealing with the daily realities of such a large inner-city high school. He had done Augie's department head job for eight years, but when he saw no discernible evidence of the value of any of his administrative work, he went back to the classroom where he clung to an illusion that he might make a difference for at least a few students each term. Yet these latest threats by radical racists admittedly bothered even Gerhardt, and he hadn't been called to be out on the front lines as Augie had been.

Perhaps it was a function of aging, of diminishing patience for adolescent hormones, of desire for a richer inner life, of a Sisyphean despair about making even one more child's life better for all his passionate teaching. More likely, it was a combination of all those. He often wondered what kinds of teachers would replace him and how long they would be able to teach. More, he wondered how they would learn to renew themselves each day—to begin again.

His own struggles made it possible for him to recognize all the danger signs of Augie's new inability to start fresh each day, of her potential professional demise. He had seen some remarkable people pitiably reduced at various stages of their teaching careers. Perhaps it was time to take her to dinner and to a concert. Then, over a late latte, he would tactfully suggest she was in serious trouble and ought to do something about it, for her own sake as well as her students'.

Augie Bricoleur was also one of the few people he was "out" to in the system, and when he'd lost his long-term gay partner to a heart attack five years earlier, she knew his deep grief and watched out for him more as a friend than a colleague. Gerhardt and Augie both had made a personal policy years ago not to be socially involved with people at work, but she'd recognized his need and made him keep going to operas, movies, and bookstores. She made him see the sense of taking a semester's leave the end of that awful January to travel while he knit up his grieving wounds away from the penetrating eyes of students and unknowing barbs of ordinary days in a high school staff room.

He had not forgotten her remarkable kindness and would stand by her, gently nudging her toward care of herself as she began this steep descent of a clearly serious, inner fall. Augie wore her "mantle of power" well, not succumbing to the usual petty tyrannies of middle-management positions in educational institutions. Her attitude had always been one of intelligent respect and good-willed responsibility. She had always taught by learning with her students, by being the best student in her own classroom and inviting the other students along—often for quite wonderful results. She was compassionate, direct, helpful in curriculum matters, supportive in disciplinary and political matters, and generous with her time and materials. That's why her current behaviour was so bizarre and why several of her peers were very concerned about her. It seemed more than just the stress of this swarming thing. Granted, others were a bit anxious too, but really!

Although she was still his department head and had a particular kind of personal dignity about her and implied boundaries of privacy, he resolved to speak to her before the day was over. No one else would. It was a peculiar habit of teachers not to extend the same care for their colleagues as they did to their students. They may mutter, muse, and gossip amongst themselves, but few ever went directly to a teacher in difficulty and spoke their mind or offered assistance. It may be the reason due process had to be written into the union's code of ethics for teachers. To be seen to struggle with teaching seemed to be perhaps a contagious incompetence, which might be the death of your professional career. How odd, for a helping profession dedicated to learning and education of its citizenry!

. . .

After Ms Bricoleur left the staff room, she dissembled through the afternoon. Just dealing with the usual gauntlet passage through the maze of lockered hallways on the way to the school cafeteria would defeat any who were faint of heart. She seemed to watch herself from a distance as she chastised an over-eager young man about groping his reluctant girlfriend: Why does the work of feminism and "no means no" still have to be done every generation? She prevented a "turf" fight between rutting lads, and farther along the corridor took a quietly weeping little soul to the counsellor's office. All that happened as she controlled her gag reflex enough to allow her to pace in the green and white cafeteria tiles, bantering with students about putting their empty lunch bags into any one of the dozen huge garbage bins, calling impertinent youngsters back to clear their tables and to return their chairs to the proper place, and maintaining public relations by responding individually to every "Hey, Ms Bricoleur, how's it goin'?"

Every day it was the same and never the same. She knew one never stepped into the same classroom, the same school, twice. Two thousand students, eighty teachers, dwelled—it seemed—in opposite camps. Today she wished for "Joshua" and his trumpet to bring all the walls of public schools down, to return to the original difficulties of education, to begin again.

Ancient Joshua was no help to her today while she waited for some unseen army to attack and tried instead to think about how she would teach short stories to her English classes this afternoon. Ever since the memo, her lesson-planning had gone to a hot place in a basket. Her non-academic Grade 10 class fortunately came first, and then she had the Honours Grade 12 English, with whom she always looked forward to finishing the day.

Good Lord, she thought, how did such an inner bureaucratic class system develop in her brain? She used to like teaching folks who have a rough time in school, victims of those old rigid row classrooms, with weekly multiple-choice testing, and policies of "five-absences-and-you're-out." She used to like beginning wherever the students were in their lives, developing a class constitution and bill of rights with them on the first day. She always laid out the course outline for them and the provincial curriculum, saying, "Okay, how can we do this together and help you get on with your lives? What DO you want from your life at this point and what is it I can teach you that will be useful to you? Let's do some real work together—we don't have much time—and since you didn't choose to be here, well, let's at least make it meaningful, friendly, and engaging." It usually worked.

So how was it this afternoon, she reflected, that she heard herself orally droning out the same old comprehension questions her own English teacher had used for "The Sniper"? Even though she remembered being shocked and moved the first time she'd read Liam O'Flaherty's narrative, she also remembered being surprised that all the talk seemed to be about the craft and structure of the story as well as a bit of the historical context of the story and of the storyteller. She had been left alone to make what sense she could of her own deep emotional reaction to the story, working it over and over in her head, rereading it to herself. She thought of that story every time she met a student with an Irish last name, saw a television news clip about the latest IRA attack on Harrods in London, or saw a movie about Ireland, such as *In the Name of the Father*.

But here she was asking the same questions that probably had appeared in student notebooks for almost a century, in classrooms ostensibly concerned with literacy and critical thought. Over and over teachers ask students: What is the setting for the story? Who really is the sniper? Draw a plot diagram of the main events using your notes from last day about exposition, rising action, complication, climax (yes, you can snicker—you know I mean the turning point), and the conclusion and denouement. Is there a clear protagonist is this story? Who or what might the antagonists be? If you say that the point of view is "third person objective," defend your answer with evidence from the story. Most importantly, what is the theme? All asked as though there was only one answer. And all this strict focus on literary form and craft allowed everyone to ignore the important questions about the reasons for human sniping and the layers and layers of conflicts needing to be understood and reworked on all levels of existence.

Time after time, story after novel, after play, after poem, responsible teachers with honourable intentions ply students with classical comprehension questions, thoughtfully planned on Bloom's (or somebody else's) Taxonomy of Cognitive Development. Augie realized mid-question that by now she was no exception, making do with weaving bits of ancient practice into structured activities that would keep the kids quiet and busy until the clock released them at the end of classes. So much work by all, and lost without a whisper of grief at the sunset of each session. And yet today, even she returned and returned to those schoolish questions, which had little to do with reality. Perhaps such habitual practices had the illusion of some comfort, especially on a day like this where chaos and violence were such an imminent threat.

She rather liked the fact that such questions were frequently derailed by the reluctant or "weaker" students who were streamed one way or another by the enduring academic class system. They insisted on reading in "the human heart" to any story they encountered, trusting the story: "Man, can you imagine realizing somebody you have been shooting at, thinking they're the enemy, is actually your brother? Makes you think."

"Yeah," another student once commented, followed with a respectful pause. "Isn't it in Matthew, Chapter 10, about 'A man's foes shall be found in his own household'?" "Yeah, and Matthew wasn't the first guy to notice that; in Micah 7:6 it says about enemies of men being in their own house. My father says that all the time and says, 'I'm going to watch you kids.'"

Why hadn't they spent the rest of that class on those comments? But such talk is rarely taken up in school in the interests of hurrying on so they can "finish" the questions that day to move on, if they are to "cover the curriculum." Cover indeed! If they could answer those questions about enemies, the whole world could change.

Memories of those previous classes faded as she began to worry over the safety of her current students this afternoon. Were some of the young men coming in the swarm today "sniping" brothers of any of her students? Why were they coming? What HAD happened? She had seen stories of atrocities in South Africa, read Nadine Gordimer, heard the British (yes, part her own gene pool) and their epics of cruel imperialism all over the world, but until now she personally had not experienced what had been going on for centuries. She was on the benefactress side of Amnesty International, and that had been a position of privilege. Now she and those most dear to her were being threatened in real and concrete ways: she knew that the person these angry young men were after dwelled in her own Thursday afternoon classroom. Suddenly she had an overwhelming surge of comprehension and bone-wracking shock-stall as all of violent history caught up with her entire personal field-of-self. In that state-changing, atomic recognition she understood swarming, made possible because of all their (and her) stories full of fear and hatred, lack of power and fragmentation of information, so that completing a meaningful life together with others could not be possible unless old things were smashed. So much in her own life and in the way schools and societies did things needed smashing, so that something better could grow. Difficulty and conflicts merely called deep attention to those hard places.

Augie needed to get her mind back on the teaching at hand. How could she shift her thinking (and perhaps theirs) to talk differently with her academic students about the power of narrative, which had been her passion and mainstay for a lifetime? They were coming to her last class this afternoon, having read *All Quiet on the Western Front*. Ironic timing, given her own feelings and the situation at hand just now, but where were the lost critical human entry points? What stories lay beneath the stories? Why did students and teachers never begin with their own stories before looking at stories of others in text? What if only the students asked the questions? If there were no authentic questions, they could move on to another story, instead of beating it to death for five or ten more completion marks to be totted up on ledgers of students' individual records in the marks program on Augie's computer, which weighted, averaged, and printed a summative evaluation by the mere pressing of a key. She would think more about this on the weekend when she was doing her prep for the following week. Maybe some curriculum changes would help her feel less overwhelmed. Everything felt too difficult to solve right now.

During the postprandial class with her "10s," she sighed and watched the clock as they worked through the questions. Would they get through this teaching day safely? There were fifteen minutes left over so she read "The Sniper" aloud to them and they were spellbound, asking her to finish the last paragraph after the bell had gone. She reminded herself to read to them more often.

One more block to get through today.

Ms Bricoleur's last-block students were so well trained in school life, she was able to leave the room to phone for a teacher-on-call and jot abbreviated plans in her daybook for the following day. When she returned to the classroom, twenty-seven heads were bent over texts, reading, and writing. She worried briefly that each of them suffered from the "too-good-child" syndrome. Perhaps she did as well. She stepped back into the south corridor and walked slowly along the row of windows watching traffic.

That's when she saw them advancing.

They drove toward the school at funeral procession, slow-motion speed and a formal six-foot distance between bumpers. She whisked out her opera glasses and could see baseball bats in the first three cars, with each car containing six large young men. She ran to the staff room, phoned the office and Bruce, and then went to quietly close each door and lock it along both corridors as the announcement came over the loudspeaker. "Please excuse the interruption: Would Winston please come to the office immediately. Thank you. Winston to the main office, immediately." She laughed. "Winston," as in Churchill. Perhaps she was too Anglo-Saxon for her own good.

Bruce, the school policeman, earned his whole year salary that day. He met the first car directly, just as it parked. Before they could get out of the car, he arrested the driver for consuming alcohol in a motor vehicle. His backup arrested eleven cars that day, and he got numbers and names of the others. That was the end of it. No further news stories. No further reports of swarming. An anticlimax. The student in her class whom she knew was the target made arrangements to move out of the city a few weeks later. She gave him her modest dirt-bike motorcycle to get the forestry job that had been arranged for him.

She never heard from him again.

. . .

Gerhardt was back in the staff room that Thursday afternoon waiting for Augie, with a fresh cup of steaming coffee with cream and sugar poured into her personal mug with Van Gogh's Starry Night image. All she had to do was drink it. She gratefully sank into the staff sofa and stared out the window, cupping her hands for comfort over the surrogate fire of the dark beverage.

Without looking at him, she said, "Gerhardt, I know why you are not already driving homeward in your Mercedes to play your beloved piano. Thank you for your thoughtfulness, but I will be fine."

"It's great you spotted those jerks when you did. Bruce said your timing was amazing, and it's all been taken care of, Augie. But you are not fine at all. I get to leave this chaos soon, take the easy way to renewed mental health; you don't. I walked by your classes this afternoon—where were you? Even when you were in the room you weren't present. You are disconnecting more every day."

Augie giggled and then choked out, "Oh Jesus, Gerhardt . . . and no need to pardon my language; that's an invocation." Tears welled up, ignoring the lip biting to stem the flow. "I can't do this any more, G. I can't. Everything is getting away from me and I can't pull things together anymore. I can't make do with all the odds and ends and insufficiencies of teaching life. Everything is too difficult. I cannot do this, any of it. Not administrate, not chair committees, not teach, not supervise. I don't have the constitution for the endless difficulty of school life. Even Rhoda thinks I'm losing it. You heard her at lunch—'Maybe you should see someone,' she said."

"Maybe you should. It might help. You should be at a peak time in your career. Give yourself a break. You have been under a lot of stress lately, but things also seem to be building up. You should have heard yourself talking to that parent, Augie."

"Oh bugger off, Gerhardt. This, from you who always has your bloody life in such Teutonic routine and financial, mannerly order. Oh, God, I'm sorry, that was uncalled for. I am just coming apart at the seams, that's all, unravelling in front of your eyes. Sorry."

"Augusta, what are you going to do about this, besides taking tomorrow off?"

"How should I know? See someone? Like whom? And tell them what? I can't cope with the stress of a teacher's life; I cry at self-esteem workshops for my staff; I want to break out my karate skills in the school parking lot when some kid 'beaks off.' That I would like to take a flame-thrower to those swarming people who have held the city hostage for two weeks, but that I deep down understand why they do what they do? You really think I should tell some 'fifty-minute hour' that I might have no control over myself, forget meetings with parents and swear at them when I do remember? Tell them that for the safety of my students, I have started to send any discipline problems down to the office. Shall I say that I snap at the secretaries who work their buns off for me, recite 'I have a little shadow that goes in and out with me' in traffic, watch five videos in a row on a weekday evening to forget life, sleep eighteen hours a day on the weekends, weep in the shower every morning, think compulsively about the end of June and death, that I continually wonder how in God's name I can transform myself enough to keep my feet on this planet day after day, figure out what it is I need to learn and why I am here, teaching? Ha—isn't that rich? Me, teaching . . . like this. How very unbecoming, Gerhardt. I am in deep difficulty. How can I reweave the narrative of my life-cloth and try to make sense of what's important by now? Until I can understand what's going on with me and some of the baggage I seem to have, maybe I should not be teaching. I need a teacher right now. Maybe I will ask for a sabbatical. I need to rest, before I can recreate the world. I need to begin to understand more about my self before I can go on teaching."

Chapter 5: Third Orbital— Psychotherapeutic Ethics

Minotaur

Once a minotaur,
a secret revealed becomes a rock,
a tree, a cow like any other.
Only the one who once held it, seeing it
thus diminished, strong the rough bark or small ears,
leans against the silent, cold surface with sorrow,
remembers it in its former, fearsome glory.

–Jane Hirshfield (2001, p. 45)

Epistemologies of an Emergent Teaching
Self: How We Know What We Know

Psychological expression and construction serve for me as a precursor study that leads to more penetrating work of a psychotherapeutic nature as I confront my negative shadow, golden shadow, and inner epistemology and ontology of my teaching self. In a deeper orbital now I notice again projections and trans-ferences, which can so limit or alter relational and ethically intentioned exis-tence. Narrative research is a cold minotaur, rock-ink that does not lie about how I know what I know. While I acknowledge abundant formal discourses in psychology and psychiatry around psychotherapy, that is not the domain of this study. However, the psychotherapeutic enterprise requires thought and inter-pretation around the inner (teaching) (wilful) self. It is an important orbital in narrative, hermeneutic research about difficulty because it calls into question intimate foundations of who we are and how we have become what we are.

Gaston Bachelard (1964) finds that psychotherapists tend to focus on the fertilizer to explain the phenomenon of flower, and by doing so, they fall short of the philosophy and poetics toward which we are inclined. Still, as all farmers and horticulturalists know, the kind, amount, duration, and application of fertilizer can have enormous significance for the life (of a plant). In this section, in a similar way, the "fertilizer" of a (teaching) self can account for some of the blooming, or lack thereof, later in life. The ethical path is to notice the fertilizer and adjust it appropriately so the moral self can bear nutritious fruit.[1]

Here is the point in my research at which, as writer, I pay attention to the motivations of the characters, problems, wounds to the psyche, existential problems, attractions and desires, interpersonal power relations, tensions, dialogue, dangerous liaisons, patterns of connections to other, and issues of intentionality (Pinar et al., 1995, p. 551). Necessarily I implicate myself in all narratives. Most importantly I pay attention to possibility for wrongdoing, for stumbling blocks to the ethical self, temptations and shadows, darker inner landscapes, and labyrinths with hidden minotaurs. These difficulties become significant points for the teaching self to learn and reconstitute itself. The refusal to know the dark side of the teaching self is what seems to be unethical—if not evil, as Noddings (1989) describes that which causes "pain, separation, and helplessness" (p. 118). Particularly as educators we must be alert to that which interferes with the good of the greater being in one's ever-more conscious self, able to recognize its own potential for harm and be vigilant to keep unethical motivations and deeds in check.

In two early stories, "Discovering the Shadow" and "Power Can Be Sweet," as well as in later stories about Dr. Mercanfract and Miss Tofelize, I became concerned with questions of the con/textual epistemology and ontology of the self that one brings, often without awareness, to teaching. In writing I began to re-understand the knowledge one has constructed—tacit and practical—that is embodied in the teaching self. Openings presented themselves for studying why the self developed as it has, as old patterns and projections fell onto the storied page and floundered against the fractal fingers of fickle philosophies. Wonderment developed about personal histories of the soul, mind, persona, and body of an individual—the ontology of a being that has come to be called *teacher*. Difficulties unacknowledged seized the knitting needles of even my sleeping and dropped me into consternation and amazement. Between dreaming and awakening, I arrive at self-knowledge about my own capacity for projection onto and interference with others. The Ms Bricoleur story especially opened these harder difficulties. With what deeper desires, needs, and transgressions should/can the (teaching) self be concerned? What is appropriate teacherly distance? Each narrative of the self in difficulty opens these kinds of questions, invites the moral self further into textual openings for the work of reconstitution.

Every teacher must get in touch with his or her own fascist and recognize the potential for one's self to colonize the Other, to do harm, to use and exploit to meet one's own needs. The nature and function of the shadow in projection, transference, and introjection must be dealt with. One must recognize the need to amend portions of the self, a constant positive disintegration of that which is unethical by that which is ethical behaviour, intentionality, and affect. How we integrate the self into authentic being in professional practice is an enduring difficulty for all helping professions. How do we come to every meeting, class, and appointment as a responsible self?

Ontological Work on the Teaching Self: How We Be/Come Teachers

Narratives like "The Anger in Our Miss Maple," "The Abysmal Performance of Miss Tofelize," "Learning to Lie," "The Small Brown Duck" lay bare a more vulnerable, raw self in difficulty, asking about alternative ways to meet those needs. They require us to ask what in our teaching can be put into our own gunmetal-gray garbage cans and set fire to? What in ourselves needs to be rejected? In what ways are we complicit in questionable ethical (professional) territory? What exactly is it that we project onto our students? With whom do we or do we not identify and what might be the concomitant ramifications for our teaching work? How is it possible to reconceptualize ourselves and change our lives in teaching and learning? Where in our systems of meaning might there be openings for more light? How can we reconstitute ourselves from the ashes of old classrooms? What wisdom is necessary for us to consider how we shall write our curricular narratives along with our students in the future? I leave these questions open. I study difficulty in the interest of becoming an ethical, integrated, conscious knower of self, redefining the denotations and connotations of the professional self.

In Jungian terms, the concepts of an *adapted* self and an *authentic* self may be useful as interim linguistic referents until the self has begun to deal with introjections from childhood and questions about how to become adult as an autonomous, individuated human being with gifts differing. For example, teachers especially need to learn how to control their own "devouring mother/devouring father" instincts toward students. Miss Tofelize shows in an exaggerated way how such devouring teachers might consume others' lives— their work, their energy, their essence of being—and prevent positive learning and maturation. It is important to attend to the hidden truths in our selves, because of the ways they may affect our teaching relationships and curricula.

Grumet (1988) is strikingly direct about this issue with respect to "traditional teachers":

> For the first time I understand that they themselves are struggling to recover their losses. Must we perpetuate this economy of psychological poverty of "bitter milk"? Must we observe the skewed rule of pedagogy, do unto others as was done unto us, withhold from others what has been withheld from us?
>
> –p. 128

We must as a profession and as individual teachers pay attention to losses, difficulties, and hidden truths, if we are to move forward into understanding, meaning, and even poetics in teaching.

As an individual teacher I had to pay attention to two difficult truths that lay buried under the texts I was producing. I kept trying to work around them, resisting when my mentors relentlessly asked me to situate myself autobiographically. It took a long, painful time and new-found courage, which still falters, to write of difficulty in my own personal history. I worry about the consequences of telling such truths and yet desire to reveal truth.

Some Inner Metaphors of Difficult Selves in Teaching

Having written autobiographically in some of the narratives that appear in my anthology (see "The Difficulty of Breathing" and "Learning to Lie," especially), I am forced to see, for instance, how I "allowed" my body to become ill with multiple allergies, persistent asthma, eczema, and frequent bouts of bronchitis and pneumonia that threatened my childhood life, a good portion of which I spent inside an oxygen tent, struggling for breath. Being ill, oddly, became a part of my survival strategy for the child-and-sometimes-adult self. It will always be difficult for me to know of these early difficulties, and I must pay attention to how my too-early losses of innocence and negative experiences might affect the knowledge, practice, and alliances I construct in my teaching/curriculum.

I must be vigilant about understanding how personal issues influence what and how I teach. It is critical self-knowledge for me as a teacher. The story "Learning to Lie" ultimately shows, I think, an example of awareness helping with reflective, appropriate practice. Instead of further silencing a student through chastisement, the teacher chooses to pay attention to what might lie beneath a transgressed school policy of punctuality, to help the student. The ability to pay that attention and choose wisely in the moment comes directly from doing one's own inner work, breaking with the past in some important ways to attend to the present.

As I persisted in writing (and reading) these narratives of extreme difficulty, issues of self-esteem, rage, lack of personal boundaries, loss of a sense of personal entitlement, excessive compassions, suspicions, deep shame, arrested psychic development, and unhealthy personality traits were continually revealed. The pain and profound grief for losses in my own life are always present when I hear of any human being's frailties, injustices, and trauma, particularly, unnecessarily at the hands of another. Those experiences of my own have also taught me appropriate compassion.

The knowledge of difficulty revealed through research with personal narratives teaches me the further importance of doing deep psychotherapeutic work toward understanding that enables me to teach and live with more reliable, ethical care and trust. These are some very hard places of the self, and we must do this per/sonal work for our own good—yes—but also for the extensive good of our students and clients. They are a vulnerable population; teachers and other practitioners often have a great deal of power. Psychotherapeutic work makes it possible to use whatever power is conferred upon us, in the trusted position of teacher and mentor, with kindness, care, caution, and ethical relationships.

Yet another difficulty in this orbital of psychotherapeutic ethics, revolves around questions of teachers' identity, sexuality, and orientation. I grew up in an extremely homophobic part of this country, where hostility, derision, violence, shunning, punishment, and religious castigation were a "normal" part of people's language, attitudes, beliefs, and actions toward those with a same-sex orientation. Homosexuality was and still is viewed as a sin by many people's belief systems. Gay and lesbian teachers often end up being at risk in a profession very uncomfortable with marginalized orientations. Even *liberal* people who tolerate or accept gays and lesbians within the culture at large often do not want us teaching their children. Such attitudes give me deep personal pain: I mindfully stand careful guard *in loco parentis* over all my students' safety because it should be a main condition of learning in education. Homosexuality in teaching is not the topic of this study, but it has been a personal difficulty in my own teaching life, because the profession has been silently censoring of this taboo subject. My own life outside teaching has been silenced and invisible. The problem of being doubly ethical (if one can speak that way) is something every gay or lesbian teacher has to come to terms with. I have known many remarkable, wonderful teachers who remained in the *closet* their whole lives, and it is always a difficulty about how to live well, with dignity, and integrity in those awkward spaces. Fortunately, there are now many who do this work in law, education, and sociology with far more scholarly eloquence than I do here.

Like the demographics of the whole population, it is my experience that about ten percent of teachers I know are gay or lesbian: Those are the ones I know about. The same percentages of my students have been gay as well. Where I now make my home, as in many places, it is not such an issue any more, thanks to the work of many, many people—often writers and filmmakers.[2] Over the past six or seven years I have known a dozen or so teaching colleagues and students who are openly gay or lesbian and unconcerned about their orientation and just busy becoming the best teaching or learning human being they can among ordinary days. What kind of person I am, the ethical work I do, the contributions I make to any of my communities at large, are what matter to me and others. The revealing work in the narratives and in my psychotherapy has made it possible for me to break my silences, acknowledge who I actually am, and realize that I am a valuable human being engaged in important generative and humane work. I want the planet to be better for my existence, creativity, and responsible stewardship wherever I find myself situated. At this point of struggle, in spite of that kind of shift in my own understanding, stories like "Dr. Mercanfract and Heidi" are too new to be "polished" to the literary level I desire. Just to story naively and work on psychological and psychotherapeutic ethics around that narrative took enormous courage to write. That work, though, helped me to come to non-judgmental and non-defensive ways to teach and work generatively with those struggling in similar ways.

Attractions between students and teachers have historically been fairly well documented in literature and film and biographies, but I have not heard or seen much published work around same-sex student-teacher attraction (except for a song by Meg Christiansen and Chris Williams about a physical education teacher) in spite of hearing informally from gays and lesbians about their attractions to teachers. "Dr. Mercanfract" although not worked narratively to my satisfaction is a conscious attempt to open that particular place of difficulty and consider how we might work ethically with dignity, compassion, and kindness toward our students as they form their own independent, healthy, and loving bonds with peers. Gay and lesbian students should have the opportunity that all students have: to have a variety of positive, productive, ethical teachers present ways of being that will help them in their own individual development. I often wonder what pain and failed attempts against one's life might have been avoided if there were teachers who are clearly and comfortably homosexual.

Along with racism, sexism, age-ism and able-ism, this judgment, condemnation, and discrimination against Other is still one of the most difficult places in the (teaching) self.

Enlightened Witness: A Question of Non-Attachment, Stewardship, and Responsibility in Educational Research

Relational power issues around how any situated self dwells generatively with others in a balanced, integrated personality are also hard human work. If we are attentive to self and Other, we witness much that is difficult, perhaps even too difficult to bear. It is, however, necessary to lifelong preparation of the self for the work and responsibility of teaching. Issues of boundaries, respect for the individual lives of those younger and more vulnerable, always must be attended to as teachers claim their self-authority while teaching students to claim their own self-authority. To move toward a healthy balance of self-entitlement with ethical concern, care, and respect for others requires diligent attention.

Paying attention to the emotional and intellectual psychic[3] domains of others, negotiating boundaries, trying to notice assumptions in a renewal of relationality are crucial professional issues. Children ought (not often do I use that word *ought*) never to be "at risk" from their teachers, and our collective inner work will never be done until that is true for all students and all teachers. For instance, in the "Dr. Mercanfract" story, Heidi is able to envision a liveable and meaningful future for herself because her science teacher always engages in an adult, teacherly way, acknowledging what is going on and steering her student away from dependency upon the teacher and looking toward meaningful work and love in Heidi's own (soon-to-be-undergraduate) life. Miss Maple sets symbolic and literal fire to the "old baggage" in her teaching. Augie Bricoleur requests a sabbatical. All these teaching characters in difficulty learn to take responsibility for their psychic selves brought to the classroom. They (begin to) realize that through lack of self-understanding, they carry more potential for harm to their students. The characters withdraw themselves in order to learn their fields-of-self in much deeper ways. Fiction and autobiography merge.

The two newest stories toward the end of this collection, "Dr. Mercanfract and Heidi" and "The Abysmal Performance of Miss Tofelize" (about the consummately *evil* teacher who "stalks" her students and inveigles her colleague to become complicit with her unethical enterprise) relate to more recent teaching difficulties and require even more courage than ones from the distant past. At the post-secondary levels such relations can grow even murkier, and teachers must also be safe from students. Some teachers, I among them, socially have been stalked by students.[4] I do not suggest that the person being followed is in any way responsible, but I have found that setting professional boundaries earlier—clearly, kindly—can reduce such difficulties. I have a personal policy to have no social contact with students outside the classroom until long after assessment and evaluation have occurred and the student-teacher relationship is over. Students should not be part of teachers' lives to meet their ego's social or intimate needs. Doing interesting intellectual work together can be compelling and sometimes raises questions of potential intimate difficulty, which must be cautiously avoided while being navigated with care, dignity, and wisdom. I must, as a teacher, make myself continually mindful of the ethical, educative quality of relationship with my students who are becoming teachers themselves. The relational lessons are often the most powerful ones.

Yet another way of learning relational lessons for me is by being fully engaged in ongoing psychotherapeutic work in private counselling, concomitant with demanding narrative, hermeneutic research. Personal counselling also contributes to living and writing the (teaching) life into self-renewal and a balanced self-entitlement. I have created new metaphors of self, found inner anodyne for pain, learned forgiveness of self, and cut loose some of my psychic burdens. I have begun to notice others more unselfishly. There is a peacefulness inside, a more Zen-like being in the present.

I rewrite my narrative of being into a new, integrated, lighter, and more durable field-of-self. Freedom within existence becomes an invigorated state of creative and meaningful engagement, and laughter and play are possible with all of life's difficulty—even in the face of the mortal abyss.[5] That freedom has allowed me to move beyond my own psychic needs to produce stories like that of Miss Tofelize, which begin at levels of narrative craft not evident in early stories such as "Getting Clearer Vision" or "Home Run." The stories I have in mind to write next are more concerned with issues of teacherly texts, curriculum, pedagogy, and exploration of the poetics of teaching. I feel I have developed a competency at my first interpretive orbitals of naive storying, psychological re/construction, psychotherapeutic ethics, and even at the narrative craft and pedagogical spheres of research. I struggle still at the edges of comfort in hermeneutics and poetics of teaching. That will be the lifelong stuff of educational research.

And then I reach for my pen again.

Internarrative: The Power of Naming:
A Sixteen-Year-Old with a Dodge-Ball
in a Large Dayroom

But that child's sadness never left him. He swore he'd never seen a creature so alone in the world. He lived a long life and made a million dollars and loved his wife and was a decent father to his sons, but he grieved about that baby all his days, the curse that hung over it, its terrible anguish.

–Shields, 1993, p. 261

There is a story that I think explains why I always start the first class of any course by learning student names. The effect of my adolescent work experiences with people with severe mental and physical handicaps taught me the power of naming and is connected with the roots of my understanding about teaching as primarily an act of being in relationship.

My first adult job began in my sixteenth summer. The first morning I arrived at 7:30 and had tea and toast with the other staff while we "did report" from the night staff of the previous evening. I was issued a new cotton uniform of ultramarine blue pants with a white stripe down each leg, white shirt, whistle, and set of keys. It was important then to have external accoutrements to distinguish myself, a recreational therapist, from the inmates at a provincial training school.

The "charge," Dave Picklesport, handed me my class schedule for the week, showed me on a little map where my classes were to be held, and toured me around the gym facilities and equipment rooms. All my morning classes (each fifty minutes long) were to be held in "villa" dayrooms and afternoon classes in the gym. He handed me a large red ball of inflated rubber, a dodge-ball, and so I wouldn't get lost, marched me to my first class, explaining as we walked. (What went on there then was certainly not typical of any schools "on the outside," and probably would be considered barbaric by today's standards, but it also functioned as the only home and family for most of those misfortunate dwellers.)

Arbutus Villa housed about seventy-five to eighty inmates (also known as patients, residents, trainees, feeble-minded, mental defectives, disadvantaged, developmentally delayed, mentally challenged, or clients) with IQs below forty. Most were completely without language and considered only trainable, not educable. Many were barely able to move, bodies rigid except for idiosyncratic, self-stimulation patterns of rocking, patting, hitting, rotating the head, or bouncing—but still considered self-mobile. My job was to try to involve them in any range-of-motion activities and exercises I could.

The structure of this villa, like most of the dozen others, was U-shaped with dormitories either side of the main nursing station. Dayrooms, dining rooms and bathrooms, quiet rooms, utility rooms, and medication and supply rooms were all located in the middle. There was an A side for the forty "brighter" ones and a B side for the others. If a patient was "bad" from A side, he could always be sent to B side or even "down the road" to a "lower-grade" ward. If he was bad on B side, he was put into the QR (or "quiet-room") which was a solitary padded cell where the offender was contained until he calmed down and no longer was a danger to himself or others and was more "manageable." There was one "official" QR per villa.

Those quiet-room policies made me careful about reporting misdemeanours because the consequences were not as simple as a few shameful minutes spent outside a principal's office, waiting for a five-minute tongue-lashing that was designed to inveigle a contractual promise of better behaviour. To be sent to the solitary confinement of the QR was a thing to dread, and of course it was often used as a threat. (Perhaps this is the reason I have always managed directly with any "discipline" difficulty that arises within a classroom. Sending a student to a "higher authority" is something I never do. I have never relied on principals, department chairs, boards, tribunals, or hearings to solve behavioural disputes: I stay directly with the difficulty with only those involved until something shifts enough for all concerned to live with. Conflict resolution and peer counselling issues making their way into the curriculum these days are old and familiar processes to me.)

"To break me in gently" my first shift was to be on A side. Dave and I got there at 10:00 a.m., where he left me with the charge nurse and told me to return to the gym by 11:00 a.m. The nurse in starched white cap, white uniform, white apron, white stockings and white shoes, which squeaked heavily on the waxed and polished brown linoleum corridor, led the way two feet ahead of me, as we approached two locked doors, one on the right and one on the left. I thought of the story in our Grade 8 literature reader "The Lady or the Tiger." The charge opened the heavy door on the right from a large ring of keys and solemnly said, "You only have the key for the front door; if you want out of the dayroom, just rap on the glass at the nursing desk and someone will let you out."

The dayroom, where the inmates went in the mornings, afternoons, and evenings between meals, was where they spent their days. As the door first closed behind me, I saw forty males of "low-grade ability" who sat, sprawled, stood, stooped, huddled, slept, paced, masturbated, gestured, cried, slobbered, howled, whined, scratched, seizured, drooled, stimmed (repeated self-comfort motions), and stared in a room with only two wooden benches. Welded metal grating covered the light bulbs. Those who could stand, and who were over five-feet tall, looked out one of two narrow, oblong windows. The floor was a polished conglomerate of black stone and concrete, mopped at least fifty times a day to remove urine, feces, semen, saliva, and vomit—not to mention microbes. (The conjured memory of that smell still shocks my senses as I write this thirty-one years later.)

There were multiple mental and physical and certainly emotional handicaps in that room where I held my first "class" with those forty Dickensian souls with only a dodge-ball as the curriculum display. The educational aim was to organize recreational activity for them—for fifty long minutes. The inadequacy of the ball I had to offer struck me as remarkably ludicrous. I nearly laughed with the profound shock.

After a few seconds of disorientation, trauma, and nausea, as I took in each of the people in the room, I set the ball down quietly on the floor in the corner. In my horror, it did not occur to me to flee. Or fight. I did rap on the glass for the charge nurse and asked her if they responded to their names. She said that most of them did.

I began to learn their names: Freddie, Mark, Murray, Stephen, Benny . . . . I started to talk to them, to make a connection somehow, to see them as somebody's brother or son, to begin relating to them because I knew it was my job to work with them and teach them as their recreation therapist.

During the first week I worked there, I did not eat and vomited often. The minute I got home from work, I laundered my uniforms and took long hot baths to remove the smell. Every night as I lay in wait for that "sleep which knits up the ravelled sleeve of care," I felt ill, first from shock and revulsion, then from pity and despair, and finally with the burden of the tremendous work that could and should be done. I struggled with a Faulknerian "sound and fury" pounding somewhere between my middle and inner ear. I wept with awe for the miracles and with grief for the aberrations possible in the human body. I wondered with reverence at how I was physically made: How was it that MY neurons and muscles and enzymes and blood and cells functioned as they did, given the visible genetic anomalies with which I was daily confronted—the horrific mutations and mutilations that result when biological, biochemical, environmental, or mechanical accidents occurred. I suffered with a strange guilt at having a whole body and mind, still too young to find Viktor Frankl's meaning in the experience of survival and suffering. I did begin to find meaningful work.

One day after a month of intensive naming labour, I mentally stepped back and noticed something I shall never forget. As I came through the door with the dodge-ball, I called out in my usual ways. "All right John, get ready for this," and "Aaron, I hope you'll be starting the ball rolling today," and "Jacob, I hope your breakfast is settled in because we have some physical work today," and "Hi, Harold," and "Good morning, Charlie, I have come to see you,"—and then I listened and watched as all forty of them began to exclaim and gurgle in approving nonverbal grunts and happy-shrieks as they crawled, walked, limped, slid, and rolled toward me like the drift of iron filings in an electromagnetic field.

My first teacher evaluation occurred one day in early August: One of the boys was to go home for a week with his family on Monday. The boy was told that his folks would pick him up at nine o'clock in the morning. He began to howl and point at the nursing station wall. He howled and pointed, howled and pointed. Finally someone noticed that he seemed to be pointing at the day roster, unhooked the clipboard off the wall and brought it to him. He managed to control his left hand by using his right hand to grasp his left wrist and pointed first to himself then to the ten o'clock "gym staff" notation. Back and forth, back and forth he pointed, shrieking "Eeeee." The staff asked him: "You want to stay for gym class and go home after?" One quiet little affirming grunt-sigh "Aaaa," and the furor stopped. The phone call went home; his family came at 10:30 and waited until he finished his class with me.

The only way to bear the work of those four summers was to find the human soul, the child, the human heart buried in the broken, distorted, and incomplete bodies in those dayrooms. In that way they became individual people and we worked together toward a word or a skill. Even the simple act of rolling the ball back so that it would be returned again became tangible evidence of a meaningful connection, evidence of another being with sentient presence. But above all, I felt a deep need to acknowledge and be witness to their existence, to guard over their safety and solitude for an hour at a time (Rilke, 1985, p. 13). The staff sometimes told me quietly, individually, that it was a relief for them to have me there for an hour because for that time they didn't need to worry and watch and could do their own reports then, prepare medications, and get ready for lunch without interruption or concern. They knew the children were active with me and happy just being. On rare occasions—usually rainy afternoons—when they raised their voices together in a sustained note in invitation to me, I sang or told stories to them. If they were engaged, I often stayed past the end of my working shift.

Through that gym work and the summer camp work (where we took busloads of twenty children for a full week's lake holiday), I learned the meaning of *in loco parentis* that continues to follow me. I "learned" the children well; I lived with them, ate with them, walked with them, swam with them, held them when they cried, spoke harshly to them when they were bad, helped them resolve conflicts, bought them treats, watched television with them, listened to their problems, patched them up when they were hurt. We struggled together, fought together, and became fond of each other. They confided or clung to my shirt or pant legs or keys; they challenged or crumpled; they asked or answered; they responded—as I did to them. Regardless of the degree of physical and mental damage those mortal human beings sustained, they were individuals with whom I developed relationships and did meaningful work, with or without language.

And while I have described the physical setting and the institutional context of the classes and pupils I had, what most strikingly stays etched in my memory are individual faces and gestures and forms: Mary, with one eye removed and her tongue cut out. Alba, a little girl who died from eating too many live spiders and mice. Derek. Willis. Catherine. Dora, who every week would whip off the thin cotton dress from her three-hundred-pound body and bounce naked on the train to express her disappointment that the train ride she lived for was over too quickly. Each week three staff members from the villa would have to come out and get her from the train. Jessie, who asked every day, "What's for supper, Miss?" and no matter what she was told, she'd reply, "Oh, my favourite." I never heard her utter any other words in the four years I knew her. Melvin, who could only recite the filthy lyrics to the nursery rhymes the male staff taught him. Laura, the spastic baby. Robyn, the hydrocephalic with the huge head, who lived in a wheelchair. Blind Daria. Shy Clive, who liked to dance. Danielle, the beautiful and violent schizophrenic. Byron, the self-destructive autistic three-year-old. Sarah, the mathematical "idiot savant". . . .

I think especially of Joey who turned out not to be mentally defective at all, but who was "only" visually impaired and hard-of-hearing. Perhaps my roots in teaching emerged because I was partially instrumental in his being correctly diagnosed and placed in a loving home.

My "report cards" of those children, which were my interior anecdotal notes about their habits, their histories, their medications, their prognoses, also stay with me. I was closely connected to dozens and dozens and dozens of people, half of whom could create an articulated version of "Miss Fowler" and half who could not.

Until writing about these experiences in reflective writings during my doctoral studies, I had not realized the profound, long-lasting influence they had on my teaching. Indeed I probably suppressed them from conscious memory because of the pain and grief associated with them, and yet my lessons there were essential to the kind of teacher I am today. Regular classrooms do not have the power to "rattle" me if I compare them to those early days. The severity of even difficult or challenged public school children never reached such extremes.

A pilot program I developed for kids at risk did have some students in the early 90s who twenty-five years ago would have been institutionalized. Adolescents with fetal-alcohol syndrome, polio and meningitis victims, severe epileptics with mild mental and physical handicaps appeared before me. I unconsciously reached back to my earlier experiences to assist me in building a relationship first, before trying to teach a provincial curriculum set for high school students. I often wonder what other teachers without similar previous experiences do and think and how they manage as more students with special needs cross the thresholds of public classrooms.

Still, from lessons of those days, I enter any teaching situation with that rudimentary notion of relationship at the base of everything. I assume the ball or lesson plan or artifact or talent I bring will NOT be precisely their need, so I need to "be with" them to "learn" them before I start to "teach." I have been accustomed to any currently prescribed curriculum just being the "emergency kit" of the classroom. Everybody eventually learns what's in the first aid kit, but the bulk of the real learning and teaching arises out of the relationship and work between us.

In that institutional place at sixteen years of age, I learned to "be" with "students," building relationships between us that were meaningful, that mattered. I watched them grow and develop: some very, very little, some remarkably, even on the very low-grade wards. No classroom since in the public system has ever been as daunting as those early dayrooms. *Kids at risk* is a relative term to me, with relational answers involving care, attention, and diligent work useful to them.

In some ways I never did choose teaching; instead, it chose me before I was aware of it. And I have returned again and again to those original difficulties in teaching since first writing this story. I want to keep the questions open about what the life situations are for my students and what it is they need. Those first questions remain in all teaching: Who are we? Why are we here? How do we work together, teachers and students, in the time and space we are allotted? What IS the curriculum when we come together in an educational setting?

We learn each other's names and begin. It is the naming of myself as teacher that remains a difficulty.

Internarrative: Black Oxfords by the Quilt—A Significant Death

Cousin Beverly was someone in possession of terrible stories, but still she managed to walk around in the world and be cheerful and smart.

—Shields, 1993, p. 177

A Factual Report

On October 10, 1984, at 18:50 hours, Neva Leone Fowler died of a myocardial infarction at the age of eighty-eight years.

Three Grief Haiku

That October's loss!
Crabapple jelly in glass
Outlives those old hands.

. . .

Soft cinnamon fur
Old dog near, winter-napping
Loving bears great risk.

. . .

Wood-smoke near mountain
Winter afternoon alone
One chickadee sings.

—Leah Fowler, 1997

A Narrative Account of a Well-Remembered Event

Early on the Wednesday morning of October 10th in 1984, I announced that I was making an impromptu trip to visit my grandmother a hundred miles away. When asked why I was going and when I was coming back, I answered that I did not know but that it was urgent I go.

Wednesdays I had no teaching at the college and usually planned classes and graded papers. Even if I had had appointments or teaching, I would have gone that day: A strong, nearly audible, inner voice made it clear that I needed to go immediately.

Driving excessively fast, I, and the car, arrived "out of breath" before 9:00 a.m., in time to catch my grandmother on her knees in her regular hour of prayer and morning worship. My feelings of foolishness at being so anxious and intense dissipated the moment she came into the kitchen for her post-worship tea and welcomed me with open arms and her lovely warm smile, delighted at my surprise visit.

"Dearie, how wonderful to see you. Are you able to stay for the day—I will take an extra hamburger patty out of the freezer for dinner at noon? Come, let me show you the quilt squares. I just need to sew four more, and I could use some advice about what colours to use."

All morning we studied combinations of patterns, laying them out in multiple configurations on the spare bed in the north room, returning and returning to the boxes of scrap silk materials cut from blouses, shirts, and dresses, familiar scraps that reminded me of years, incidents, and people from before I could remember. The emerging patterns were complex, a log-cabin kaleidoscopic whirl of dark, patterned, and light colours, amid which she sought artistic balance, weighed against what was available to work with, since she had no money to buy new materials, except occasionally for the backings. Her arthritic hands floated over the six-inch squares in continual motion, where subtle (chaotic to the unaccustomed eye) shifts of a few pieces changed the entire mood and construction of the quilt, and just as quickly she accepted or rejected the visual result.

She didn't appear to need me to say anything. Years ago I had abandoned attempts to offer advice or to converse. Once in a long while, if she looked directly at me, I would utter "Mmmm," and that seemed to keep things in progress. This morning, however, for the first time—ever—while quilt-deliberating, she sat down a little too firmly in the cherry rocker and said, "Dearie, my head feels like a block of wood today. I can't seem to figure this out just now."

"Why don't we have an early lunch, just this once?" I suggested. "You have a 'lie-down,' and then we can go for a nice autumn drive. On the way home we could stop at the library for some new books and then look at the quilt again before supper."

She laid the loose squares down on the small table and agreed. We worked together at table settings, a cabbage coleslaw (with extra raisins and lemon juice: "That's what really gives that exquisite sensation to the palate, Dearie"), rhubarb-onion relish, flour gravy, carrots, and of course, the wonderful meat-loaf hamburger patties with spices and lemon peel.

She asked me to say grace that day. I launched into the familiar combination of Shakespearean and Quaker-Methodist language appropriate for invoking divine assistance for each member of the family, each friend, the ongoing work of the church, the sick, the lame, the halt, the blind, those in need of inner healing, and of course, the leaders—civic, municipal, provincial, national, global (and in that order). I concluded with the traditional expression of deep gratitude for the gifts and provisions of the day, making us truly thankful for what we were about to receive, mindful of the "gift of Thy son," and the possibility of forgiveness and redemption in "not my will but Thine, in Thy Holy Name. Amen." Her resounding "Amen" followed swiftly and firmly on my own, and for a moment I had a strange Doppler effect of a spiritual kind, but I shook it off, and we began one of our typical gastronomical conversations, which spanned the breadth of centuries.

Grandmother moved effortlessly from stories of awkward births and deaths of distant relatives, to civil and uncivil wars, from the "doings" of the local missionaries building hospitals or schools out in the field, or the call for local social work of poor, unfortunate souls, to the crop of Pyracantha berries, which foretold of a particularly brutal prairie winter, from the demise of a misguided robin, to the degenerating quality and morality of the language used on the Canadian television, from the local bylaws surrounding saving an historic building, to her concerns about global patterns, and her recognition that mortality was a heavenly gift because one's life ultimately becomes too heavy, and hers was ready to go to her "heavenly Father whenever he should require it."

I told her again I would miss her when she was gone, and she nodded but said that soon it would be time. We both brushed away tears, smiled at one another, and "tucked" into our dishes of home-canned raspberries. She asked me if I had read in her devotional readings for the day and for the next, October 11. When I said I hadn't, she invited me to read that passage of text before leaving to go back to work at the end of the day. I promised I would.

She also reminded me that I had promised I would let her go when it was her "time" without heroics, without CPR, and without wild medical interventions. I reiterated my commitment to that, having no idea how near that requirement lurked.

She napped while I did the dishes, and then we got into my sturdy blue Volvo to tour the circumference of a twenty-mile radius (for what was probably the 912th time together), noting the finish of harvests, the absence of birds and mammals elsewhere readying for a difficult winter, the ability to see the bones of the trees, the lovely skeleton of the landscapes, the pale autumn light of an early dusk, and "the marvellous way God puts the earth to sleep each winter."

We stopped at the library, where I chose an even dozen books from authors she enjoyed, such as Grace Livingstone Hill or Lloyd C. Douglas— uplifting stories of the triumph of good over evil tendencies of the human spirit. While the librarian stamped the date on the little white due sheet pasted inside the back of each book cover, she inquired about my grandmother and asked that I take friendly greetings to her, and "due back in two weeks, please."

As I came down the library steps and crossed the road to where she sat in the parked car, I noticed she watched me carefully. The nearer I got to her, the more startling the remarkable blue-grey clarity of her eyes, which seemed to watch me from some infinite new distance. There was a look of understanding, resolution, and profound, calm, quiet wisdom I shall never forget. It is the look of someone at peace with their soul, already on their way to a better and desired place than this earth. I recognized in that moment that she had completed her life and was deeply aware of it.

When I got in the car she returned from that great distance, laid her warm hand on mine and said, "I wouldn't do anything differently another time, Leah. I would choose to believe in God even if I am wrong, battle against evil, work hard, love as much as possible, and try to understand the lessons of pain when it appears. All the difficulty and struggle of this life is worth it. Do you fancy a chocolate malt before supper?"

We both laughed, got our malteds, and drove home to supper prepared by my aunt and uncle who had been winter-dwelling in the basement for Grandma's last couple of years so she could remain in her home, even after two mild heart attacks and the increasing physical infirmities of a more than eighty-year-old body. I lived with her in the summers when I did not have to teach, travelled with her to her beloved mountains often and had her visit for "holidays weeks" several times a year.

Of course the actual supper that followed has been erased from my memory because of the events that followed. We had finished supper, dishes were being done, and I was gathering my things together to drive the hundred miles home. Grandma had gone into the basement storeroom to get down a box of additional silk so she could finish the quilt and move to her usual winter project of hooking rugs. She came rushing out of the room into the foyer near the basement bedroom, saying something about needing to lie down quickly, and began to fold in front of us. I instantly knew she was dying; this was why I was here. We caught her before she fell and laid her on the bed. There was a bit of flurry and confusion finding her nitroglycerine tablets upstairs and phoning the right number for an ambulance (9-1-1 gets you the fire department), stumbling over the precise address. I kept hearing CPR rules in my head and our so-recent lunch conversation about not interfering when it was clearly her time to die.

We shouted that we loved her, while I remembered that hearing is the last of the human senses to go at death (how do they know that?) and concentrated on her shiny black oxford shoes, backs unscuffed from always standing on her feet working. She gave two great last gasps as that great loving heart finished its work. I had the sensation of a tremendous magnetic force condensing from her head to her feet, concentrating itself in a shimmering energy about eighteen inches in diameter, just above her chest, and then a whispering of that energy field upwards and away, pausing briefly at the door as if taking one last look and then drifting toward its destination. I still have no "rational" explanation for that experience, and yet it is more true, more vivid in a concrete, sensate way than any other experience I have ever had in my life.

In that moment something nervous in me stilled itself for the first time in my thirty-three years, as I said to myself, "Ah, so that is how to die. I have learned and know how to do that now. I can manage whatever else comes along between now and then."

And the ambulance attendants were far too late, but it did not matter.

Death is not an emergency.

Chapter 6: Fourth Orbital— Narrative Craft

The *histoire* is the what
and the *discours* is the how
but what I want to know, Brigham,
is *le pourquoi*
Why are we sitting here around the campfire?
—Ursula Le Guin (1980, p. 192)

Authors of Our Teaching: The Stories We Hold, Tell, and Censor in Education

The community of mortals (Caputo, 1987) consists of individuals (historically and currently), persistent storytellers attempting to make sense of our human condition. They languaged Being in the world, even before the advent of papyrus and ink and certainly before ballpoint pen, celluloid, home videos, and DVDs. Aesop, an (alleged, sometimes) early sixth-century Greek storyteller who lived as a slave on the island of Samos, seemed to know that truths about human beings, their relationships, their "dark-side" vices, and their virtues needed to be characterized, or once removed from "fact" in stories, to avoid blame, scapegoating, and serious conflict. Refuge could be taken in the phrase "It's just a story." Still embedded "lessons" and "reflections" of human experience were told through moral fables of personified animals. That tradition of changing the "facts" to "fiction" in order for the teller to be free to tell truths has remained. Narrative fiction continues to be one of the tremendously rich places to learn about the structure and nature of ourselves and others as we live through time.

Perhaps the greatest danger inherent in that narrative craft is the developing illusion of control—control over lives, others, and events. It is seductive for a writer to rewrite events, a deity-like power-lust to alter endings, change the course of history, create, repair, or destroy. And yet one's writing and rewriting of the past and present and future is, I would argue, a necessary assignment of development. Narrative craft is a method of research that reveals our relationship to language and sense-making and that inform our lives, our work, and our relationships.

Academically, narrative landscape has been well studied, theorized about,[1] and now is opening its doors to "tourist researchers" from disciplines other than literature, composition, and language, who see new merit in the narrative for its revelations.

> Studies ranging through sociology, psychology, philosophy, semiotics, literary theory, and historiography have taken up this interest in narrative, and it has become increasingly evident to numerous influential theorists and practitioners that narratives are a primary embodiment of our understanding of the world, of experience, and ultimately of ourselves. Narrative emplotment appears to yield a form of understanding of human experience, both individual and collective, that is not directly amenable to other forms of exposition or analysis. It is generally acknowledged, for example, that our understanding of other cultures and persons is gained from, and in the form of, narratives and stories about and by those peoples.
>
> –Kerby, 1991, p. 3

Because of my own exploration of the narrative landscape (through lifelong avid reading, fiction writing, and many years of teaching English literature and composition), I find myself wanting to (re)trace some epistemological trails. These trails lead back over the evolution of narrative conventions, structures, functions, and literary craft. They are part of the process of coming to knowing through stories and developing my discourse about the "narrative teaching self."

Kerby (1991) suggests:

> The reason for [understanding ourselves and others in narrative] has to do with the way narratives articulate not just isolated acts but whole sequences of events or episodes, thereby placing particular events within a framing context or history. This form of contextualizing has, especially since Dilthey's hermeneutics and also gestalt theory, been recognized as crucial to any form of understanding. In hermeneutics this circular dialectic is seen as one of parts and wholes: the parts can be understood only in relation to the whole they comprise, and vice versa. In light of this insight we are perhaps justified in concluding that it is especially through the unifying action of narration that temporal expanses are given *meaning* ... . Isolated events need to be placed within a developing network of other acts if their broader significance is to be grasped.
>
> –p. 4

Events (often public-historical ones, as well as personal-historical ones) and who "caused" them, attended them, or was celebrated (or victimized) by them were the focus of the earliest stories. Concern was scant about point of view, symbolism, irony, or conventions; and without the self-consciousness of postmodern, poststructuralist questions of subject/object, signifier/signified (*signifi-catum*), "genre-busting," deconstruction, perspective; or the problematics of "defining" fiction, generally, or authorship in narrative autobiography specifically.

Things change. In the late 60s and early 70s, the ambiguous and problematic nature of narrative (structure) began to be explored, and in the period of time between 1972 (Gerard Genette's seminal work, *Narrative Discourse*) and 1988 (*Narrative Discourse Revisited*), discourse about narrative changed dramatically. From 1970 to the present, there has been a change in the nature of the questions about narrative (craft), the ways of thinking about narrative, and our way of talking, writing, and interpreting narrative, which in some ways parallels the progress of my own narrative and teaching work over the same period of time.

One of the main casualties of postmodern work is an old and comfortable sense of speaking about things with certainty (Doll, Jr., 1993, for example), and educational research and narrative discourse are no exceptions. Certainty has fallen away, especially in the past thirty years, as the once-established genres, patterns, boundaries, conventions, and language of narrative have been sliding, shifting, and blurring. I can almost smell the acrid ozone of boundaries burning, as orbital shields around the core of story decompose into a lighter, more cohesive energy of multiple interpretations and understandings.

There is increasing difficulty in defining narrative and in explaining narrative method with certainty and clarity (and why I resist trying to offer a stable definition), but it seems to me that five main shifts in thinking about narrative in that critical, paradigm-shifting time have to do with

1. *Literary questions of structure* (see the work of Champigny, 1972; Genette, 1972; and then, for example, Chamberlain 1990; Ricoeur, 1981);

2. *Philosophical and psychological questions of authorship*—for example, Foucault's (as cited in Rabinow, 1984) essay, "What Is an Author?" and conversations about relationship between autobiography and fiction in narrative);

3. *Political questions of two main feminist concerns about notions of mastery of a canon and of appropriation of voices of the Other*;

4. *Hermeneutic questions of reader response* (beginning with Louise Rosenblatt in the 40s) *and interpretation of text*; and

5. *Pedagogical, ethical, and professional questions of narrative use in educational research* (especially my questions for purposes of this book).

Those five main shifts in narrative discourse are also important in my own long history of being a teacher. Once upon a time as a literature and composition teacher, I used to be able to talk with modern confidence (as opposed to postmodern uncertainty) in my secondary and college English classrooms about story (*histoire*) structure. It was expected that a literature curriculum held me contractually responsible for teaching the standard elements of fiction as though they were completely unproblematic. I had overheads, notes, handouts, and clouds of yellow and white chalk dust as archival evidence of our diligent work together, learning definitions of plot, setting, point of view, characterization, theme, irony, and symbolism. Confidently we memorized terms, hunted for examples in everything we read, and wrote multiple choice, matching, true-false, short-answer, and essay tests to illustrate our knowledge. Narrative conventions were rigidly designed and adhered to, and the work of any good literature teacher also included histories of the grand narratives from early Greeks, Norse myths, German and French fairy tales, through to modern British, American, and Canadian short stories and novels.

Unfortunately, I must confess my first students in the late 70s only got my version of those works—notes cribbed from teaching sources, passages excised equally from great and lesser critics alike and woven into my choices for what they would read, how we would read, and for what purpose—primarily looking at a main element of structure. Even the questions were contrived ones, often at the back of the story or in teaching guides, which I dutifully photocopied and handed on to my students. Consider this a public apology, now. And yet structure was a large focus in the discipline of literature in schools. Until the reader-response theories trickled down into teachers' literature "binders" (!), this was the traditional, impoverished fare across North America.

That was the beginning, however, of my own ability to re-examine what I was doing with literature in my classes, and Rosenblatt first caused me to see the need to melt down old structures of analysis, question things I had taken for granted, and rebuild my classroom work to match the change in my own and my students' reading and thinking practices.[2] Questions about the nature and meaning of being such a teacher are taken up again in the curriculum pedagogy and poetics of teaching sections closer to the end of this book.

The wonderful thing is that all those marvellous literary works survived such battering. Returning to them now, with fresh eyes, deepens the pleasure and value of reading them again and waiting for students' questions, for "teachable moments" (which frequently arise amid our focused conversations about structure), and for better connections through interpretation and meaning-making.

In the "Ms Bricoleur" story, I wanted as author/writer to pen the events around *swarming*. The Augie character kept dragging me into the murk of comprehension questions about short stories in the classes. The difficulty of being thoughtful about what you bring and "plan" for each class, against the backdrop of historical, personal, and community dramas, is often a paradoxical place, where the teacher splits from the personal self and thinks pedagogically in the midst of a multiplicity of living plots. That place can invite a disorienting dissociation. In another story Miss Maple is vomiting at the break but at the same time she is planning her next class. As structures break away regularly in the classroom and plots unfold where the endings or even the direction is unknown, teachers attempt continually to author the living texts of the classrooms, as *bricoleurs*, using the scraps of nothing to knit up sense and meaning within self-organizing chaos.

Included in the evolution of narrative theory, neologisms and translinguistic definitions offer more accurate ways to describe understanding and explication of such narrative texts. Terms like *metissage* and *bricolage* appear, along with a call for "situational self-reflexivity" and "anti-models" as textual mirrorings, to deal with questions of difference and marginality, "braided" in with mainstream, dominant voices in a more consensual and equal way without being compromised or watered down. These deeper textual concepts provide new entry points and ways of reading pedagogical narratives that reveal places of difficulty. They also reveal possibilities for (re)constituting the author and the reader. We move beyond any particular story toward a more encompassing understanding of what it is to teach, to write about that teaching without traditional constraints, and to read per/sonal narratives. Understanding and interpretation from those stories inform the apprenticeship of beginning teachers and the thorough, intensive professional development of continuing teachers.

Chambers (1984) describes that profound responsibility that is passed onto our understanding of the narrator: Becoming narrator means a reconciliation with time and work, while being subject to the "danger of loss of experience in telling" and attending to "residues," that task of "reconstituting something lost," knowing that "self-knowledge and self-acceptance is not enough—validation is needed by others. . . . To have others accept the story is to have others accept one's self" (pp. 105, 116).

What of the difficulty if the story is rejected as too difficult to know, or is unwanted?

My preconceptual writing becomes conscious research as I work toward deeper understanding, including myself and beyond into educational enterprises. By this fourth orbital I begin to feel I have gone too far, cannot turn back, except hermeneutically. I feel scholarly and pedagogic imperatives to stay with the difficulties I have opened through narrative. Intensive work in narrative craft is called for: that of attending to issues of *muthos* (the arrangement of events) and *dianoia* (the faculty of saying what is possible and pertinent in given circumstances).[3] This writerly reflection establishes conditions that enable the next orbital of analysis—engagement with hermeneutics, noticing what is possible and not possible to say, what is being both revealed and concealed.

Narrative research, then, requires a reconstitution of the individual self within the spatio-temporal structure of a community of mortal narrators. Each life story occurs in relation to all the other life stories. Autobiographical writing in narrative form keeps open key questions of serious inquiry in the writing, reading, and interpreting of any story: Who holds the *pen?* What and how is she writing, and why? Who am *I* holding this pen? How am *I* writing? Why do *I* persist with stories of teaching difficulty and the self? What is my role as teaching author and researching reader of my own stories?

Grumet (as cited in Chamberlain, 1990) offers a way for me to think about those questions—whose answers continually shift—by taking up her notion of dialectic in narrative perspective as she describes the

> dialectic of written communication[4] as an interaction of distanciation and appropriation [that] offers us a way of understanding how these texts of educational experience may serve as wedges that we drive between layers of that experience. Distanciation is achieved as the written text edges away from the original intention of the author and the reception of his [her] original audience, and makes sense without being limited in reference to the original context of the dialogical situation from which it emerged.[5] Appropriation is achieved by the reader who takes to himself [herself] what was once alien.
>
> —p. 14

Grumet explains:

> The text projects the possibility of new worlds by offering a sense that, though drawn
> from the dialectical interplay of actual contexts, transcends them, leaving the reader
> with the possibility and option of finding within himself and his community the capac-
> ity to realize the world the text signifies.
>
> –p. 19

Who indeed "Holds the Pen" which signifies *the* world? The position of the
"I" in questions of author/narrator, the (signified) story, and the
reader/audience lead us into the craft of writing the self, of auto/biography,
without an intermediary narrator holding the pen for us, someone who might
misrepresent us, who might lie, who might not serve our best interests, who can
never really know what it is to be "this I." But when "I" comes to write itself,
what then is the point of the narrative? What does it mean? How shall we
interpret it? How shall the "I" (personal eye) come to write itself?[6]

In feminist critical theory, one of the vital issues focuses around the need to
situate the "I" of the (female) subject. Behind that issue lie questions of perception, personal history, central consciousness, voice, authorial intent, point of
view, and the multiple relationships among those questions in light of the
writer, the reader, and the reading—all these have become explicitly problematic as I develop my narrative craft, as I see and am seen in autobiographical
and often fictive work.

Chamberlain (1990) sets a question for himself at the beginning of his text
Narrative Perspective in Fiction: "Can narrative perspective provide a medium
through which to disclose potential meanings and through which to share the
lived experience of narrative texts from both familiar and culturally different
worlds today?" As I continue to narratively write my way through difficulty in
the (teaching) self, my answer to Chamberlain's questions is a consistent and
resounding *yes*. In narrative there is often a hermeneutic *turn*, where the familiar
becomes strange and the strange, familiar. That narrative process continues to
move me toward understanding of both difficulty and self.

French feminist Hélène Cixous addresses some of these points of entry
into difficulties of self and narrative (and its craft) in her essay of "Coming to
Writing," which begins with a very early, primal description of coming to know
and respond to the face of her "[M]other," and the other "Faces" that "give
birth to me, contain my lives." She describes her fear of separation, from birth,
and claims that "at first I really wrote to bar death. . . . I write the encore. Still
here, I write life" (as cited in Jensen, 1991, p. 5). Cixous writes poignantly of all

the difficult things Caputo pointed to in his (cold) radical hermeneutics.[7] She continues:

> Writing: a way of leaving no space for death, of pushing back forgetfulness, of never letting oneself be surprised by the abyss. Of never becoming resigned, consoled; never turning over in bed to face the wall and drift asleep again as if nothing had happened; as if nothing could happen.
>
> —as cited in Jensen, 1991, p. 3

My own teaching/writing self must not become resigned, consoled. I do not want to turn over in my pedagogical bed to face the educative wall and drift asleep again. I need to be absolutely attentive to the abyss, to what could happen, to life. Writing one's teaching life calls for noticing the desire for consolation, the need for sleep, the fear of the abyss, the anger against nothingness, and then consciously living beyond those constraints.

In "The Laugh of the Medusa" Cixous pontificates that once a (teaching) woman has "come to writing" out of a psychic need, more social and political functions can be attended to:

> Woman must write herself: must write about women and bring women to writing, from which they have been driven away as violently as from their bodies—for the same reasons, by the same law, with the same fatal goal. Woman must put herself into the text—as into the world and into history—by her own movement.
>
> —as cited in Hoy, 1990, p. 481

Cixous also warns women who write to beware, but implores us to keep writing ourselves as the signified and signifiers of our own narratives: "Everything trembling when the question of meaning strikes" (as cited in Jensen, 1991, p. 6).[8]

She imagines languaging/languaged women narrators: "Ourselves in writing like fish in the water, like meanings in our tongues, and the transformation in our unconscious lives" (as cited in Jensen, 1991, p. 58). For Cixous, writing is the main way to (re)constitute the (woman) self.

In 1992 while reading *Writing a Woman's Life* (Heilbrun, 1988), and after reading the invitations to women from Woolf (1929) in *A Room of One's Own* and from Cixous to write their lives, I began to imagine what it would be to write a woman's teaching life. What would it be like to write my own (hidden) life as a fiction writer with hermeneutic and feminist grounding who teaches "for a living"? The question of ethics and fiction/autobiography definitions of truth began to emerge. How much "can" a storyteller tell? How much *may* the storyteller tell?[9]

Partial answers about how and what might be written came from Heilbrun (1988) who discusses three of the four ways[10] to write a woman's life:

1. The woman herself may tell it, in what she chooses to call an *autobiography*.
2. She may tell it in what she chooses to call *fiction*.
3. A biographer, woman or man, may write the woman's life in what is called a *biography*.
4. The woman may write her own life in advance of living it, unconsciously, and without recognizing or naming the process. (p. 11)

But any way "she" writes it, there is some risk involved. As Nancy Miller (as cited in Heilbrun, 1988) says: "To justify an unorthodox life by writing about it is to re-inscribe the original violation, to re-violate masculine turf" (p. 11).

This talk of "turf" needs to be called into question. Writing a life truthfully need not violate person or space. It will be added to the vast collection of human voices—yes—but for me to say that it must be either man's voice or woman's voice is to fall back into reductionist dualism. I agree with Mary Jacobus that there is a question about "the nature of women's access to culture and their entry into literary discourse" (as cited in Heilbrun, 1988, p. 12), but all of us, women and men, need to write in spite of the original, social, and political difficulties in pursuit of understanding through written, self-languaged narratives.

One of the main historical turning points in women's autobiography (at least for Heilbrun) occurred between the publication of *Plant Dreaming Deep* by May Sarton in 1968 and her subsequent book *Journal of a Solitude* in 1973, where she "deliberately retold the record of her anger [and that] what has been forbidden to women is anger, together with the open admission of the desire for power and control over one's life" (Heilbrun, 1988, p. 13). Heilbrun claims that not many women before that had written truthful autobiographies. At the time I first read her work, I balked at what I took to be a corpus of "lying" texts constructed by women, but having struggled with narrative craft intensively for years now, I think Heilbrun raises important problematic questions about accessible, *acceptable*, and too-difficult truths with which "woman-I" must engage and find courage to keep writing with more open accuracy about the truths of experience. The phenomenological veracity required in narrative form is what is required for rigorous narrative scholarship.

Feminists have been taking that task on as a critical, political need within narrative craft: "Feminist ideology is another word for trying to understand, in the life of woman, the life of the mind, which is, as Nancy Miller has noted, 'not coldly cerebral but impassioned'" (Heilbrun, 1988, p. 265). There is concern that "Women have been deprived of the narratives, or the texts, plots, or examples, by which they might assume power over—take control of—their own lives. The women's movement began with discussions of power, power-lessness, and the question of sexual politics" (p. 17). Heilbrun takes as one of her main projects the examination of

> how women's lives have been contrived, and how they may be written to make clear, evident, out in the open, those events, decisions, and relationships that have been invisible outside of women's fictions [and she wants to] suggest new ways of writing the lives of women, as biographers, autobiographers, or, in the anticipation of living new lives, as the women themselves.
>
> –p. 18

In my work throughout this text I have been particularly interested in ways of (re)constituting the (teaching) self by narrating that self in a theoretical and practical feminist undertaking "to articulate a self-consciousness about women's identity both as inherited cultural fact and as process of social construction [and to] protest against the available fiction of female becoming" (Miller, as cited in Heilbrun, 1988, p. 18).

Reader of Our Teaching: Witnessing Difficulty

The narrative craft of the writer is obviously tantamount to such projects, but the narrative craft of a reader is also a critical part of the life of a narrative:

> The ways we read women's lives need to change as well; unlike the reading of the classics—or of men's lives, or of women's lives as events in the destinies of men—which always include the frames of interpretations that have been elaborated over generations of critical activity, reading women's lives needs to be considered in the absence of a "structure of critical" or biographical commonplaces.
>
> –Heilbrun, 1988, p. 129

We are reminded, "It all needs to be invented, or discovered, or resaid" (Heilbrun, 1988, p. 19). Heilbrun cautions scholars, writers, and readers concerning an ethical and political attention to differences in intellectual and theoretical agendas, warning "We are in danger of refining the theory and scholarship at the expense of the lives of the women who need to experience the fruits of research" (p. 20).

There exists a longer tradition of the confessional (naive storying?) nature of early autobiography, but there is a strong call for exploration of the blurring of lines between (auto)biography and fiction, as writers strain and struggle with language to write themselves, (re)constitute them/selves from the journeys and landscapes of their lived/imagined experiences. This is a perpetual challenge in my own work. It is clear that the

> concept of biography has changed profoundly in the last two decades, biographies of women especially so. But while the biographers of men have been challenged on the "objectivity" of their interpretation, biographers of women have had not only to choose one interpretation over another but, far more difficult, actually to reinvent the lives their subjects led, discovering from what evidence they could find the processes and decision, the choices and unique pain, that lay beyond the life stories of these women. The choices and pain of the women who did not make a man the center of their lives seemed unique, because there were no models of the lives they wanted to live, no exemplars, no stories. These choices, this pain, those stories, and . . . how, in short one may find the courage to be an "ambiguous woman."
>
> —Heilbrun, 1988, p. 31

"These choices, this pain, those stories," and finding courage are also of interest to me as I examine ways of writing my teaching life. As a researching teacher of teachers I need to hear (re)iterated the vital importance of those stories:

> What matters is that lives do not serve as models; only stories do that. And it is a hard thing to make up stories to live by. We can only retell and live by the stories we have read or heard. We live our lives through texts. They may be read, or chanted, experienced electronically, or come to us, like the murmurings of our mothers, telling us what conventions demand. . . . These stories have formed us all; they are what we must use to make new fictions, new narratives. There is no "objective" [sic] or universal tone in literature, for however long we have been told there is.
>
> —Heilbrun, 1988, p, 40

The teaching profession has been feminized by history, by society, by government, by practice, but if we are to continue to learn and be reflective about our work, we need to engage in stories about teaching lives and to tell, write, and rewrite our lives as specific individuals who are mattering fields-of-self, worthy of narrating and being narrated. Teachers carry all the stories from past lives, culture, history, disciplines so that new beings can make their own new narratives, perhaps of care, of peace, of ecology, of health, of ethical being.

Having explored naive storying, psychological expression, and psycho-therapeutic ethics, concerned for narrative craft that includes conventions of structure and authorship, style, and diction, I return to the narrative as writer again in this fourth orbital of narrative interpretation. In my return to the orbitals of analysis, I re/cognize more and more subtext emerging from the stories I have written. Behind the bravado of their language in "The Anger in Our Miss Maple," I see the frailty, despair, and fear of Maple's students. Under the roll call, contrived plans, and impromptu spelling test, the anger, fear, and sarcasm reveal a brutal desire in Miss Maple for control, as much of herself as anything. Close-up I see the dangers of living unexamined lives, think Ms. Maple needs professional and personal help, worry she will completely break apart, perhaps be lost forever like so many others I have known, because the signs are all there of a teacher at risk.

I hear the language between Miss Maple and the students and understand that there is no lingering together across their linguistic chasms. There is an attempt at carrying the curriculum without honouring the narratives of the teacher or the students or the one they construct together, and the result is disastrous. I see the generations of curricular decay in the rows of disabled desks, the routines, the bells, the scripted, crippled dialogue.

But it is precisely at those ruptures that space opens for the possibility of something more generative to emerge. The vomiting is a violent rejection of all that came before, an emptying out of the whole self to create space for some-thing new. In this narrative craft orbital, cognitively and affectively, I go back to look for consistent images of anger. I look for progressive, incremental escala-tion in the tension of the story and in matters of craft, start again to edit, to add, to rewrite, to substitute stronger words and push boundaries further and fur-ther. I re/work what happened or might have happened.

In travelling these narrative landscapes of history, recollective reconstruc-tion, and future imaginative plots, questions of *form* (genre, plot structure, analyzable features) and *content* (characters, descriptions, themes, human mes-sages) are always problematic. Questions of boundary/relationship between fiction and truth are ancient but critical as well: Did this really happen? How much of this is true? What are the facts in this story? Even more perplexing philosophical, literary, political, and hermeneutic questions emerge about perspective (standpoint, position, point of view, voice) in narrative. Ethical and political concerns by feminists and minorities about wrongful appropriation of voice ("even" in fiction) are raised, challenged, and re-asked against story texts that claim truthfulness.

Other critical questions about the function of fiction become an integral part of literary analysis: Whose story is this? Whose needs are being served? What is the usefulness of narrative? What about the (developing, changing) patterns, the (tacit, preconscious, unexpected, required) revelations, and the (inner, outer) reflections that are revealed in the course of narration? How do we make sense of our lived lives? What kinds of information do stories con/vey to the young about a troubled world in progress? Why are narratives a way of connecting the self to the world?

Such questions are foregrounded in my choice to write my own stories rather than find stories as a collecting researcher. From among the dozens of teachers I asked about difficulty in teaching, I got only two or three narratives and then became aware that I could not ethically include such stories from others, being mindful of the difficulties around appropriation. Still, once my stories were written and developed to the form they appear here, those larger questions applied to all stories also must be applied to mine. Each question illuminates a different portion of a narrative text to me as the writer of them, and I continually go back and back to rewriting, editing, reading, and rewriting. I have abandoned all these stories, perhaps with the exception of "Miss Maple," long before I am ready.[11]

As a writer who also values literature (moving from the self to universal questions about self) and who has had the kind of relationship with text that I have, I always must attend to questions of craft. How does the story shift in meaning if I change the point of view? Why do I write many of the narratives here in the distant "third-person, omniscient" narrator? What are the points of view in each story? How are the elements of short story balanced? How do modern concerns of emplotment relate to ones of *dianoia* (saying what is possible in a given situation) and *bricolage* (braiding up the threads) of one's life in a text that continues to depart into the secondary fictive world?

Beginnings and endings are altered, and I rewrite the order of things and look at what happened differently each time. I (re)member more detail, provide information within dissembling, and watch for a tiny detail that has gone unnoticed and that is suddenly illuminated just as I am about to withdraw or redraw it. What I thought the story was about takes on a different shape, metamorphoses into another story. Stories invite other stories, and I begin again, back in naive storying or ahead to hermeneutic quests of interpretation and understanding.

In my research within the narrative craft sphere, questions of difficulty emerge around my own writing abilities and shortcomings, my own writing process.[12] Even with years of reading and teaching language and having studied Latin, French, and German, I still prowl in etymological and semantic texts to explore, find, and reach further for language that might come closer to what I mean. I always struggle to find the right word, consider the nuances of connotation, denotation, and contextual and historical usage. Communication difficulties about the expressive and receptive functions of the language arts also arise, as readers find different textual entry points. Those multiple interpretations need to be laid out next to one another. Perhaps the more finely crafted a story is, the more interpretations/inquiries are possible.

The power of narrative partly has to do with the way the story is told, and that takes time and skill and practice and multiple editing. I have had a focused, twenty-five-year writing apprenticeship and still rail at the literary muse for failing me. I notice the imperfections of each draft and have come to understand that the best draft of any narrative still dwells in the mind.

The German poet Rainer Maria Rilke (1985) helps with forgiveness of such imperfections when he reminds us in *Love and Other Difficulties* that we must live the questions and resolve always to be beginning. Each new story I write throws me back to the beginning of the writing process: It does not get easier, so some of the most important work at this phase has to do with the writing self learning patience and discipline in staying with the difficulty of writing. As I mentioned earlier, I continue to struggle with an overactive censor and critic, silencing it by giving myself permission to write badly, first freewriting to separate the writing process from the editing process (Elbow, 1973, 1981). I understand that there will be at least seven or eight drafts as a minimum and in several cases arduous rewriting and editing as many as thirty or forty times through the whole text.

The raw story calls for attention to the language I use: Is that really how I sound? Are those really the words I choose as I write about my self and my work? Is this the diction I want in my teacherly self? How will reconstructing my discourse change the way I think about and understand my teaching self and the difficulties in which it engages? I am compelled through writing and reading my narratives to pay heed to and hear my own voice as though from another. This reflexive process makes it imperative and possible to stay with all difficulty I discover in my stories: My language is a just-safe-enough place to re/cognize my self in teaching. What I am unable to say is also there underneath the text. I wonder what other teachers are unable to say or do not know they can speak and yet go on teaching.

Writer of Teaching Work: Re-Quilling Narrative Truth

The very process of narrative work, as I hope is shown in this book, is the process of working on the (teaching, professional) self. My life and living are laid out for all to see, whether I intend it or not. But as a constructed narrative text, there is sense, understanding, awareness about what I am learning and who and how I am becoming.

Giving a text of one's life stories and fictions is not easy to undertake. There is a period of silence while the reader reads alone (or may hear the story), and then time seems to be required while the narrative is taken in, turned over, considered, before different conversation, comments, criticisms, and responses begin. The conversations that have ensued from some of the stories others have read have always been surprising, and often, after feedback from people, I will go back to a story to revise, edit, add, reorder so that the sense is more focused. I use readers to gauge the gap between intention and result, and even in that exchange meaning shifts as text shifts in a continual quilting bee of language. It seems at the narrative craft level of research that I shift from discovery of self revealed in the text, to the self as writer, learning from the "read" text. In this way the text begins to teach me about reading and writing the self.[13]

The second work with others is as a reader who writes. As I read the work of others I notice how they make their sentences, what words they use, how they achieve the effects they do, how they write and talk about their own narrative work, and am moved by the sheer beauty and skill of writing by writers such as Virginia Woolf, Wallace Stegner, Margaret Laurence, Charles Dickens, Nadine Gordimer, William Trevor, Jane Rule, Iris Murdoch, Peter Ackroyd, Carol Shields, Michael Ontdaatje, Aritha van Herk, Timothy Findley, Margaret Atwood. I return to my own writing craft to improve the texts I will be offering among the larger writing community to a community of readers and teachers, even though this is not the main purpose of my work on the self in difficulty.

How other teachers engage with these stories is not for me to determine, although I am interested in how people might read and work with these narratives. That is work that extends far beyond this document and may become a larger part of my work in the future. But there is some part of the writing-author-me who surely does write beyond myself for others as an invitation to enter into conversation about the self, difficulty, and teaching.

Pleasure in writing and word carpentry for me come in the creative aspect of making something good and useful. Stories give us information, but they also give us a kind of experience through the phenomenon of reading. Meaning begins to be revealed and multiple interpretations are made visible just by playing with the way a narrative might be written. Possibility of heuristic discovery exists behind every attempt at narrating. New metaphors for the self and being insist themselves as I write narrative to find out what I think and know, what my values are, and what living means. I am perpetually astonished with what is revealed as a result of careful narrative work.

I learn about the way I and other teachers speak and move in relation to students, about the way we talk about teaching, what we notice or consider important enough to contextualize in a plot, what "knowledge is of most worth," and what aims of education and pedagogic creeds we hold. The style, diction, and tone connote layers of experience against settings and (un)expected events that are the stuff of our daily lives.

There can be an affective shift in consciousness—like hearing an opus of music switch from a minor to a major key in the movement from one chord to the next. Bubbles of unplanned laughter at the self tickle the back of my learning throat, and sudden welling of tears arises when I actually understand something I never have before: writing releases an unkind tension and the warmth of hope in authentic being grows again. Perhaps some people live to write; I think I write to live and understand more fully.

Internarrative: The Abysmal Performance of Miss Tofelize

Just as a person who is always asserting that he is too good-natured is the very one from whom to expect, on some occasion, the coldest and most unconcerned cruelty; so when a group sees itself as the bearer of civilization, this very belief will betray it into behaving barbarously at the first opportunity.

–Simone Weil, as cited in Zwicky, 1992

I used to think if you fell from grace it was more likely than not the result of one stupendous error, or else an unfortunate accident. I hadn't learned that it can happen so gradually you don't lose your stomach or hurt yourself in the landing. You don't necessarily sense the motion. I've found it takes at least two and generally three things to alter the course of a life. You slip around the truth once, and then again, and one more time, and there you are, feeling, for the moment, that it was sudden, your arrival at the bottom of the heap.

–Hamilton, 1994, p. 1

"Doria? Oh good, I knew you'd be there. Ides of August again, my dear. God, I envy the steadiness of a woman like you who can live and work in the same place for thirty years. You must know absolutely everybody in this town. And teaching for all those years—well, we all know students tell their teachers far more than they ought to. They are lucky to have a trusted confidante like you. Hope you are properly appreciated. Anyway, Doria, I appreciate you and you know I still need your help again planning this year. Shall we say this evening around eight? I can't possibly work in this heat until after the sun goes down."

Mrs. Doria Gray, recently widowed teacher of language arts and school counsellor, hesitated on the other end of the school line. She always found it hard to say no to Fausta Tofelize and rarely succeeded. Embarrassingly often, Doria was flattered by this charming and lively middle-aged woman. They had taught in adjacent classrooms for three years. Fausta had even arranged that. Within days of being hired to teach literature and drama at the academic private school, she had inveigled the headmaster into giving her the large classroom next to Doria's. She confided to him that it was a selfish request for the room: With no windows and down at the end of the hall, it was perfect for teaching drama and film and for having plays and literary readings without disturbing other classes. She laid her surprisingly warm hand on his bare arm and said she knew she could count on him to understand the needs of a drama teacher and grant her request.

The headmaster thought Miss Tofelize one of the most classically beautiful women he had ever seen, with a reserved presence of self-possession rare in a teacher as young as she must be. She had a way of making any request seem reasonable. He found himself wanting to offer his assistance for anything she might want. The headmaster, like Doria Gray, began to find it difficult to say no to Miss Tofelize.

Fausta was well aware of Doria's reluctance on the other end of the phone and paid attention as the woman hesitated, "I don't know, Fausta, do you really think it is necessary?"

"Your cautiousness is becoming, Doria, but of course it is necessary. You know I count on your experience and knowledge so that I can get the school year off to the kind of start we both want for our students. Now if you will just bring the class lists from my mailbox there and say, the first ten cumulative files, we can get started tonight. I have made your favourite lobster bisque. Even as we speak, there are two lovely bottles of a private reserve Piesporter intended to remind you of your favourite cycling trip down the Alsatian wine route when you were a young woman in love with your Bernard."

"My goodness, Fausta, I don't remember telling you that story, but you don't even like light German wines . . . and I really don't think we ought to be taking . . . "

"Exactly, you see how much I will sacrifice for you. See you here at eight? You are wonderful to save me once again. I owe you. I will sign you up for the Theatre Club again this year. How's that? Remember the fun we had? Tonight, then." And she hung up.

Fausta's promise suggested she knew of Doria's weakness for theatre, probably born out of an old desire to be an actress. She loved to come and be audience to the goings-on in Fausta's drama program, was careful not ever to get in the way, and when that silly school-spirit, club-mentor sheet came around, Fausta would just add Doria's name to the list as she did last year, to fulfill both their extracurricular obligations under Fausta's Theatre Club. For that reason alone Doria was grateful. She told herself she had something to offer to Fausta as well: Her new laser printer would be very useful when it came time for producing programs and tickets. That was something tangible she could contribute to the Theatre Club.

. . .

During the bisque appetizer and the main course of scallops on spinach linguini with dill cream sauce, Fausta amused, entertained, listened compassionately, and proffered the always financially struggling Doria ample loan money so she could build herself a proper greenhouse. Images of gentle spring gardening in her early retirement floated into her mind. Although Doria was only fifty-five, she could pass for seventy. Her face seemed to wear each school year's burdens visibly—especially the last couple of years. It was as though all the transgressions of students and teachers alike, during her thirty-year teaching career, had etched themselves directly onto her body. Her students remained perpetually youthful, of course, but each September on the first day of classes, it oddly occurred to her that she might be the only one who was aging.

Only when she was with Fausta, whom she didn't really know all that well, did she feel lighter, younger, and as though her own teaching work actually mattered to someone other than herself. Perhaps it was silly, but she really felt noticed by Fausta. When they worked together, Doria stopped worrying that she might be only mediocre in her teaching. And now, Fausta was offering such lovely help so that Doria could have that little conservatory she had wanted all her life. In fact, Fausta made it almost seem as though it would be a pleasure to see Doria have something she had always dreamed of building. She didn't say no and suddenly they were making lists of varietals and best horticultural suppliers, discussing lighting and misting nozzles, and sketching diagrams for the best place on her lot with handy access to the house in case of bad weather. She had nearly forgotten the reason for dinner. She drained her third glass of wine quickly as Fausta reached out to pour from the second bottle of Piesporter.

Not until after the exquisite crème caramel and cappuccinos, sprinkled with freshly grated cinnamon and Belgian chocolate, did Fausta ask to see the register lists of the students. She resisted the urge to snatch the pages away from Doria who insisted upon taking her own methodical time about reading aloud the names of all forty-five new students who would form their three classes. None of the names Doria read meant anything to Fausta. Yet. Although she only needed to learn ten tonight, Fausta did begin to note the cultural backgrounds of the surnames, already thinking she would have to "bone up" on Japanese Noh plays, French morality plays, Oberammergau—those pieces of drama and literature that would quickly hook into the collective unconscious of her various students, drawing them in before they understood why their school work with Miss Tofelize was becoming so compelling.

"Doria, no need to read the whole list again, dear. Bring them all with you and let's go into the library, shall we? More fitting and comfortable there, don't you think? Armagnac or Courvoisier—you like it heated in a snifter, don't you?"

Doria was a little soft around the edges of common reality by this time, surprised and pleased Fausta remembered how she liked her brandy, and only fleetingly registered the understanding that Fausta had a way of asking questions that provided an illusion of choice. The sensation was almost that of being guided down a slightly too-fast river, so that when one finally took notice of the unfamiliar banks on either side, there was a disorienting shock about just how far one had drifted. She chastised herself for her appetite of the grape and made a postprandial promise to herself to be more moderate and pay better attention to her health in the future. "Courvoisier, please, Fausta. Thank you. That was a wonderful dinner. You are a heavenly cook."

"Not really." Fausta set the heated brandy on the Celtic silver coaster Doria admired so much. "Now may I have the lists, please?" She set down her ice water on a small kiln-dried wood tea table and chose the fired hemlock-burl chair opposite the leather reading recliner into which Doria had already happily settled. That way they could share the tapestried footstool Fausta had obtained in another lifetime.

"First ten names, Doria. Read me the cum[1] files first and then tell me everything you know about each of them. I want to know which people matter to them, who their parents and siblings and significant others are. You know their strengths, weaknesses, longings, disgraces, secrets, ambitions, and I don't. I need to know everything about my students—who they are and what they require. In order to meet their learning needs, Doria. You understand, don't you?"

Doria nodded wearily to her friend. Perhaps it was the nearly too-generous warmth of the room that made her wonder just how good a friend Fausta might be. After taking a sip of the startling amber liquid, though, Doria began to read and talk to Fausta about the names on the class lists she held in her hands. She felt that Fausta properly appreciated her keen powers of observation and understanding of each student's relational context. It was true, in trusted position of teacher, she had learned far more about each family than any other person in the town, except perhaps the priest, and was uniquely positioned to give Fausta the information for which she had asked.

Each student was described in great detail as Doria painted precise verbal portraits of the public and private narrative histories of every student. She didn't suppose it hurt to reveal all these things to Fausta. She was a colleague. After all, she would be teaching these students soon, and the background information could be helpful to her in her methods and lesson planning. Because Doria was aware of the rapt and engaged attention on her by her friend, she continued to read in spite of the lateness of the hour and her need for rest.

It did bother Doria a little about all this keenness for knowledge of students, but certainly the last two years showed Fausta to be very capable indeed, with her students having the top grades in the school. Only one or two young girls had dropped out of her classes the first year and then last year, maybe two or three, but probably not serious enough students for the academic pressure at Worthington's Private.

Oh, yes. There was that one awful thing last term about the Wilson boy's suicide. Doria had thought Fausta was very close to the boy and his family, but it was clear she had done all she could, and ultimately managed to take the tragedy incredibly well. After that horrid ordeal, mid-February when the rest of the teachers were flagging, Fausta seemed to get her second wind and organized good ideas from other people into accomplished activities and events for the benefit of every one. It somehow didn't matter that she got the credit for all the ideas too, since she created such a "lift" to the school and managed in a remarkable way to remove the dull gray from each of their winters.

The Wilson family had moved away, not long after, probably to get a fresh start.

Perhaps that was why Fausta wanted to know so much about her students, to prevent anything like that from happening again. It must have upset her more than she'd let on, Doria supposed. If, as Fausta's friend, she could help, she supposed it was all right that she had transgressed policy and taken home the confidential files from the school office. In the middle of her reading, she glanced over at Fausta for reassurance of friendship and was rewarded with a lovely warm smile and gentle encouragement, "Continue, Doria; your astonishing knowledge about my students is more helpful to me than you realize. I can't say how much I appreciate your working with me."

Time whispered past midnight, and in her growing fatigue Doria did not notice that with each name completed, Fausta became more animated. Doria begged to quit for the night, but Fausta insisted that they finish the first ten "case histories," as she liked to call them. It was well after two in the morning when Fausta walked Doria to her car, aware of the woman's nervousness about being out alone at night. When Doria was safely locked in her car and had rolled down the window to say goodnight, Fausta handed her a signed blank cheque and said, "When you are ready to order the plants, let me know and I'll give you another cheque."

"Oh, Fausta, my goodness. You are far too generous. Really. Maybe I shouldn't . . . "

"That's what money is for, Doria. Write in the amount you want and enjoy it. Now then, tomorrow—again at eight? I want to finish the list by the end of the week. That gives me time to arrange to see each of the parents and interview each student individually before school starts in three weeks. No time to waste, friend, so bring on the next ten souls."

Doria faltered at the slightly too-wide smile, but she gratefully accepted the cheque because it could also make a couple of overdue payments on her credit cards and allow her to buy materials for constructing her beloved greenhouse. Of course she would pay it back as soon as possible. "Well, Fausta, I am not really comfort . . . "

"Splendid. How about chicken yakatori and a light rice dish and just a boysenberry sorbet for dessert? I know you want to be healthier in your eating. Only one fine bottle of Chardonnay tomorrow, I promise, and I wouldn't dream of tempting you with brandy again. Perhaps just a tiny cup of warmed sake. Settled? See you at eight, sharp. Oh, and thanks so much, Doria. The privileged information you possess about our students is such a help to me, so I can get on with my planning for the year."

Doria laughed nervously and, not quite against her will, agreed to come the following night with the next ten cumulative, confidential student files. "Honestly Fausta, I don't know where you get all your incredible energy from. You seem to be the same age as I am and I am exhausted."

Admittedly, the evening air was torrid, but it was the uncommonly hot breath from Fausta's sibilant words, "See you soon, my dear," that imperceptibly singed the delicate downy hairs along the edge of Doria's ear. She involuntarily drew away and anxiously glanced up at the lithe, standing figure of her teaching friend clad in black, but her apprehensions were dispelled once more by the glow of Fausta's persistent smile directed almost intimately toward her weary confederate.

As Doria's old Mercury eased away from the curb, Fausta smiled again, this time to herself. She relied with certainty on the knowledge that her new students also would have difficulty saying no to Miss Tofelize.

Chapter 7: Fifth Orbital—
Hermeneutic Enterprise

The returning of life to its original difficulty is a returning of the possibility of the living Word. It is a return to the essential generativity of human life, a risk, and ambiguity that such generativity entails. Hermeneutic inquiry is thus concerned with the ambiguous nature of life itself.

–Jardine, 1992b, p. 119

Hermeneutic Philosophy as a Companion Lens

Once I have analyzed the narrative craft, working with the four language systems,[1] I reach further, for hermeneutic philosophy to interpret, explain, and understand much more, as painful and as necessary as that can become. Cold hermeneutic shudders ensue as I confront the essential difficulties, not just of teaching but also of *being*, which are at the centre of teaching. Hermeneutic philosophy deepens my interpretive thinking because it involves a way of working that includes the messiness of human daily life while searching for the rich, layered qualities of meaning and understanding about what it is to be fully engaged in worthwhile projects. Hermeneutic approaches are

sensitive to both purposive and unintended covering up [and] openly dialogic in nature: the returning to the object of inquiry again and again, each time with an increased understanding, and a more complete interpretive account . . . [which] is more modest in its aims than is a formal set of rules or causal law, but . . . subtle and complex, intellectually satisfying, and more appropriate to human action, embracing the historical openness, the ambiguity and opacity, the deceptions, dangers, and delights that action manifests.

–Packer, 1985, p. 1092

Reading hermeneutics, both as a discipline of thought and understanding and as a mode of seeing and interpreting human action, has changed how I research narratives and conduct narrative research in education. Hermeneutics has influenced the way I become aware of questions, how I deal with "conceptual baggage" (Kirby & McKenna, 1989, pp. 49-53), the way I "do research" (emergent, recursive, living in the "margins"). Using a hermeneutic lens as part of every narrative analysis has altered forever the way I interpret texts and create meaning. I pay attention to Shelley Davis Finson's point (cited in Kerby & McKenna, 1989, p. 33) that interpretation of data "requires a critical consciousness which recognizes the systemic nature and ideological dimension of oppression . . . [not] in regard to the words of the women, but rather in regard to the context within which and out of which [we] are functioning."

The roots of early hermeneutics, with its essential concern for the multiplicity of meanings, can be found in philosophy, theology, and jurisprudence, all disciplines deeply concerned with the nature and purpose of interpretation.[2] The first recorded reference to hermeneutics appears to be attributed to Aristotle's *Peri Hermeneias*, which was a treatise on the "logic of statements" having to do with the "grammatical structure by which subject and predicate are united in human speech to reveal the character of things" (Mueller-Vollmer, 1985, p. 1). The "character of things" is the main characteristic in the language of every narrative. Even in 350 BCE the inextricable relationship between language and meaning was being systematically and deeply explored. That strong thread/theme of the insistence/reliance on the relationship between thought and language is one that has remained, even in the most radicalized forms of post/modern hermeneutics.

The other important ancient root of hermeneutics lies with the etymology of the word itself. Hermes was the messenger of the Greek gods. The task of such a messenger was formidable: one who must first of all be conversant with all the words and referents of the gods, as well as their idiom and intent. Hermes had to be capable of understanding and interpreting for himself what the gods wanted to convey before beginning to "translate, articulate, and explicate their intention to mortals" (Mueller-Vollmer, 1985, p. 1). The task that faced Hermes also faces post/modern educators everywhere, as messengers of society's curriculum to its youth, of the wise to their innocents. That task requires linguistic competence, excellent communication, lucid discourse, and profound understanding as we position ourselves as translators and questioners of human meaning and interpretation across all disciplines. The second main thread that has remained central to the hermeneutic enterprise throughout its lines of development and change has been the attention focused on the question of the complexity and multifaceted network of interpretation and understanding that may be possible.

Teacher as Hermes: Trickster Messengers of Curriculum

The Hermes[3] character is always present in the writing me, the reading me, the curriculum planning me, and the teaching me. From that Hermes character, I learn to hold multiple interpretations while always being aware of the trickster factor in any text—especially my own—where belief and intent can interfere with truths revealed and (un)covered.

Lather (as cited in Packer & Addison, 1990) describes interpretive research as "inquiry that seeks reciprocity; . . . that requires 'self-disclosure on the part of the researcher' . . . and discussions of false-consciousness" (p. 277). Furthermore Lather declares:

> Interpretation is far from being an undisciplined guess. And if an interpretation is not a guess, then evaluating it need not be like testing an hypothesis [but rather an uncovering of truth].

–p. 278

For my purposes I have selected those hermeneuticists whose questions most closely relate to my own. Heidegger and Gadamer, for instance, thought hermeneutics was part of philosophy "because it transcends the confines of individual disciplines and deals instead with their foundations" (Mueller-Vollmer, 1985, p. 4). Historically the study of hermeneutics was acknowledged to be interdisciplinary and concerned with completeness, truthfulness, and sincerity. Hermeneuticists are still concerned with "truthfulness" in interpretation, but by the end of the seventeenth century an important shift began to happen with Schleiermacher and others in the Romantic period. The individuality of the author, in Caputo's (1987) term "the messenger," began to be a critical consideration in any explication of text.[4] That holds true especially in feminist research where the writer declares her or his contextual being so readers may know who holds the pen and be more aware of the identity of the messenger.

Interpreting Difficulty

Historically speaking, one of the earliest thinkers in "modern" (post-modern?) hermeneutics is Friedrich Schleiermacher, whose work challenged the Sophists before him.[5] Schleiermacher's discoveries relied heavily on the linguistic dimensions of human understanding and its importance, rather than the performance of oration and argument. Objectivity in language was replaced for him by a sense of relativity in all languaged acts.

As early as 1795 Schleiermacher advanced the notion of the organic unity of a work and the symbolic nature of art that allowed for the possibility of infinite interpretations of a text. He insisted that understanding was not just a decoding of a "given" meaning or a clearing away of obstacles to "proper" understanding, but an enterprise of illuminating interpretive conditions, such as the development/history of the author (and the reader), context, symbolic subtext, the ability of both the writer and reader to decode and express language, the purpose of the text, the format of the text, the political agenda, and other audience. These essential conditions for the possibility of understanding and its modes of interpretation were substantial alterations of the "ancient" work in hermeneutics of tran/slating and ex/plicating texts. This concern for these conditions—which are shifting, changing, never the same twice—implies a deeper consideration of the inherent relationship and context embedded within every text. Like Schleiermacher, for me, all texts are relational.

The old assumption that a reader could understand everything until a non-sensical passage or contradictions by the author were encountered "went out the window." For Schleiermacher, understanding was a never-ending, (re)constituting task that always contained elements of ambiguity. This perhaps is even truer in the twentieth century. Schleiermacher challenged his readers to approach the meanings of language with both the tacit and the conscious knowledge that what is read and understood will always be only partial. One can interpret and explicate *an* understanding of a text, but there will always be space for other readers and knowers with their (differing) interpretations. Such an orientation influences the way researchers and critics read everything (narratives, historical accounts, semi-annual financial reports from banks, case studies, and so forth), keeping in mind those *Momenten* (described below) of the author, the context, the symbolic subtext, the ability to read, the political agenda, the purpose, other audiences—always rereading and returning and returning to the text(s). Discourse

> has a two-part reference, to the whole language and to the entire thought of its creator, so all understanding of speech consists of two elements [*Momenten*]—understanding the speech as it derives from the language and as it derives from the mind of the thinker.
> –Schleiermacher, 1978, p. 2

For Schleiermacher the primordial author is not fixed but fluid and dynamic, in "flux," something mediated in an act that synthesizes the two planes of the (outer) system of language and the inner system of thought. Speaking/text must be understood as a moment in a person's mental life. For the analyst/critic of other people's writing, the claims that can be made are limited, but even within that framework of "moment," of mental "snapshot," many interpretations are possible.

Schleiermacher insisted that hermeneutics is a "commonsense endeavor" that requires "linguistic talent and a talent for assessing individual human nature" (as cited in Mueller-Vollmer, 1985, p. 4). From grammar to psychology, poetics to allegory, from exposition to interpretation, the work of hermeneutics is a demanding one—linguistically, ethically, philosophically, practically.

Schleiermacher's work (first introduced to me by my teacher Tetsuo Aoki) is particularly helpful in the development of my own thinking about working with the texts of others as a mediator/interpreter/translator. Schleiermacher viewed hermeneutics as the "art of understanding," as I do. The presentation of one's understanding is also the art of interpretation, but the concept of a basic ambiguity, or uncertainty, is an inherent part of all interpretation. Knowing this makes me infinitely more "care-full" in my readings and interpretations of the narratives I use and present in this book.

In any process of understanding, the parts must be understood in relation to the whole, just as the whole can only be understood in relation to its parts, including the form and style in which that happens. For a researcher in education, this relational concept inherent in the work of interpretation is critical. Teachers' writings, students' report cards, school reports, notes to parents, and so on must be understood in relation to the whole educational context in which they exist, and the whole of education and its aims must be understood and interpreted in light of the parts. I bring this assumption, this perspective, to all language I encounter.

Another German influence in hermeneutics as a way of opening my relationship with language and Being was Heidegger's semantic usage of certain persistent concepts that are an integral part of the hermeneutic project. Learning his usage of originary German words, such as *Verstehen* ("understanding," as opposed to *Kenntnis*, meaning "knowledge"), *Dasein* ("being, life, existence," and more), *Sprachkraft* ("linguisticality"), and *Gerede* (which commonly translates as "talk, gossip, rumour," but which Heidegger interpreted as "alienated speech"), has deeply enriched the way I think about things.[6]

This idea of *Gerede* has interesting implications in analyzing narrative texts. I also take Heidegger's concept of *Gerede* as evidence of *Erleichterung* ("desire to make things easier"), which signifies removal from the original difficulty of being.[7] That process (easy way out) with facile, unsatisfactory answers to complex questions seems to lead to a sense of meaninglessness and to non-relational existence. It is also why essential questions of philosophy and theory ought to be understood as rooted in everyday, concrete life and yet not understood.

So part of my own self-conscious hermeneutic work is to keep in mind the layers of interpretation in my own writing and reading process, my personal and cognitive sense of the difficulty of semantic differences. These semantic, grammatical, and syn/tactical differences are concrete evidence of the problematic nature of the common ground that "lies" in the "between" of the multiple perceptive, cognitive, and linguistic relationships between writer/text/reader.

What I also borrow from the early, more idealistic Heidegger includes his principal concepts of *pre-understanding* (common ground), of *Dasein* (being) and of *Zeit* (time). Struggling early in my readings in curriculum studies, I accepted most everything Heidegger wrote, but Caputo helped me to circle back for a more critical look. Heidegger, as Caputo (1987) explains,

> means to get a fix on the flux by inscribing a circular pattern on it in the *logic* of movement . . . in the sense of logos as letting be seen, . . . a movement of "care" [which] involves a tendency to fall in among things and to fall outside the proper concerns of Dasein's own Being. . . . We tend to drift farther and farther away from ourselves . . . toward dispersal and dissipation.
>
> –p. 62[8]

In an attempt to resist dispersal and dissipation, in both teaching and in my interpretations, I circle through the seven research orbitals, keeping in mind Heidegger's central hermeneutic task of "uncovering" that which is not immediately apparent.[9] His sense of "lived horizons" was a particularly compelling theme as I studied difficulty in teaching. Like Heidegger, I always wanted to include past, present, and future, the "hermeneutic circle," of understanding in relation to the whole of which it is a part and vice versa.[10] Very useful in narrative analysis of difficulty in teaching are his three "modes of engagement" distinguished as "ready-to-hand, unready-to-hand, and present-at-hand." Packer (1985) renames these three and further describes the "practical, reflective, and theoretical . . . hermeneutic method [which] is the appropriate approach for the study of human action" (p. 1085). I also, of course, borrow Heidegger's concern about "What Is Called Thinking?", especially in the "difficulty of teaching" (as cited in Krell, 1977, p. 29).

Before Heidegger the philosophical enterprise concerned itself largely with questions "metaphysical, ethical, epistemological, aesthetical" (as cited in Mueller-Vollmer, 1985, p. 32). Heidegger's work, especially in *Being and Time* (1927), seemed to change the focus of philosophical hermeneutics to "understanding, interpretation, and explication" from text created in pre-understanding (p. 33). My own naive narratives were created in pre-understanding, which I have come to refer to as naïve storying (especially early life incidents I have written about, as well as early teaching stories, such as "Getting Clearer Vision" and "Home Run"). Interpretation and understanding come much later through hermeneutic work with the narratives that have gone through editing at the psychological, psychotherapeutic, and narrative craft orbitals, or spheres, of researching engagement.

This partly explains why narrative research can be such a rich place to look for "grounded," relational knowledge and understanding. Narrative and auto/biography often "say" in advance—before there is an awareness by the author of meanings and interpretations embedded in her own words. In telling a story, one kind of understanding evolves; in reading and rereading by the author another understanding emerges. Then in the hands of self as reader and other readers, more understanding and interpretation also gather and reveal meaning and truth. This process of the human action of narrative construction, and then of mining it for meaning, is an essentially hermeneutic project. My main reason for studying hermeneutics is to assist with interpreting narratives in researching teaching difficulty at the site of self.

There are two more influences from Heidegger to which I want to draw attention and which inform my work in thinking about educational relationships in a practical sense: one, revisiting the concepts of his "modes of engagement" and, two, reconsidering what Heidegger said is the "difficult work of the teacher."

The basic mode of engagement is "ready-to-hand," when we are actively engaged in practical projects in the world (preparing lesson plans, taking attendance, answering a student's request for a pen by loaning one). Our skills and abilities are associative rather than cognitive or unconsciously competent, as Tetsuo Aoki would say. In this mode, as Martin Packer (1985) describes this state:

> We are aware of the [whole] situation . . . as a whole network of interrelated projects, possible tasks, thwarted possibilities. . . . Distinct entities [draw] and "withdraw" from our focal awareness of ourselves and our "tools." Both become fused with the activity. . . . The manner in which these aspects of a project are experienced is in turn structured by the personal and historical situations. . . . My action and my situation fit each other, structured on the one hand by my personal concerns and on the other hand by social and personal styles and habitual practices. . . . The skills and practices we bring to our

everyday activity are, for the most part, so over-practiced and familiar to us, so taken for granted, that we are simply unaware of their existence. We act within them, and they rarely, if ever, become problematic. We are not even aware of our ignorance of them. Indeed if we *were* aware of them we would be overwhelmed and unable to continue to act. [When one] very occasionally becomes explicitly aware of the various skills one is putting into practice . . . one's performance deteriorates rapidly. Generally, it is only when we reflect on what we are doing, prompted usually by confronting a problem, that we begin to see the network of interrelated practices, skills, and habits that supports all our apparently simple everyday actions.

–p. 1083

Much of an experienced teacher falls into this first mode of being. Having student teachers is one way to jolt us into thinking about our practical knowledge as we attempt to deconstruct and make visible our taken-for-granted professional skills and habits.

The second mode of engagement Heidegger describes is the "unready-to-hand." As Packer (1985) continues: "The *unready-to-hand* mode is entered when we encounter some problem or upset in our practical activity" (p. 1083). When our expectations, predictions, familiar patterns break, our attention shifts and what calls to our awareness, changes. We can no longer engage in a holistic, dynamic way because something has gone wrong. In teaching this happens often in everyday work. The difficulties come to the fore. Our meaningful work is diminished. Our experience, our actions, and our reflective thought shift. The important part of this hermeneutic way of interpreting what happens is that the difficulty is still "an aspect of the project we are involved in" (p. 1084). This is quite different from the empiricist or rational traditions of wanting to "isolate" abstract, theorize, and decontexualize the object of inquiry amidst real-life difficulty and other concomitant aspects of a complex real situation. In the "unready-to-hand," the real hermeneutic work begins: uncovering what we do not understand and discovering what has "gone wrong." For instance, we begin looking for what has happened so that what we were doing is no longer working very well or has stopped completely. Teacher burnout, or sudden inability in teaching, is a painful example of being unable to work through (in meaningful and useful ways) the experience of the "unready-to-hand" mode in pedagogy.

Heidegger's third mode of engagement is the "present-at-hand" and entered only "when we detach ourselves from ongoing practical involvement in a project at hand" (Packer, 1985, p.1085). We need, as part of our process of fuller understanding, to "step back" to reflect on the more general and—yes—abstract aspects of our engagement. The sense we make, our interpretation, our experience changes yet again in this more thoughtful mode.

The theories of behaviourists and cognitivists seem to function mostly in this "present-at-hand" mode of "objectivity,"[11] but even they do not, as the hermeneuticists do, appear to take fully into account the complex knowledge that participants have about the "will, self-deception, or the ambiguity and polysemy to interpretation that every [human] action shows" (Packer, 1985, p. 1085).

The "ready-to-hand" with all its inherent pre-understanding of being in the practical world is the starting place then for hermeneutic study, that semantic or textual structure of everyday practical activity. Again, "hermeneutics is concerned with meaning, as a sensibleness that can be found to be present or absent in a course of action or in an account of that action" (Packer, 1985, p. 1086). From one perspective, an action has one meaning; from a different perspective it has another. There needs to be openness to several valid, although differing, interpretations.

Another characteristic of practical activity is that it is holistic, and so the hermeneutic account includes the realization that "understanding a particular act is not possible without understanding the context within which it occurs. The 'ready-to-hand' mode involves a complexly woven network that Heidegger called the 'referential totality' which foregrounds all interpretation" (Packer, 1985, p. 1086). This is a very different and complex construction of languaged meaning, from the "findings" and "data" of empirical and rational theoretical approaches. The hermeneutic tendency of attempting to match interpretations with the contextual complexity of real action and real situation seems to be the best fit for relationships in education: knowing and doing what is called for in teaching situations. Understanding and meaning need to be developed around those moments when we "do the right thing" with students and also the results when we do not attend to what was called for and "do the wrong thing." That is what true praxis is about: an honest match in the "living out" between our theories and our practices.

Hermeneutic study of teaching situations as described in narrative accounts of educational work and relationships continues to contribute to our knowledge of the consistencies, inconsistencies, and heuristics (for example, Moustakis, 1990) of the relational truths that are possible between teacher, learner, and what is to be learned.

As Packer (1985) concludes:

> The hermeneutic method employs a detailed progressive description of episodes of social interchange and gradually articulates more and more of their organization. The

grounding of interpretation in "ready-to-hand" understanding . . . is the place to begin an inquiry with this practical everyday understanding . . . [and then] push this understanding into the "unready-to-hand" mode and make it accessible to thematic description. One way in which this is done is by attending to that which is problematic in the original understanding, the lacunae, the gaps, and the contradictions that, in our everyday practice, we habitually gloss over. . . . Our understanding of a person's action (like written text) is never comprehensive or straightforward at the outset. Some sort of articulation and correction of our understanding is necessary, and a hermeneutic inquiry undertakes this in a systematic and coherent manner. The resulting interpretation has the potential to be what Giddens (1976) called "revelatory." It can go beyond what our original, unreflective understanding showed us and also beyond what the agents report they were doing.

–p. 1089[12]

Revelatory research is critical to the educational enterprise and is at the core of what learning is; it keeps the teacher authentically engaged in learning. Perhaps that is the way we continue to earn our ability and right to be with and teach others. It de-privileges the teacher's relations of power toward a more consensual, relevant, and democratic form of education.

Original Difficulty in Teaching

Teaching is even more difficult than learning. We know that; but we rarely think about it. And why is teaching more difficult than learning? Not because the teacher must have a larger store of information, and have it always ready. Teaching is more difficult than learning because what teaching calls for is this: to let learn. The real teacher, in fact, lets nothing else be learned than—learning. . . . The teacher is ahead of his [her] apprentices in this alone, that the teacher has still far more to learn than they—he [she] has to learn to let them learn. The teacher must be more capable of being more teachable than the apprentices. The teacher is far less "sure" of the material than those who learn are of theirs. If the relation between the teacher and the learners is genuine, therefore, there is never a place in it for the authority of the know-it-all or the authoritative sway of the official. It still is an exalted matter, then, to become a teacher—which is something else entirely than becoming a famous professor. . . . We must keep our eyes fixed firmly on the true relation between the teacher and taught—if indeed learning is to arise.

–Heidegger, as cited in Krell, 1977, p. 356

I still believe in that kind of importance of teaching work in society. The demands on teachers ought to be among the most stringent regarding wisdom, knowledge, justice, ethics, and kindness. The distinction Heidegger makes between teacher and "famous professor" is critical, especially in a teacher-education faculty. Some professors are true teachers, but the layers of understanding (personal, academic, humanitarian, philosophical) required of excellent teaching are not reflected in the "popular" view of teaching as an easy job with lots of holidays, or as a job one gets if other professional avenues are closed. Part of my inquiry is an effort to uncover deep, "problematic" areas around authentic educational enterprise that has so much to contribute to the potential quality of living.

My readings of Heidegger are by no means inclusive or complete (as they never could be). Instead I concur with John Caputo (1978): "Heidegger's writings must be for us not a body of texts to be subjected to a learned exegesis, but a voice which calls us to set our own reflection into motion" (p. 270). That is how I read Heidegger and, like him, attempt to develop consciousness with care!

Hans-Georg Gadamer (1975) is another voice for me fundamentally concerned with the central question of "not what we do or what we ought not to do, but what happens to us over and above our wanting and doing, [making it clear that] what we are concerned with here is not a difference in method but a difference in the aims of knowledge" (p. vii). Gadamer, rather like the idealistic Heidegger, believes that the aims of knowledge have to do with understanding and interpretation—and not with control issues or the balance of power between those in dialogue. He seems to imagine a positive world where the goal is "good and equal discourse," recognizing, as Aristotle before him, the situational "good." And it is inviting to dream of "the model of hermeneutics [which] is the reciprocal understanding attained in the relation between the I and the Thou. Understanding a text carries with it the same possibility of perfect adequation as the comprehension of the Thou" (as cited in Rabinow & Sullivan, 1979, p. 127).[13]

Those "aims of knowledge," which also concerned Gadamer, do need to be questioned deeply and are a topic of ongoing debate central to curriculum studies. The hermeneutic question often invoked is "How is understanding possible?" and both (early) Heidegger (1927) and Gadamer (1975), respectively, thought that the "movement of understanding . . . lies in the very nature of things," in "Dasein's very mode of being," and so "self-understanding is an integral part, perhaps a starting and returning point, of the possibility of understanding" (as cited in Rabinow & Sullivan, 1979, p. 128). Good narrative analysis is one way of approaching understanding of the nature of things. Stories constitute interpretations that inform that knowledge.

Gadamer (as cited in Rabinow & Sullivan, 1979) asks, "How does the original significance for life pass over into the reflective experience of significance for culture?" (p. 129) and, as a way of addressing a basic question of deep concern for my research, "How far does the aspect of understanding and its linguisticality itself extend?" (p. 133). That invites the question about the ability to access factical life of teaching, partially through language that could move its writer toward self-understanding and then exercise a hermeneutic "turn" of the Heideggerian sort. An understanding can transcend the "effective historical consciousness" of the writer/speaker toward a larger and collective consciousness about education and curriculum theory. As Gadamer and so many other hermeneuticists speak about history, I reject the possibility of reading, writing, understanding, and interpreting history objectively. All accounts and all reader responses are merely interpretations, some more valid than others. That hermeneutic "turn" could allow critical play between practice and theory, thought and being, consciousness and action. This is a reflexivity so important in development of our understanding of "experienced knowledge" as a relational knowledge.

As Gadamer (1975) further explains:

> Play goes beyond the consciousness of the player and is in this respect more than a subjective behavior. Language goes beyond the consciousness of the speaker and is in this respect more than a subjective behavior. Precisely this can be described as an experience of the subject, and it has nothing to do with "mythology" or "mystification."
>
> —p. viii

It could be argued, in a parallel way, that education (and more specifically, teaching) goes beyond the consciousness of the teacher and in this respect is more than a subjective behaviour, which can also be described as an experience of the teacher. A natural extrapolation from this is that interpretations of an individual narrative can exceed the consciousness of the writer and that such interpretations enrich our understanding of teaching and education.

> The hermeneutic work of Gadamer is not only a persistent posing of ultimate questions, but also a sense for what is feasible, what is possible, what is right, here and now. In my view, one who philosophizes must be all the more aware of the tension between his own claim and the reality in which he stands.
>
> —Krell, 1977, p. 174

Gadamer's studies also extended the work of Heidegger, especially in *Truth and Method: Outline for a Philosophical Hermeneutics* (1975) and *Philosophical Apprenticeships* (1986). He summarizes (in the latter book) the significance of Heidegger's work: "In my view, Heidegger's great achievement consisted in shaking us out of a nearly complete forgetfulness by teaching us to ask with all seriousness: What is Being?" (1986, p. 187).

Another critical teaching of Heidegger's, according to Gadamer, is a hermeneutic suspicion of given "doctrine." Gadamer (1986) writes: "Heidegger interprets the acceptance of the doctrine of ideas as the beginning of that forgetfulness of being that peaks in mere imaginings and objectifications and runs along its course in the technological age as a universal will to power" (p. 186).

Both Heidegger and Gadamer (1986) found it important to:

> think of truth as simultaneously exposure and concealment . . . a way of experience. It insists that there is no higher principle than holding oneself open in a conversation, . . . [a kind of] unending dialogue of the soul with itself, which is what thinking is, and is not to be characterized as an endlessly continuing determination of an object-world waiting to be recognized.
>
> –p. 188

Curriculum studies, and especially the seminal work of reconceptualists like Bill Pinar, Madeleine Grumet, and Janet Miller, call educational doctrine and "truth" into question and call for remembering knowledge and understanding that includes dialogue with the lived Being of the knower. Pinar's (2004) call for international complicated conversations is a directly intentional hermeneutic endeavour to approach transnational interpretations of enduring questions of methods, designs, development, implementation, and evaluation of education of ourselves and others on this planet. We could/should/may be in a process of continually (re)constituting ourselves in dialogic thought through language. So, for example, languaged (as opposed to dramatic or visual) narratives of teaching experience then become a medium between subject and the object-world, where the original difficulty of being, "truths" of experience of being in teaching are both revealed and concealed in literary description, enriching our individual and collective understanding about the experience of being a teacher in the everyday world.

One other "good" I appropriate from Gadamer involves his sense of "horizon" (a contextual fusion of past and present and future) and his work with "effective-historical consciousness," which I think will be useful as I work with narrative texts. Gadamer (as cited in Rabinow & Sullivan, 1979) comments:

> The historical consciousness that characterizes contemporary man [sic] is a privilege, perhaps even a burden, the like of which has never been imposed on any previous generation. Our present-day consciousness is fundamentally different . . . a full awareness

of the historicity of everything present and the relativity of all opinions. . . . Having an historical sense signifies thinking explicitly about the historical horizon which is co-extensive with the life we live and have lived. . . . Historical consciousness no longer sanctimoniously listens to the voice that reaches out from the past but, in reflecting on it, replaces it within the context where it took root in order to see the significance and relative value proper to it. This reflexive posture toward tradition is called *interpretation* . . . . Historical consciousness is interested in knowing, not how men, people, or states develop *in general*, but, quite on the contrary, how *this* man, *this* people, or *this* state became what it is: how each of these *particulars* could come to pass and end up specifically *there*.

−pp. 111−116

Here, my interest in knowing revolves around not teaching "in general" but how this teacher, this student, this class, this curriculum, this education became who or what it is: how each of the particulars could end up "specifically" here or there.

I have wanted to believe that by studying past particulars with a larger pattern in our lives, we can indeed learn from experience, and I used to take that for granted. After conversing with Deborah Britzman (personal communication, March 18, 1997), experience as a learning that might help in the future (once upon a time inherent in our beliefs in learning about the past) has been called into question: "Suppose our experiences don't help us with the future?" Fighting with this question, which remains open, is another example of reconstituting my thinking about interpretation of narratives and about preparedness and planning in educational work.

The most important source of my current understanding of hermeneutics process, humility, and interpretation that I take to my self-constructed narratives has come from John Caputo's work in *Radical Hermeneutics* (1987). (I look forward to reading his new book at this writing.)

The goal of deconstruction is neither unitary wholeness nor dialectical resolution. The goal is to keep things in process, to disrupt, to keep the system in play, to set up procedures to continuously demystify the realities we create, to fight the tendency for our categories to congeal.

−p. 236

Caputo (1987) is one of the recent hermeneuticists who carefully examines his predecessors and situates himself in some interesting ways. His thinking contributes to my ways of reading texts against texts in my research in relational education. He is preoccupied with the theme of "flux," and he shifts his focus from the traditional hermeneutic attention to the message and concerns himself more with the messenger. What the role of the messenger is, what decisions the messenger makes, and the multiple relationships of the messenger that contribute to "understanding" are of primary importance to Caputo. He speaks of the uncomfortable things first: chaos, the abyss, withdrawal, struggle, uncertainty, individual insufficiency. (Common conversation in teachers' lunch rooms everywhere.)

Gone are the gentle probings of an early Heidegger or the idealistic, "good" Gadamerian hermeneutics of a kinder age. A new attentive, aware consciousness emerges into what Caputo (1987) calls a "cold hermeneutics":

> A hermeneutic moment in which we recover, discover, retrieve the movement by which we are transfixed. In this moment a shudder of recognition resonates through our (non)selves leaving us temporarily speechless, suffering from another bout of Unheimlichkeit.[14] . . . It is in this shudder, this trembling, that I locate a cold and comfortless hermeneutics which I think it is the special virtue of [the mature] Heidegger and Kierkegaard[15] to have expounded.
>
> –p. 200

The resonances here are deep. When the ground upon which one is/has been resting falls away, there is no feeling of comfort, but a brutal sense of falling into a nauseating,[16] black nothingness, a terrible groundlessness. When "the center cannot hold,"[17] there is a deep interior shudder and our "thrownness" of Dasein cannot be languaged away. I have not really found many who do "own up to the difficulty we are in" in the physical and immediate way that Caputo does. He has great courage at getting at the meanings in the territories beyond where most hermeneutic philosophers have been willing to tread. He goes beyond the grammatological (deconstructive) reductions of Derrida to authentic concern about "what organizes, nourishes, and directs in the understanding of Being that matters, and that is the *Woraufhin*, the 'upon which' of the projection" (Caputo, 1987, p. 172). He distinguishes between two types of projections (primary and secondary) to approach the meaning of such Being: the primary, "the being which is to be understood (projected)" and the secondary, "the meaning of that Being" (pp. 172–173). This distinction (founded upon Heidegger's work) enables Caputo to think about meaning: "Meaning is not exactly the object of understanding, *what* is understood by the understanding, but that *in which* what is understood is suspended, held up" (p. 173).

In my own existential, pedagogical "fall," I tried (and failed) to find meaning by thinking about "the what" and the "in which," as Caputo says, of my praxis. Reconciling what I try to teach with real, live students in front of me, with the world-at-large and its myriad interdependent systems, often is over-whelming: It is what drove me back to learn more, to return to teachers of my own.[18]

But in spite of the danger of the territory Caputo works in, he plays (and by example teaches me to play) with the language, which informs our knowledge of seemingly negative entities, and for me, succeeds in reframing things so that I can go on in a cooperative spirit of generativity amidst all kinds of difficulty. Caputo (1987) more than all the rest reveals the *Gelassenheit[19]* possible in the (radical) hermeneutic project of understanding and interpreting original difficulty, which does liberate the spirit and the mind to

> learn openness—which means at once graciousness, for one knows that has always to do with gifts and giving—and we learn a sense of transiency, for one knows the powers of withdrawal. . . . We learn to come to grips with *kinesis*, with coming to be and passing away, and with the mysterious powers which govern that movement.
>
> –p. 175

Caputo positions himself somehow "between" Heidegger and Derrida:

> Derrida's deconstructive work issues in a grammatological exuberance which celebrates diversity, repetition, alteration. Heidegger's deconstructive work issues in a meditative stillness, which could not be more alert to the play in which all things are swept, but it is stunned by the power of its sweep and culminates in a deep sense of the play in which mortals play out their allotted time. And what I call radical hermeneutics will not let either the Heideggerian or the Derridean gestures win the day, will not entrust full authority to either . . . but keeps subverting one with the other. Just when thinking is lost in solemn stillness, when it is beginning to take itself seriously, dissemination bursts upon the scene with its disruptive laughter.
>
> –p. 206

It is that laughter (often in response to Chaplin-esque slapstick of daily life) and play that assist us in keeping the existential balance we need. As teachers, learners, human beings, we regularly "take a leap[20] off the stability of the ground, the solidity of presence—terra firma—and we land in the flux" (Caputo, 1987, p. 206). Noticing that flux can put us into a severe case of post-traumatic stress syndrome, or we can learn from it and deal with it. How? Caputo says: "The play is all. Beneath, behind, around, to the side of all grounding and founding, in the ground's cracks and crevices and interstices, is the play" (p. 225). That stance gives us the ability and perspective not to take the "thrown-ness" of existence personally, feeling picked on by some malevolent force of Fate, ruining our lives with difficulty.[21]

That kind of play, that acceptance and understanding of the "flux," has enormous implications for the way we (re)constitute ourselves as teachers, requires us to address ancient and current educational "difficulty" and questions teaching praxis in very different ways than the nineteenth and twentieth centuries have prepared us to do. We need to shake our own ground and read our understanding, theory, and experience.

As Ted Aoki (Professor Emeritus) wrote:

> In my view, Caputo has helped readers shift hermeneutics from those interpretations in which hermeneutics is rooted in metaphysical ground to another interpretation in which instead of roots we find in the origin nothing but difficulty (no roots, no ground, no foundation)—scary but lovely in the Heraclitean flux.
>
> —Personal communication, February 1994

That is an intriguing "pre-delineated" tracing of nothingness in which to consider the way "things fall apart"[22] in teaching/schools/education, not with fear of loss of "control" but with curious interest so that "the progress of experience is not a matter of continually being amazed by what is ever new, or of being confounded by the flux, but rather of filling in already pre-delineated horizons (or, alternately, of revising expectations when we are indeed surprised)" (Caputo, 1987, p. 41). Caputo reminds us of Husserl's early observation that flux is the only constant and to remember that the "principle of principles is a principle of suspicion that there is more to what is given than it gives itself out to be" (p. 40).

This could raise the question of an inability to ever be "satisfied" with "knowing"/"understanding" anything that requires us to completely suspend defining the concepts of *knowledge* and *experience*. Caputo seems to have a radical concept: that any "given" ought to be more accurately perceived as "thrownness" of being and that one must ever return to that groundless flux of being, in the lifelong work of the (re)constitution of the self.

Caputo (1987) concludes his exploration (*Radical Hermeneutics: Repetition, Deconstruction, and the Hermeneutic Project*) by (re)turning to the task of thinking, which is conducted in the ground of the soul, to keep open to the mystery, to keep the play in play. My task of thinking from the ground of my soul about education is about exploring the mystery of relationships between and among the teacher, the learner, and the "learned." And one of the ways to approach keeping "open to the mystery" in teaching acts and in teacher education is to play as well, to play with educational conventions, with expectations (of those teachers and students and the knowledge they produce between them), with language, with multiple interpretations, with stories, with each other within the chaos of (daily) life. We are, as Caputo says, bound together by the mystery of our mortality and midnight shadows.

The Austrian child psychoanalyst Bruno Bettelheim (1975) claims a similar affinity between the I and the Thou. By virtue of our individual helplessness and by the uncertainty of things, we require one another, are "bound to" each other, indissolubly linked. It is part of the nature of Being that we attempt to provide anodyne for it, in a kind of Kierkegaardian conquest of the flux and the abyss. We must resist the temptation to overcome the flux—as though it were possible—and dwell in the middle of it, laughing and talking and thinking all the while.

Interpreting Texts of Difficulty in Teaching Work

Reading hermeneutics has profoundly influenced me as a teacher and curriculum researcher. As teacher I am a Hermes as an instructor-messenger of the curricular gods, trickster trader in artificial power, interpretive truth-sayer of the "bodies of knowledge" in the disciplines, corrective mentor. But these are archaic and dysfunctional models for the kind of educators so needed for our "kids at risk," "our differently-abled," our "learning disabled," our "advance placement/international baccalaureates," and all our other, "ordinary," "normal" students who fall into none of the "categories." They all need teaching from those "a little ahead" of them, all of us caught together in the Heraclitean flux.

Amid that flux how shall I reconstitute my self and my metaphor of self in teaching?

Am I a postmodern Heraclitus, dwelling on the fact (weeping?) that we "can never step into the same teaching situation twice"? Education, like all life-grounded endeavours, is in a state of constant flux and requires of us to make new combinations and permutations of our wisdom and action in each case. Perhaps a good Buddhist, Heraclitus had the "central belief that all things are in constant transition. His views on the mutability and fleeting character of all things led also to his partly humorous label as the "weeping philosopher," or the "dark philosopher" (Benet, 1987, p. 443). But why DO we weep if things are always shifting, since that IS the way life is? Can we not learn that the flux is the "constant" in the education "formula"? A newer, lighter, post-structural quantum self that is both mass and energy can endure and dwell generatively in such a flux. Through the process of reading Caputo, I first conceived of the self as an electromagnetic/nuclear field-of-self that can stay with all difficulty, being influenced and influencing without being destroyed. Remember the law of physics: Matter and energy are neither created nor destroyed. And what is the implication of this law for the teaching self? Perhaps teachers do need to break down or burn out, but we will have to change: Life requires that continually. Although we experience teaching as a routine, life in teaching perpetually changes, second by second.

The hermeneutic approach accounts for continual flux as we return in an ever-recursive enterprise of adding to our deep knowledge about any human action and situation. This is what is really at the root of "lifelong" learning: to continually reinterpret as we add new wisdom to the meanings in our existing cognitive constructs of the world. And my work as a responsible educator is continually to learn and "notice," with Gadamer's (1986) hermeneutics of suspicion of the whole question of the foundations of our insights into "truth." I also need to play as I (re)constitute myself to sense and interpret and be attuned to what is called for in ever-changing daily life in teaching and writing about that teaching. And to interpret, according to Ricoeur (1981), "is not to discover an intention hidden behind the "text" but to unfold a world in front of it" (p. 94). But interpretation can get much more dramatic than (un)folding a world:

> The autonomy of the text already contains the possibility that what Gadamer calls the "matter" of the text may escape from the finite intentional horizon of its author; in other words, thanks to the writing, the "world" of the text may explode the world of the author.
>
> –p. 139

On Staying with Difficulty in Teaching

So we come full circle to original difficulty, to having worlds "fall apart" (Yeats, 1920), explode in front of us, finding ourselves groundless—full circle to the hermeneutic enterprise of interpreting original difficulty. And I step into the hermeneutic river of education again in this conclusion; it is not the same river the second time, with some temporal distance on my part. I find a way to travel my own landscapes and territories, especially in radical hermeneutics. I agree with Caputo (1987) that (radical) hermeneutics is a deep lesson in humility, which "slips into the ethical," and a deep relational lesson in compassion, which "arises precisely from the sense of a common fate, from suffering (*passio*) a common (*com*) comfortlessness" (pp. 258–259):

Radical hermeneutics comes away chastened from its struggle with the flux. It has wrestled with the angels of darkness and has not gotten the better of them. It understands the power of the flux to wash away the best-laid schemes of metaphysics . . . . The moral of radical hermeneutics for mortals itself is to sharpen our sense of the contingency of our schemes, of the dissolubility of the metaphysical world. The moral for mortals is that none of us occupies a privileged place of insight, none of us has access to a god (or goddess) who passes on to us any hermeneutic secrets . . . . There is nothing to do but face the worst, the play of the epochs, of the temporary constellation within which we live out our historical lives, to wade into the flux and try not to drown. . . . That inspires caution. It makes one proceed in such a way as to keep as many options open as possible. It deflates pretension . . . . Such authenticity, which means owning up to our shortcomings, inspires a certain compassion. We are, after all, all siblings of the same flux, brothers and sisters in the same dark night. We all have our midnight fears, a common mortality . . . . And so I envisage, as the moral upshot of all this, a "community of mortals."

–p. 259

Central to all education is the learning of being in a community of mortals. If we understand this alone, our pedagogy will shift dramatically, because priority and what is really needed in learning come to the fore among us differently than giving total authority to a syllabus or extant detailed set of objects or course outline. Government can make generative decisions in support of the work in education, but each community is different, and every teacher interprets that community's *texts* and places them between the teacher and the student to interpret together.

Finally, Caputo (1987) asserts:

Our own concern is to keep the conversation moving, mobile, and to trust the dynamics of the *agora*. We do everything we can to see to it that the debate is fair, that no one's voice is excluded or demeaned, and that the vested interests of the powerful who usually end up having their way are restrained as much as possible.

–p. 261

With these cold hermeneutics I return to the landscape of narrative I created . . . with as much humility, caution, sensitivity, and compassion as I can. I approach cautiously, more aware, alert to interpretations I, and others, have not yet noticed. I feel nervous and write a haiku to try to name the narrative flux.

Hermeneutic Haiku

Text as sleeping bear
Desiring relationship:
How do I wake it?

—Leah Fowler

Along with the hermeneutic question of original difficulty, meaning and truth always snapping at my heels, my earlier concern for ethics arises again. I want the truths of the story uncovered, revealed without writing explicit factual detail that would harm/misrepresent anybody in my work. Verisimilitude without violation. Essential. Difficult. Stay with it. Attempt to lay out the narrative truths in this foundation of personal pedagogy, even (or especially) when I seem to lose ground. Pay attention to what else might be noticed about the narrative, question what the plot, characters, conflict, setting are really about. Search for more of the difficulty that calls to be written more explicitly. Learn how to write in such a way that the narrative reveals and shows, rather than tells directly in factual didactics. A story is not a report, and a plot is more than a story, and a narrative is more than a plot.

I pay new hermeneutic attention to questions of diction, style, tone, colour, specificity of nouns and verbs, of adjectives and adverbs to align them with what seems to lie beneath the text. As a hermeneutical writer, I add words here and there, subtract at other places, notice other interpretations and play in words as their meaning shifts and changes as I re-read. Even after interpretive orbitals of naive storying, psychological construction, and psychotherapeutic ethics, I am unable to let go of the story, yet. And what did happen at the end? Does it go too far or not enough? Is it literal, figurative, magic realism? Perhaps . . . Well, now I leave the questions open.

What are the truths revealed through hermeneutic work with the text? What other interpretations might be constructed, offered, reconstituted? How do I/we resist *Erleichterung* and stay with the multiple meanings of difficulty in living? How might we work generatively amid chaos? What possibility is there for the field-of-self working, living, and loving ethically with compassion, humility, and joy at the edge of the mortal abyss? What should I be paying attention to in life texts? What are my hands doing, as Carlos Castaneda so often asked, doing in my research and in my (teaching) life? What about that unfolding in a field-of-self that is unwittingly revealed through auto/biographical narrative texts? Why am I here, now, in this place and what is my work and meaning in living that is both relational and solitary, both "wave" and "particle"?

And of course, difficulty continues to reveal itself:

> The returning of life to its original difficulty is returning of the possibility of the living Word. It is a return to the essential generativity of human life, a sense of life in which there is always something left to say, with all the difficulty, risk, and ambiguity that such generativity entails. Hermeneutic inquiry is thus concerned with the ambiguous nature of life itself.
>
> —Jardine, as cited in Pinar et al., 1995, p. 119

And when the living-words of my life appear on the page, as both writer and reader of self-constructed narratives, there can be re/cognitions and discoveries of such a proportion, that I attempt (as Shakespeare's Lady Macbeth advised) to "screw courage to the sticking point." I practice continuing my life, even when I don't "know" how to carry on. The difficulty is sometimes volcanic as the rock surface of the text cracks, crumbles in archi/tectonic shifting plates of words, and from underneath, the lava of meaning in old pain, broken relationships, unkept promises, grief for lost possibility erupts and threatens my very existence. Perhaps this is the deepest reason Virginia Woolf put the stones in her own pocket and waded into her river-water death, in an effort to keep the volcanic pressure of her reconceptualizations sufficiently weighted, the water cool enough to put out her own lava of understanding, because it was too painful to bear any longer.

Hermeneutic work on self-texts is terrifying work, which has an unstoppable way (perhaps because it is so unpredictable) of leading one deeper and deeper into truths that may be difficult to know and impossible for which to provide anodyne. Still, one faces up to original difficulties in one's life and being through the very process of hermeneutic research.

Out of the hermeneutic themes/ projects of "restoring life to its original difficulty," "repetition," "recollection," "kinesis," "(re)constitution," *Verstehen* ("understanding"), *differance,* and "staying open to the mystery with humility and compassion," I appropriate the threads with which I weave my "thought cloth" (Kirby & McKenna, 1989, p. 154) for my inquiry around difficulty in the existential, mortal (teaching) self. Caputo calls for facing up to original difficulties and suddenly I plunge into "cold hermeneutics of the self," where I have not nearly enough compassion, humility, courage, or laughter. A covenant is made as I commit to staying with the difficulty, to continue to write even when my thinking and being has neither the clarity nor the focus desired. I make an ethical promise to myself and become trustworthy in this hermeneutic process. I look for others who share this kind of work too.

In the hermeneutic sphere of my research in the narrative process, I call into question my thinking and my interpreting as I attempt to make meaning from teaching stories. As a member of the community of teaching mortals, I wonder what it is that I can contribute, what I can stay with for the benefit of us all. I look yet another time in the shuddering-cold, hard mirror of my own narrative texts, tremble and reconstruct meaning as I (re)constitute myself with every reading, every rewriting. It is the most honest and most painful professional development I have encountered; I am surprised at the effect on me and more importantly on my pedagogy. (This is taken up more fully in the next chapter.)

The place (function) of hermeneutics in education needs to be explored and expanded. Educators can still consider Husserl's (as cited in Mueller-Vollmer, 1985) contention that "the essence of meaning is seen by us, not in the meaning-conferring experience, but in its 'content,' the single, self-identical intentional unity set over against the dispersed multiplicity of actual and possible experience of speakers and thinkers" (p. 28). This community of (speaking and thinking) mortals (Caputo, 1987) in which we find ourselves, always was and continues to be at the heart of narrative. The human condition is a familiar theme for authors, life's difficulties the basis for "plot," "groundlessness" as the entry point for a setting where struggles with the flux begin *in medias res*. In such narratives we play and laugh and grieve and think about and understand and interpret the essential/existential mystery of life.

By reading and interpreting narratives that do confront the difficult places in teaching, together we can consider why we are teaching and how we might Be as we are teaching. This is work that extends long past the event of this book. I begin certain conversations here by describing my own specific way of working narratively as I research difficulty in teaching: the directions, outcomes, and effects of these textual and narrative conversations are impossible to predict. I can only speak to the effect on me.

> "Come to the edge," he said.
> They said: "We are afraid."
> "Come to the edge," he said.
> They came.
> He pushed them . . . and they flew.
> –Guillaume Apollinaire, 1880–1918

Hermeneutic study of texts, such as self-constructed narratives like "The Anger in Our Miss Maple", constitutes a recursive self-pushing to the edge of one's fear and knowledge and comfort, and yet the flight of understanding about that which is difficult to know can support our consciousness about being mortal, temporal, spatial, and contextually situated, embodied beings. When as a reader I am arrested or startled by text, especially my own narrative texts, hermeneutics helps me think "well" as a textual and philosophical way to stay with all lived difficulty and contributes to a profound sense of the meaning I carry as a languaging being.

Again, the perpetual goal of hermeneutic projects is toward conscious, deeper, and more complete understanding. As Pinar (Pinar et al., 1995) writes: "In its contemporary form, hermeneutics is faced with three interrelated concerns: understanding, explanation, and critical assessment" (p. 642). Germane to my research, I hope to contribute to the understanding, explanation, and critical assessment of difficulty in teaching. Doing that work seems essential to teachers and human science and social practitioners, especially when we work with vulnerable populations of students or health clients.

When I began studying hermeneutics in 1994, the topic of difficulty arose from my beginner readings of John D. Caputo. Although I did not have formal training in philosophy, I have read often and widely in that discipline, but in returning now to Caputo's work, I find even more resonance with his humane and ethical approach to radical, cold hermeneutics. A rebuilding of hermeneutic philosophy may be an important companion as we try to rebuild and reconceptualize yet again in the field of education.

In the next chapter, I bring this hermeneutic understanding to all of my teaching and research. I turn the focus of my inquiry toward difficulty of the self in orbital of curriculum, pedagogy, and teacher education, mindful of humility, play, fear, mortality, laughter, and community.

Internarrative: The Difficulty of Breathing

Water. Then air, I suppose. The inorganic compounds were the substrate first. Oxygen, hydrogen, nitrogen were "givens" before I was born. First—after birth, breath.

I must have chosen to breathe. All teachers started life by breathing and there are still lessons to be learned about that. But my own breathing, from infancy, has been a difficulty.

"Take a deep breath and learn to slow your breathing."

"You will probably need to take three aerosol sprays for the rest of your life, to control your asthma"—and the alternative to that is neither attractive nor long.

This has called for me to pay deep attention to breathing.

"When you inhale, take in the yoga energy of the universe and let out the breath very slowly, as slowly as possible."

"Just step into this drum . . . we are going to cut off your air for a few seconds intermittently and test the strength of your breathing response."

"We are testing your vital lung capacity." "Hold your breath. Again, again."

Nitrogen is 79 percent. And oxygen? Almost never enough.

And wasn't there a novel by Anne Tyler called *Breathing Lessons*, and don't pregnant women learn breathing exercises to help them when they are giving birth? What about breathing lessons for writers?

What about breathing lessons for teachers?

How are breathing and silence connected? Breathing and language?

"I can't breathe."

"I can't breathe with you on me: grandpa, cousin, neighbour, boy-next-door, boy-who-sits-behind-me-and-dips-my-braids-in-his-inkwell . . . ."

I can't breathe. I don't have voice to tell people I don't have voice. I can't tell.

Artificial respiration can revive people, but how do you rescue yourself?

Air is inorganic, so they say, but breathing is a miracle.

What about breathing lessons for this teacher?

Chapter 8: Sixth Orbital—
Curriculum and Pedagogy

Being aware of oneself as the instrument of one's teaching and aware of the story that makes one's life sensible allows for greater change and growth as well as greater intentionality in teaching choices.

— W. Ayers, cited in Sears & Marshall, 1990, p. 20

Curriculum and Pedagogy in Narrative Research

Never do I forget that we are mortal: Every student, colleague, every teacher, parent, caretaker, psychologist, nurse, social worker, child care worker, secretary, librarian, audio visual technician, administrator, board member, trustee, politician, courier, mail person, loved one, family, friend, like me, is mortal. To continue to work and love and try and learn and teach and expedite and care and problem solve and think and attempt to "improve," given the death sentence that finishes each physical life, is itself a remarkable kind of miracle inviting a deep reverence for life, for the tremendous power of Being.

I look into the eyes of the people I work with and for, live with and love, knowing there are constraints of time and physical ability. Carol Shields (2002) talks about how narratives reveal that conditional quality of our lives:

> Novels help us turn down the volume of our own interior "discourse," but unless they can provide an alternative, hopeful course, they're just so much narrative crumble
> . . .
> Unless is the worry word of the English language. It flies like a moth around the ear, you hardly hear it, and yet everything depends on its breathy presence. Unless—that's the little subjunctive mineral you carry along in your pocket crease. It's always there or else not there.
> Unless you're lucky, unless you're healthy, fertile, unless you're loved and fed, unless you're clear about your sexual direction, unless you're offered what others are offered, you go down in the darkness, down to despair. Unless provides you with a trapdoor, a tunnel into the light, the reverse side of not enough. Unless keeps you from drowning in the presiding arrangements . . . . Unless is miracle of language and perception . . . . It makes us anxious, makes us cunning . . . But it gives us hope.

–pp. 224–225

I see novels, library books signed out, and think about how books outlive us and wonder if the borrower will live to read the books. I remember taking my grandmother's unread books back to the library days after she was buried in the ground and winter had frozen the earth against life. Often I say to my classes, "If this were your last day, would you be here learning and why?" I often think of the difficulties that arise continually: All seem to pale next to the difficulty of dying. Our experience of difficulties in life seems to culminate in the finishing of a life, but paying attention to imminent mortality focuses and refines curriculum in the way no other parameter can. There is so little time together: What shall we do and why?

There is an urgent precision, a sharpened clarity, and a diligent focus when we know our time is limited. And it is. Keeping that in mind helps me from being overwhelmed by minor difficulties, able to maintain a healthy perspective that allows one to sort and choose what is most important in learning and teaching. The time-bound curriculum, by its very chronicled nature, may be a blessing that contributes to heightened consciousness in learning. There is always too little time in teaching.

I have come to understand that difficulty will occur, that chaos is natural and self-organizing, and that ruptures in teaching practice should be expected if not well loved.

A teaching life is subject to the laws of physics and chemistry and biology: gravity, uncertainty, matter, energy, states, change, chaos, relativity, probability, philosophy, language. As well, "external" difficulties of a physical, political, economic nature in educational systems are part of the normal course of being, often and oddly blamed for what is "wrong" in teaching. However, the most important (wisdom-developing) lessons about teaching have come at places of rupture in my inner difficulties of practice, signposts of what is "unready-to-hand." In those interior difficulties in this analytical, reflective orbital of curriculum and pedagogy, I have the responsibility to attend and be aware of much—difficulties of perception; paucity of conceptual thought or understanding; insufficient inner psychological work; unattended ethical "sinkholes"[1]; and imprecise language in (always insufficient) communication in relational (educational) contexts. This is not to take a martyred "it is all my fault" approach at all but rather one which assumes these difficulties are at work in each of us and requires each of us to be a wakeful steward of our own consciousness and Being.

Troubling Pedagogy and Implications for the Teaching Self

If I can teach myself to stay with those dynamic tensions of difficulty in teaching, then I maintain conditions for my own persistent learning. One way of managing unbearable sites of self in teaching is through narrative. If what Noddings (1989) says is true, that "stories have the power to direct and change our lives" (p. 157), then teaching stories have the power to direct and change our teaching lives. My research work around the teaching stories I have written about difficulty inclines me to think this is true. Researching as "author," as "reader," as "editor," and as teaching practitioner I ask: What do these stories have to say about teaching and what do they mean in terms of a teaching life? I notice other ways the stories have worked on me. They have allowed me to uncover ruptures in my being as teacher. Issues of power and control, feelings of inadequacy and poor self-esteem, are revealed alongside vices of vanity, criticism of "other," facile disapproval and dismissal of ideas and practices in students and teachers alike. I notice an outmoded insistence about driving "the curriculum" with (terrible) inconsistencies between theory and practice. The stories call for hard work in my practice.

"Dr. Mercanfract and Heidi" flags the sensitivity, awareness, maturity, and kindness required of teachers to lead in a healthy, non-devouring way, as young people form their own identities, orientations, and meaningful relationships. "Getting Clearer Vision" re-minds me to pay attention to what is going on in the present, to watch the faces of all my students all the time, and to respond in ways that foster agency and dignity in their struggles. Stories also suggest forgiveness, anodyne, understanding. Compassion is appropriate in my own struggles as a necessary part of learning in front of my students, making some of my lessons visible to them when appropriate. The "Home Run" story keeps me humble and reminds me to take my students out of the classroom often and level the teacher-student hierarchy to a community of mortals (Caputo, 1987). "Black Oxfords" invites me to live in the present as if every day were my last, so every moment (with students) "matters." Even in daily terms this can mean a deep reduction in "dead-time" or "lost time" that exists in so many classes, waiting for the bell, which "tolls for thee." I am also reminded that I do not know the many griefs of my students and colleagues. I have no business judging (without knowing) the actions of others, although I may ask out of concern for their lives and well-being to know if I can share the work or help alleviate any suffering so we can emerge together into our communities and worlds.

And each story I write nudges, prods, provokes, pinches, abrades, bites at my (professional teaching) self. It requires me to pay attention to the language I use in talking about my experiences as teacher and assists me in multiple constructions of meaning about the nature of (my) teaching as a reflective practitioner, without expecting easy answers to difficulty. I continue to stay with the problematic nature of difficulty. As Oberg and Artz (1992) write:

> Through the careful analysis of our language, we have become aware of subtle influences on our thinking . . . . We have come to realize that the expectation for a resolution of the issues we have raised must remain unsatisfied, that we must learn to live with the tension that arises from the uncertainty of unanswered questions. This is the nature of .

> –pp. 154–155

If narratives have been explored in the earlier orbitals of naive storying, narrative craft, and hermeneutic orbitals of research as readerly and writerly texts, it is educationally useful to think also of narratives as teacherly texts that can reveal pedagogical "entry points" into the curriculum of teacher education and teacher development, professionally and personally. In this interpretive sphere, I return to the narratives I wrote with the eye of the teacher (and the learner) that I am. I want as both the writer and the reader of these narratives of difficulty to consider implications for personal pedagogy and learn more about what it means to teach and to be a teacher.

Any teaching story certainly does not end after the writing of it. I keep going back to reading and re-reading. Once I have told a story to you, I begin to think hermeneutically in terms of teacher education, of professional development, of therapy for experienced teachers, of a space in which to reconstitute the meaning and interpretations of curriculum and narrative. I read the stories again and then the story of these stories and the not-told stories. Each time, as Emily Dickinson said, "There's a certain slant of light." There is a hermeneutic turning and turning as the narrative becomes the falconer training the reader to go a little further in the spiral to return to the centre each time with a little more force of mind. One has the experience of John Caputo's radical hermeneutics of confronting the abyss, trembling within this community of mortals, considering the very hardest questions, struggling to notice what is called for in those spaces of insufficiency that occur in curriculum and in narrative. In life. Please see John D. Caputo's (2000) book: *More Radical Hermeneutics: On Not Knowing Ourselves*. For practitioners and researchers this work has compelling ideas and edges to inquiry approaches to begin to work and know differently than ever before.

Narrative research is a critical philosophical and analytical process of interpretation and thought at the tensioned site of self in the reflexive praxis of teaching and curriculum studies. I begin by attending to what the teaching self is doing or how it is being affected in each of the writings I include here. What kind of teachers *are* Fowler, Maple, Bricoleur, Mercanfract, Gray, Tofelize? How *did* they/I become as they are? How do teachers speak and what do they not say? What do they do and what do they refrain from doing? How are they in relation to their students? How do they contribute to the learning of themselves and their students and colleagues? What are their character flaws, psychic motivations, and sites of insufficient self-work and understanding? What are their pedagogical intentions—what do they want to teach and why? How does each of them understand curriculum? I look to what and how I have written about these questions. Through my breaking of these silences (see Miller, 2005), I begin to return myself and my research to the classroom, as I always must.

This phase, concerned with issues of curriculum and pedagogy in the narrative research process, focuses my attention on what is being revealed about the teacherly words and actions and on what information we glimpse about that which trans/pires inside the doors of teaching. What can I notice about the contextual teaching situations? What difficulties emerge for students and teachers? I want to understand how each stays (differently) with those difficulties day after day. Thinking more deeply about what teaching and learning means, what multiple realities co-exist in acts of education, I notice differences in the work of novice teachers and experienced teachers, in my own former and current teaching. I want my writing in this curriculum orbital of analysis to port/ray (teaching) life, rather than simply describe, and to ask my (teaching) eye to notice what my pen might have missed. Persisting with hermeneutic traces, I become tacitly aware of learning about the underside of teaching, notice the trickster teacher with the public persona marginally/holographically outside the inner self. Professional maturity develops.

This curriculum and pedagogical narrative analysis work has become a complicated conversation (Pinar, 2004) involving autobiography, narrative, professional education, and curriculum knowledge. Habitual practices in teaching become strange, unfamiliar in much the same way an anthropologist regards an unfamiliar clan. As a researcher, I am both participant and observer and must consider in what ways I am complicit with all that emerges from the narratives. The teacher-in-me is looking in a textual mirror when I read the stories I write about teaching. I see reflections of what I also must teach myself.

The teacher-in-me who is writing these narratives goes back and looks for places to write in explicitly what has been-taken-for granted and not written. In that sense, none of these stories is finished yet or ever can be . . . . They are working narratives, yes, for information and experiences, but for the teacher-in-me who is researcher, they teach something different each time they are encountered. How the story means is perpetually shifting, like electrons in their orbitals around a magnetic nuclear core, where Heisenberg's uncertainty principle is at work: that of not locating the actual place of being at any given time. I live and teach amid perpetual flux.

I persist in questions of the teaching self again. How is it that I am the kind of teacher I am? How do I understand myself as a teacher? What is the meaning of my teaching self in the world? Who is the self that teaches? In what ways might my teacherly work contribute to the project of human history? What is difficult about my work and being as a teacher? Is *educare* an appropriate metaphor for teaching? How might I continue to uncover my unknowing and convert what I learn as a reflexive educator to lived experience in a relational world of teacher preparation and teacher development? Palliating experience in some important ways—relieving pain and anxiety without curing—(one does not *cure* existential difficulty in the natural world), the narratives of self I write require me to pay a particular kind of focused and explicit attention to how I am living those questions in the daily vicissitudes with students, colleagues, administrators, significant others. As a result of such narratives, concentrations of difficulty reveal themselves to show where thoroughgoing work is still needed. Janet Miller (2005) encourages because she too has

> struggle[d] to create spaces within reconceptualized versions of curriculum theorizing that could enable me to explore, for example, "the personal" and "the political," not as a binary but rather as reciprocal, interactive, constantly changing and (re)constructing influences on my own and other teachers' conceptions of curriculum, pedagogy, and research.
>
> –In preface by Bill Pinar, p. x

From Contract to Covenant Through Curriculum of Narrative Research

Labour-wise, teaching has been negotiated contractually between a teacher and a community, school board, principal, headmaster, or directrice. But if we research the original difficulties of teaching and the teaching self, we come to a different relationship with our career and work of education. As professionals, we move from the contractual business law toward a more enduring covenant, focused on the good of students and their communities. That quality of engagement fosters deeper capacities for meaningful work in an ongoing stewardship of the whole learning project of education, locally and globally.

At this place of examining covenant-quality of research on difficulty, I think about how teachers might reconceptualize and reconstitute what we understand by teaching. I keep asking what is it for the self to be teaching and what is difficult about being in teaching. Rather than receiving answers, more difficulty is illuminated, and fewer places of certainty stay still. Instead, in a cold hermeneutic gesture, I stay with the teaching difficulties laid bare in the text, hopeful that understanding and multiple interpretations about my work in education will follow if I trust the narrative of my (teaching) life. It is a task that involves faith in the hermeneutic capacity of a writing and reading self amid groundlessness and flux continually to keep open the questions about what is possible in teaching and what is difficult about living as a teacher.

As each difficulty is illuminated and understood and recedes again, another is revealed elsewhere in the existential palimpsest of being. Penchants for power are revealed. I can no longer blame my schooling, my experiences, colleagues, students, or administrators. It is after all my text there in print: *my* aims or intentions and words are (un)covered for all to see. The displays, materials, and texts I choose and use are called into question as I ask again and again whose interests and needs are being served. Questions must be faced about learners in my care who need fairer or more challenging, relevant activities and projects.

I stand quietly in front of the narratives I have constructed about my teaching experience and behold the (never intended) images of myself as teacher embedded in the text. I am unable to ignore any longer the ruptures in my practice and relational networks, mis/takes of teaching and being, because they are laid bare here on the page in (visible) ink. In this place of humility and honesty can I be fully mindful about participating in theorizing and thought that is more "transgressive work that is not only different from what has come before but also different from what either of us, individually, might have imagined"? (Miller, 2005, p. 262).

The curriculum of difficulty for the teacher has multiple *display* sites and (re)sources often in the relational texts of being with students. There are the (un)bearable relational (self) sites. They are sites that involve

1. *Emotion* (anger, grief, transference, attraction, scorn, joy . . .);
2. *Power* (personal and titular authority, control, assessment and evaluation, culture, class, race, power, sexual orientation, age, status ...);
3. *Personal narratives* (experience, dreams, beliefs, working principles, situated historical auto/biography, life-timelines, traits ...); and
4. *Discourse(s)* (language, dialect, fluency, intertextuality, synchronicity, interpretation, cognitive linguistic schemata, semantics, syntax, diction, style, purpose, disciplines, subjects, topics, syllabi ...).

These are only four (of many more) tensioned relational difficulties to which teachers must attend and which teachers must learn, understand, and work with generatively. Life for the teacher, inside the classroom and out, offers many "texts" to study existential, psycho-social, political, administrative (organizational, bureaucratic) cultural, philosophical difficulties that arise unexpectedly on a daily basis in the normal flux of teaching.

We need reflexive knowledge, skills, and attitudes to create meaningful work as trickster (hermeneutic) messengers of curriculum.

The curriculum of difficulty for the teacher requires the *activity* of deep, committed engagement, no matter the difficulties that naturally arise in the course of time and being. Narrative research is one way to rethink and rewrite the educational narrative I live as a teacher, toward new and poetic images of self that at once startle and teach, challenge and satisfy, entice and create meaning.

The curriculum of difficulty is continuously and continually assessed and *evaluated* formatively and summatively in the classroom and long after, in the living. Especially amid difficulty we need to ask how we are doing, whether or not our (pedagogical) aims are being met, if the displays we use are of the most worth, and how our activities of being with students are engaging to them and to us.

While forgiveness of self is not needed for the ontological nature of being, my narrative research is one compelling confrontation of all that one is and claims as a teacher. As a researcher in this pedagogical orbital, I revisit my path through naive storying, psychological construction, psychotherapeutic ethics, narrative craft, and hermeneutic philosophy over and over, looking for lessons I want to, and must, learn at every phase. I pay attention to the curriculum each suggests and seek the texts of others to enhance what I am doing. Over and

over I go back to Caputo and Pinar, Grumet and Greene, Polkinghorne and
Kerby. I follow endless etymological, literary, and psychological trails, never far
from hermeneutics with its concern for interpretation and how that influences
and moves me in my understanding of curriculum studies, teaching and difficulty, and personal being. I notice the effects on my professional practice.

I need to "get smart" (Lather, 1991) about what I am doing as a teacher,
understand the ways "I answer with my life" (Casey, 1993), what "bitter milk"
(Grumet, 1988) I offer to my students, why I often "teach to transgress"
(hooks, 1994) towards a practice of freedom, and how the "counternarratives"
(Giroux, Lankshear, McLaren, & Peters, 1996) I hear and write and tell and live
influence my teaching self in relation to others.

My work as a teacher is to learn even more than the students with the goal
of making myself redundant to them in their progressive path toward inde-
pendence and educated citizenship. I stop matronizing, actively encourage
authentic conversation, and notice opportunities for development of personal
agency in each of us. As I do that I need to look back and forward while dwelling in the present, with a need for care/full constructions to em-
body/contain/reveal the curricula of difficulty in my work with student
teachers, experienced practitioners returning to university, and graduate students as they pursue their inquiries into theory and practice. Narratives are one
answer to my own inquiry into difficulty in the (teaching) self and lead me in
ever-widening, different lessons.

As I begin to approach the conclusion of this book, I notice that the most
inviting site to work now is the nexus between teacher-readers and teacher-
writers as a generative place to reflect about our selves and our practices in the
community of other educators. My solitary narrative work has led me to see the
need for teachers to narrate our teaching together, to write our experiences and
then study them as a place from which to work to improve our practice and
understand more about the nature of difficulty in teaching as a normal and
useful part of education that keeps us alert, engaged, and maturing toward a
wisdom and a poetics in teaching. Talking about these things with each other
develops our professional literacies.

Like Heraclitus and the river, we never step into the same classroom twice
because of the tremendous flux of life. Every day, every minute is different.
Anything might happen. We have a professional choice about whether or not
that "uncertainty principle" closes us down with anxiety, a sense of continual
burden, and perpetual frustration at having so little personal control. It could

engender a lightness of being and mindfulness in teaching amid difficulty and change.

By the time I had con/trolled the narratives as writer and reader through all the previous orbitals of interpretive struggle, research, and thought, I came to conceive of the teaching self as a quantum field-of-self, as physical, atomic matter, as well as a complex electromagnetic field of psychic and existential energy. It is a postmodern, post-structural metaphor of a self in keeping with new or quantum physics and fractal mathematics. The meaning of that is that I now understand the self as a more durable, cohesive field, not subject to old structural risks of breaking. If "the centre cannot hold," perhaps it will shift as it needs to shift. The centre could move to where it is most required.

Seeing the (my) self as both matter (particle) and energy (wave) (rather like light), it is possible both to (re)construct a teaching self and to be constructed by the narrative of a teaching self, living at work. I can claim a cogent, authentic "beam or ray" of my being, and at the same time dwell in relation with others lightly, flexible but present, with appropriate boundaries, much like the electron clouds in orbitals around the core of an atom with its neutrons and protons. The probability of *fixing* that self at any finite point in space also will be subject to Heisenberg's uncertainty principle. That is precisely the quality that allows us to enter the teaching and learning space day after day.

We are matter and energy subject to all the bio-physical laws of a genetics designed for infinite recombination (especially through our narratives). Teaching becomes the chemistry and physics of (relational post-Newtonian mass, gravity, and energy of) each orbiting field-of-self who is engaged in individual projects of *currere,* all within the collective common reality of oxygen, water, carbon, and space. It is a durable self that I can constitute, using all the knowledge I construct, as I learn more about the difficulty of living my way into being a teacher and studying the nature of being a teacher of teachers.

The curriculum of difficulty for the teacher to learn has the professional, ethical, intelligent, and personal *aim* of reconstituting the self to be the best teacher possible at every moment in a state of pedagogical poetic being. Narrative methods contribute to that kind of practice and reflection of that reflection in very important ways.

More lessons lie ahead. The places I want to look now involve those ruptures where I am startled by text and life. I wish to develop more of my notions of a "field-of-self" in teaching. Study in self-narratives explores the metaphor of story as the double helix of human consciousness and experience, thinks about the place of narrative research in teacher education and difficulty, and creates a self-forgetting, embodied poetics in breathing and teaching. As teacher and researcher, I am not a contractual being, but I do construct a covenant with my students, my self, and the study with a consciousness of hermeneutic *educaritas*. Through my curriculum research and study, I create, develop, and refine pedagogical literacies that I can bring to my students.

May we be interested in answering Pinar's (2004) invitation in curriculum and pedagogy for reconstruction:

> Subjective and social reconstruction is our professional obligation as educators in this nightmarish moment of anti-intellectualism and political subjugation. Alone and together, let us participate in complicated conversation with ourselves and with colleagues worldwide. Let us construct an increasingly sophisticated and auditory field of education, one worthy of those schoolteachers and students who, each day, nearly everywhere on the globe, labor to understand themselves and the world they inhabit. May our "complicated conversation" complicate theirs—and yours.
>
> –Pinar, 2004, p. 258

Internarrative: Dr. Mercanfract and Heidi—
The Unbearable Likeness of Teaching

While my response [to a text] may be philosophically irrelevant, such a judgment is pertinent itself only inside a philosophy class. Educationally the significance of [the text] is my response to it, it is the way I use it to illumine my darkness, and so lighted, move into unexplored rooms.

—Pinar, 1981, p. 340

"Good morning, everyone. Welcome to Physics 12. On your desk you will find a course outline, a laboratory report book, and a student-interest inventory page. Please set aside the lab book and the inventory sheet and focus at the top of page one. Young man, this is a class for scholars and unless you are prepared to come up here and teach today's class, I suggest you have two options: you are welcome to join our community of scholars, which requires your undivided listening attention. On the other hand, you are welcome to take up Shakespeare's ancient invitation: 'There is the door: there lies the way'."

Polite laughter rippled quietly through the class, and the young man, blushing to his roots, muttered, "Sorry, Dr. Mercanfract; it won't happen again."

"Quite all right, we are each allowed an error or two. You have gotten yours over with quickly and you've inadvertently taught others proper behaviour so we can get on with the business of becoming scientists. Now, let us study the course outline together. You should make note of your questions as we go, and I will provide time at the end to deal with each question in turn. After all, that is the purpose of true science—is it not—to answer important questions about our world?"

Dr. Mercanfract placed her right hand in her lab coat pocket, held the course outline in her left, and launched into her beloved orderly world of physical science, tacitly pleased at the way she had handled the ruffling interruption. The student's quick acquiescence served her purposes well and got the class atmosphere off to a proper start. It meant she would need to brook very little adolescent silliness in this lot, because the pressure of disapproving peers, wanting to appear adult-like, already was at work.

. . .

Heidi West, the girl in the first row by the windows, was particularly stirred by the intelligent rhetoric of this tall, patrician scientist before her. She had never heard a woman talk with such erudition before, about important things like the meaning and purpose of philosophy and ethics in science. Doctor Mercanfract's serious passion about the work needed on Earth called to something awakening deep inside Heidi. This teacher's whole way of being, from the certainty of her starched, heavy-cotton lab coat, to her no-nonsense penny loafers, to her sensible, close-cut, salt-and-pepper, silver hair, provided an image of an interesting life for a woman that Heidi never had been able to see in her mother or her mother's friends. Their lives seemed entirely circumscribed by husbands, children, shopping, cooking, and cleaning—all those daily, mundane activities that seemed so alien to Heidi.

How like an outsider she felt when recipes were exchanged, stitches in knitting corrected, or new wallpaper patterns enthused over. She had worried quite a bit lately about what would become of her in the next crucial five years. How would she ever manage what seemed to be expected of girls: to attract some boy "with prospects"? The boys in her neighbourhood always seemed so rough and physical and mean, fighting or near-fighting in their games. She had never been attracted to them in any meaningful way, even though she knew she was supposed to be. Other than for a good game of baseball catch, she never chose to spend time with them. It wasn't that they were unpredictable, but rather that they were predictable. Maybe she felt this way because she didn't really know any boys whom she could call "friends" yet. But the likelihood of romance seemed impossibly remote, given her complete lack of interest in them as potential partners.

Heidi also had learned, the hard way, to keep some of her feelings about her girlfriends carefully hidden. She often felt like an outsider when she was with them as well, listening to their giggles as they passed a blush of boys on the sidewalk or to their talk about their dates, "how far they went," and who had broken up with whom, so "he was fair game now; you should go after him, Heidi." These days she experienced an inner mist of loneliness and was often silent with too many puzzlements.

Given what she could see of the marriages in her neighbourhood, understanding eluded Heidi about how other women, her mother included, had become attracted and then attached to their husbands. The adult men seemed to disappear out of the house for eight to ten hours a day to their important jobs, then come home, and sit down to the table for an already prepared good dinner just like their mother used to make. They seemed to spend their evenings watching television sports, reading the paper, or tinkering with their cars. They were to be deferred to, managed, cared for, paid attention to—especially if displeased or annoyed—and asked for constant approval for everything from school grades to haircuts to baby-sitting jobs. Meanwhile, the women and girl children in every home in her community washed and tidied up, did laundry, ironed, finished their homework, did needlework, and occasionally broke up arguments among the boys. After baths and reading and bedtime snacks were accomplished, the adult women planned what was for dinner the next day, made lists of what needed getting, bought, repaired, phoned, made. Communication, friendship, or care between those men and women, contractually bound before God and the law, wasn't apparent in any way to Heidi. The whole pattern was sometimes a depressing mystery, one that seemed to exclude her.

It troubled Heidi in her images of her future self to think of growing up to do exactly the same, missing only the face of the man who would be in her own adult household. When people asked her what she wanted to be when she grew up, she always said, "A doctor," and then tried to ignore the indulgent smirks of the inquiring adult. "I do have the grades, you know, and there are women doctors now," she would assure them. But her confidence faltered because she didn't know any personally, had only read of them, and at just eighteen was aware only that would-be-doctors went to university and did medical school and then an internship. How she would get there herself had not been worked out, and the closer she got to finishing high school, the further away the possibility seemed.

Now here, in the first fifteen minutes of this Physics 12 class, Heidi saw the white video blank of her own future begin to take shape. She would show Dr. Mercanfract that she was a very serious scientist. Dr. M. would know how to get into medicine because she had talked about a special few people in this class who would go on to be doctors and scientists. Heidi vowed then and there she would be one of them, and she planned to stay after school to tell her plans to this teacher with the formidable presence and reputation.

. . .

Dr. Bertha Mercanfract really liked to teach physics to her three classes of Grade 12 students. Behind those seventy-five pairs of eyes might well dwell the one mind that the country desperately needed. Certainly she could have been teaching at a university, but she believed young people needed passionate scientists in the school system to kindle students' scientific curiosity. Medicine, physics, genetics, chemistry, astronomy, engineering—all the sciences—needed upcoming, dedicated minds for ongoing work. Why the teaching of beginners in an academic discipline was left to the newest and youngest teachers was beyond Dr. Mercanfract. She took her teaching work very seriously. Through careful planning of the curriculum, rigorous lectures and assignments, and challenging assessment, she knew that many students would come up to the task and see the value of living a life committed to important scientific work. High school was the critical time when people often made life choices about careers.

She did notice one interesting and serious-looking girl in the front row by the windows, saw that undivided glitter in the eyes fixed as she began to lecture about the history of physics and the characteristics of a serious scientific mind. The girl may just have ideas of greatness without real ability, but still she seemed very alert and keen.

Dr. Mercanfract asked the students to fill out their self-inventories next. Her purpose was to hook into the prior knowledge and existing cognitive schemata of the class members, both individually and collectively. Reviews and teaching methods were planned accordingly. Some questions about interests in books and films and television and sports were designed to set them at ease in a comfortable social way, but the real questions that Dr. Mercanfract read carefully were those about units of science they excelled at in earlier grades, who their favourite scientist was and why, along with a list of scientific formulae to see if the students knew them and their importance to society. She wanted her students to work hard and felt responsible for filling in cognitive gaps they might have.

That first day her students also were given their own lab books, along with a carefully prepared set of three sample lab reports—a terrible, unacceptable one, a mediocre one that would get them by with a C+, and a splendid one that went well beyond the requirements quantitatively and qualitatively, which taught her something that was original and had the potential for publication in a science journal. She couldn't help paying close attention to those students who asked her to clarify her expectations about the A+ example. These were the potential students who perhaps would continue in science after graduation.

Again she noticed the young woman, in this class of predominately male students, when she raised her hand along with those who wanted to attend a noon-hour seminar on lab writing. Good. That was a place to sound out how deep her real interest was in physics. She felt positive about this class, excited about initiating them into significant studies.

Dr. Mercanfract went on with the rest of her handouts for them. The well-planned course was laid out topic by topic and week by week in thorough detail. The course outline was nearly ten pages long and included assignments, weighting for each assignment, quizzes, tests, and examinations with their percentage values. It was perfectly clear to every student what the curricular demands were and what explicit responsibilities they would be shouldering to pass the course. Nine or ten students never came back after that first day with the course outline and student inventory. While she was sorry to see those students go, Dr. Mercanfract also felt pleased about the academic rigor and proper attitude that this set for the year—only the dedicated remained to study. Much was possible to accomplish with those remaining keen students.

She also handed out the leaflets about the Advanced Placement and International Baccalaureate programs and made her generous offer of tutoring Saturday morning physics sessions. The goal was to move students toward success in those extra exams that would earn them early university credits and cause their averages to soar in the first year of post-secondary education as a result of the intensive high school work. She prided herself on the fact that a few students returned to her each autumn from university to get advice and additional coaching about their freshman courses. Once again, the young woman in the first row took out a highlighter pen and began to mark various points on the two programs as Dr. Mercanfract spoke. Clearly there was at least one avid student in this year's class.

At the close of that first class, Dr. Mercanfract reviewed the procedure for correct format and content of laboratory reports, making it clear that they were about to embark upon an apprenticeship of a time-honoured discipline, using the same scientific method all great scientists used. A clear-headed knowledge and use of the facts were required as they developed a rational, objective approach to the world that worked in concert with their initiation into adulthood. It was a time to "put away childish things," and her call to them, for their minds and understanding to go to work in the service of the global community, was a passionate and meaningful one. She made it clear that they were needed, that science had some critical problems ahead that it had not yet solved. She explained to them how essential it was to educate and welcome new, disciplined, intelligent, concerned, young scholars in science. This was the key start into mature, real-life work, well beyond the realms of childhood and definitely not for the faint of heart. Dr. Mercanfract's students were stirred by her wonderful invitation to them to work hard with her.

. . .

Heidi West knew when she got home from school that first day not to mention how much she liked her Physics 12 class or her new teacher. When her mother asked, "How was school today, dear?" Heidi replied, "Okay, it's just school. I need to do my homework. I'll be in my room." She wanted to keep to herself that feeling from her two-hour morning physics class and the short, inspiring conversation she had managed to have with Dr. Mercanfract after school.

. . .

The next morning Heidi left early for school so she could sit on the cement ledge near the steps to the main teachers' entrance to the school. She was hoping to be "accidentally discovered" by Dr. Mercanfract, but she also wanted to find out what kind of car Dr. Mercanfract drove. Just after 7:30, an older, navy-blue Volvo station wagon, in mint condition, pulled into the lot, and Heidi's early rising was rewarded.

After memorizing the licence plate, she watched her science teacher collect a lovely, well-worn, chocolate-brown briefcase, a couple of videos and text-books, and a paper lunch bag. Watching her teacher cross the parking lot toward the entrance where Heidi waited gave her time to appreciate Dr. Mercanfract's beautiful full-length, navy cashmere coat, notice her steady, certain gait, and come to the startling conclusion that she thought Dr. Mercanfract was a thoroughly handsome woman. It was the first time in her life she had connected the word beautiful to a human being, and something important shifted inside, something that at once felt dangerous and exciting.

"Good morning, Dr. Mercanfract."

"Good morning, young lady. You were in my Physics 12 class yesterday, were you not, up in the front row, and then spoke to me for a few minutes after classes about getting into medical school? Lots of work to get there, but if you set your mind to it, and stay diligently focussed, you can do it. Remind me of your name, please."

"Dr., uh, uh, my name is Heidi West, Dr. Mercanfract."

"'Dr. M.' will be fine, Heidi. Glad to see you here early, ready to work. If you come with me, I can unlock the classroom so you can get started before classes begin."

"Oh yes, thank you." Heidi collected her backpack, closed the physics text she had posed on her knee, and leaped to her feet to follow Dr. M., the Dr. M. who had noticed her in the front row yesterday! The Dr. M. who said Heidi could, if she would set her mind to it. Well, she certainly could—and would. She was more than ready to begin now.

Heidi echoed Dr. M.'s "good mornings" to the principal, the vice principal, the caretaker, the secretaries, various teachers, and students, feeling very much like she belonged in this school and very much like she was walking with Dr. Mercanfract.

Over the following two hours of class, Heidi diligently took notes, listened, nodded, read in her textbook, and constructed careful, perfect answers to the questions at the end of the chapter on light.

. . .

Every morning for a full term, Heidi waited at the front door at school to greet Dr. M. and be let into the classroom to work for an hour before classes started. She also attended the Saturday morning study classes and would have stayed to help Dr. M. in the lab in the afternoon, but her mother thought going to school on Saturday mornings was nonsense and made it clear that Heidi had plenty of chores to be done Saturday afternoon at home, before the Sabbath.

All Heidi's work paid off: Her marks in Physics 12 were all in the 95–100 percent range, and consistently over 85 percent in biology and chemistry. And she was pretty sure Dr. M. noticed. She worked at being a model student to please Dr. M. and tried to ignore the new peculiar sensation beneath her fifth rib whenever she was near her physics teacher. Heidi had never been happier or more hopeful in her life. Dr. M. was even recommending that Heidi be awarded the school science exchange scholarship. It involved a nationwide science conference and a three-week course at Coast University for budding young women in science and paid for air fare, accommodation, and meals. Only private spending money was needed, and her baby-sitting money had accumulated over the years, so she could easily manage that part.

She planned how to approach the subject with her mother, sensing neither she nor her father would give permission, but somehow the time was never right. Maybe Dr. M. would help her work that out. She would ask her the next day since the permission slip had to be signed by Friday—the day after parent-teacher interviews.

After the next afternoon's dismissal bell, two days before parent interviews and three before the conference application deadline, Heidi ran out to the parking lot to wait for Dr. M. and ask her advice, but the navy car was gone! She returned to her locker in the hallway down from the lab and stood staring into the metal closet, her heart pounding. Where was Dr. M.? She had to talk to her. A classroom door opened nearby and Dr. M. came out, locking the door behind her and undoing her umbrella in readiness for the pouring rain.

"Heidi! It's five o'clock, dear, why haven't you gone home?"

"I looked for your car, but it was gone. I need to talk to you."

"You can walk me out, Heidi, but you'll have to make it quick; my ride is waiting for me and I am a bit late."

"Well, it's about the science award you have been trying to arrange for me and . . ."

They rounded the last corner before the exit and literally bumped into a woman as tall as and even more elegant than Dr. Mercanfract. Heidi had never seen the woman before in her life.

"Bert, what on earth happened to you? I was getting worried. You said to come at 4:30, and it's after 5:00."

"Sorry, luv, tinkering again, you know me. I needed to set things up for tomorrow's lab and make a few transparencies for the overhead. This is Heidi, one of my senior physics students. Heidi, this is Dr. Erincoeur. It's pouring rain. Perhaps we could give her a lift home, Jess."

"Hello, Heidi. Does your teacher make you work as hard as she does herself? Yes, of course, we can drop you off, if it's not too far. Chris and Brenda and the kids will be there at six, Bert. Remember?"

"Oh Lord, is that tonight? Jess, I have a set of quizzes to grade and tomorrow night is parent-teacher interviews. I need to look over my anecdotal notes. Never mind, we'll work it out. Where do you live, Heidi?"

Heidi had been rendered speechless until now. "Uh, about eight blocks up Rendon Street and over a couple on Monet, but you're in a hurry—I can walk. It's not raining that hard."

"Nonsense. Hop in the car, Heidi. That's not far out of our way. Besides you can tell me what you were going to ask me."

As the Volvo pulled out of the lot, Heidi sat in the back seat and stared in wonderment at these two amazing, tall, attractive women, listening to their amicable bantering. "Love" Dr. M. called the woman! What would it be like to have Dr. M. call her that? And Jess (was it?) called Dr. M. "Bert." Heidi looked out the window and imagined the woman calling her Erick. They must live together, thought Heidi. There was a deep ease, comfort, and friendliness between them, a closeness that certainly none of her friends or her mother's friends seemed to share. It was almost like they were married or something. She wondered what it would be like to go home with them instead of to her own bleak existence.

Home! Suddenly, she didn't want Dr. M. to see the little house she lived in, and she couldn't possibly let her mother see her getting a ride home because she would have to explain to her. She tapped Dr. M.'s shoulder and sputtered out, "Here will be fine. Thanks. The corner. Please just stop here. I . . . I have to stop here and get some milk at the corner store."

"Are you sure, Heidi?"

"Yes, yes. Thank you for the ride."

"Okay, but borrow my umbrella. I guess we will have to have that talk tomorrow about what's on your mind, okay?"

"No, no . . . I don't need your umbrella. I will be fine. Okay. Thanks." Heidi leapt out of the car, almost before it came to a full halt, and dashed off down the sidewalk toward her house without even a pretense of stopping at the store.

. . .

That evening Heidi lay on her bed and stayed awake for hours thinking about the ease and warmth between the two women who had driven her home. Care was evident even in the way they talked to one another. She had assumed that Dr. M. was married to a faceless Mr. Mercanfract and, like most students, really hadn't thought about her teachers' lives outside the classroom. But that night Heidi was comforted by thinking about those two remarkable women going home together to have company for dinner, doing the dishes together after the guests left, talking and joking as they discussed their day, their ideas, and their work. Perhaps Dr. Erincoeur would make a cup of tea for Dr. M. while she marked her papers and prepared for the next day. Heidi finally drifted off to sleep wondering if the two kind and confident women also shared the same bed.

. . .

Heidi awoke with a jolt next morning, realizing she had not talked to her mother about the honorary science scholarship, let alone gotten her to sign the compulsory consent form. Thankfully her mother had to pick up an elderly neighbour for an early dental appointment, so Heidi dashed off to school without breakfast, saw the navy car already parked, and rushed to the lab.

Dr. M. was preparing an electrical parallel and series circuitry experiment but glanced up at Heidi's hurried and somewhat haphazard entrance. "Slow down young lady, what's on your mind?"

"Um. Thank you for the ride yesterday. Your friend is very nice. Do you live with her?"

"You are welcome. Yes, she is, and, yes, I do, although my private life doesn't really concern you. It's not a question you really ought to be asking, Heidi. Now what is all the panic?"

"I haven't talked to my mother about the science scholarship yet, and Friday is the deadline for the consent form. I don't think she will let me go because it's almost four weeks away from home. She already thinks all the work on Saturdays is ridiculous and thinks I should get a part-time job with Dad's company so I can work up the ladder there and give up this nonsense about telling people I want to be a doctor." Heidi blurted all this out and began to cry.

Dr. M. set down the soldering gun and looked steadily at Heidi. "I see."

"I'm sorry, I didn't mean to be rude, Dr. M. I really didn't, it's just that you seem so happy together, and yesterday, well, I wish I was your friend like Dr. Erincoeur, or at least, I wished I had somebody like you do."

"I'm sure you will find somebody important in your life, all in good time, Heidi, but now what are we going to do about this scholarship business? Is your mother coming to the interviews tomorrow?"

"Yeah, I think so, but . . . "

"Would you like me to talk with her about it?"

"Oh, would you?"

"Yes, I will, but I want you to come with her, Heidi. She needs to know how serious you are about this. Now hold this wire still while I solder it to the capacitor."

Dr. M.'s lab coat sleeve brushed against Heidi's arm as she connected the wire again. As the older woman's shoulder inadvertently pressed against her student in an attempt to reach the awkward circuitry, Heidi thought she could smell grapefruit soap from the warmth of the woman's so-close, lovely face. Dr. M., deeply engaged in the electrical problem at hand, was completely unaware of her prize pupil's overwhelming desire to put her arms around her teacher's neck and never let go.

. . .

Mrs. West walked two feet in front of Heidi as they crossed the gymnasium to the small desk where Dr. Mercanfract sat in alphabetical order with the other eighty teachers at the large high school's parent-teacher night. Dr. M. rose, offered her hand in greeting to both of them, and invited them to sit down.

Heidi fidgeted nervously, tightly pressing a small eucalyptus leaf in her pocket. She watched Dr. Mercanfract and tried to ignore her mother.

"Well, Mrs. West, in short, your daughter Heidi is the best physics student in this school and has a promising future ahead."

"She certainly works hard enough at it. I hope she isn't getting any fancy ideas. Her father and I are hard workers, and there's no point filling her head with high falutin' ideas. We can't be paying for any of that university business. She needs to settle down, get a job, and find herself a husband and start a family of her own. I have been encouraging her to take typing and computer. She claims she's not interested, but interest hardly matters when you have to make a living. I'm sure a sensible woman like yourself knows what I mean."

Heidi stared at the brass rings that opened up the holes in the gym floor for the volleyball net poles to go in and wished she could shrink and slide down into one of them right then.

"Perhaps you aren't aware of the fact that Heidi is the top science student in our very large school, Mrs. West. She wouldn't need to pay tuition and board at the university. Her marks alone would guarantee scholarships, and there are lots of programs available, especially for young women who want to make a career of science. In fact, Heidi has been recommended for a three-week summer scholarship in conjunction with a national science conference this coming summer, all expenses paid. All we need is your approval for her to go ahead."

Mrs. West had been pulling on her gloves in readiness to leave, but at Dr. Mercanfract's last piece of news, her head snapped up, and she glared at Heidi. "Did you know about this?"

Heidi nodded miserably.

"Mrs. West, please, this is a tremendous opportunity for Heidi. If you would give your consent, it would mean everything to Heidi."

"You'd do well to keep to your teaching, Mrs., uh, Mrs.—Heidi, it's time to go." She gathered up her handbag tightly and started toward the door.

"Mrs. West, please talk it over with your husband and say, 'Yes,' for Heidi's sake."

. . .

"Wait'll your father hears about this nonsense, young lady. Where on earth is your head? You are dreaming, girl. Your big fancy teacher might be putting grand ideas in your head, but you are going to have to work for a living, until you can get yourself a husband. The way you carry on, young lady, no man is bound to have you anyway. Now, get those supper dishes done and get to bed.

I don't care if you are eighteen. Half the time you behave like a twelve-year-old, mooning around listening to your sentimental symphony music and writing in that little journal book thing of yours. When I was your age I had been working for two years at a law firm. That's where I met your father. He owned the furniture company that supplied all the law offices. And he can jolly well arrange a job for you this summer. You aren't going anywhere, so get that idea out of your head."

. . .

The next morning Heidi refused to come out of her room and was absent from school. Her mother barged in midmorning and said, "You have one day to sulk, young lady, and then you get back to that school and finish up your courses. Nobody is going to hire a dropout."

"Mom, please, have you talked to Dad? I have to go get that scholarship. I promise: I will work with Dad as soon as it's over. Please."

"Your Father is very busy right now, Heidi. Maybe tonight after dinner, but I really don't think it is a good idea. That teacher has put grand ideas in your head."

"She hasn't put any ideas I didn't already have. She is a great teacher. You don't even know her. Besides, this is a big honour. God, I can't believe you, mother. And don't call me young lady."

"You stay in your room, Heidi. Don't you speak to me like that, in that tone of voice. I don't want to hear another word about this nonsense. Your father will speak to you later."

What seemed like hours later, Heidi heard a light tap on her bedroom door. Her father pushed open the door and said quietly, "What's all this about some summer thing at school? Your mother doesn't think it's a good idea."

"Oh Dad, please, I have the top grades in science in our whole school, and my physics teacher recommended me for a scholarship in the summer. It wouldn't cost you any money, and it really is an honour to be sent. Please, Dad, please. This is a big chance I won't get again."

"Who is this physics teacher anyway, and why was your mother so cross after the interview?"

"She thinks Dr. Mercanfract is putting ideas in my head about being a doctor, but she's not. I have always wanted to be a doctor, if you'd pay any attention to what I say. She's just a great teacher. My marks mean it is possible for me to go to university. My mother just wants me to get a job and get married, but I am not the marrying kind, Dad. This could be my career. You have got to help me, 'cause Mom won't budge now, unless you say."

"I will have to think about this, Heidi, but I am really not sure it's a good idea, as your mother says. And don't talk silliness about not being a marrying kind. Every girl dreams of a husband and home of her own."

"Not every girl, Dad. But please say, 'Yes.' I have to get the consent form in tomorrow or it will be too late. Please."

. . .

Heidi sat at the breakfast table, dully swirling the floating raisins in her bran flakes, waiting for the inevitable disapproval.

"Your father and I have decided it is not possible for you to be away this summer. You will just have to tell that physics teacher of yours that her job is to get you to pass Grade 12 Physics and finish school, so you can get on with your life."

Heidi looked at her mother and yelled. "This is the rest of my life—now. Just because you live a stupid confined life doesn't mean I have to," and lunged out the door only grabbing her knapsack at the last minute. She had known her father would never side with her against her mother, so this morning she had already packed a few essentials in her bag, along with her school work on top. She had already determined never to come across this threshold again.

She started off toward school but couldn't face that. She skipped physics, unable to confront Dr. M., and went to the city library, seeking refuge in the familiar, silent stacks.

All day she aimlessly flipped through science magazines, signed out a biography of Mme. Curie, and photocopied an issue that featured Dr. Roberta Bondar's career from girlhood to her recent space flight. She wished she had mothers like they did who understood how important science was. At seven, the library closed and Heidi sauntered to the little cafe that specialized in paprika goulash, whatever that was, near Dr. M.'s address, which she had found in the phone book.

She ordered the "special" and, working at being adult, ordered a latte, after the woman who owned the cafe described to her what it was. By now her mother would be furious; Heidi should have been home four hours ago. She glanced out the window at the fading daylight and considered from an odd, new distance what she might do next.

The door to the cafe opened, and the woman who lived with Dr. M. entered.

"Hi, Ulricka, two goulash to go, please, with red cabbage salad." She glanced at Heidi and said, "Hello there; aren't you the student we gave a ride to the other day? What are you doing in this neighbourhood? You look bothered."

Uncharacteristically forthright, Heidi spoke directly to the woman, "My parents won't let me take the science scholarship, so I'm not going home."

"Ah, and this is the scholarship that Bert, uh, Dr. Mercanfract, has recommended you for?"

"Yeah."

"So what are you going to do?"

"I don't know, but I am not going home—ever again."

"That's a bit extreme, dear. Is there no other way? Why don't you come and have a cup of tea with us, and we will see if there isn't some better way to sort this out?"

"Oh, could I? That would solve everything."

"Well, don't jump to conclusions. You better come and have a conference with your teacher. She may have some other ideas that could help you."

. . .

Over a cup of cocoa, Heidi spilled her story through tears of frustration to her attentive teacher, including how much she wanted to live like she and Dr. Erincoeur did, in spite of the hostile homophobic attitudes and vicious language of many of the students at school. "I don't care what anybody thinks anymore. And I want to be a doctor. You said if I really wanted to, I could be. Maybe I could stay here, with you two. I really care about you, you know."

Dr. M. listened through all of it, without interrupting, without moving. When Heidi was at last spent—having been heard out—Dr. M. began to speak to her.

"Heidi, I know this award means a great deal to you. But even if you don't go on the scholarship course, it certainly does not mean you cannot be a physician, if that is the life you choose for yourself. Your parents speak out of concern for you, even though you may not agree with them. Ultimately we are all responsible for the lives we choose to live, even if we do not choose what genetics, society, and culture have handed us. If you decided to live a life closer to one like mine, there are some wonderful advantages and some difficult disadvantages, but that is the same for all of us in any community. Jess and I have made a good life for ourselves, and we both have work that matters to us. When the time comes, I trust you will make the best life possible for yourself as well—like ours, or not. But you certainly cannot stay here with us. I am your teacher, Heidi, and that is how I best can help you. It isn't that we do not like you or do not care about you, but you need to go back home, finish your schooling, and then make some decisions after you graduate. In only a few months time, after you have graduated, and if you want to, you can arrange to move and find a place of your own."

Heidi began to weep again.

"Heidi, why don't we phone your mother and father and ask them over to explain again? We will go through the award business with them one more time, then if they don't agree, you are going to have to let this go. They will be very worried about you by now."

Heidi shook her head, "It's no use. They don't understand."

But Bertha Mercanfract picked up the phone, asked Heidi for her number, and when Mr. West answered, spoke quietly to him for several minutes. When the Wests arrived, they declined tea, but before they left with Heidi, they did sign the consent form with the mutual understanding that after the conference and course in July, she would work all of August in the furniture business before she decided about university.

. . .

Heidi's plane landed and one of the science conference hosts saw that she got the right bus to Coast University. She followed the "Young Women Scholars in Science" signs at the main entrance and found the registration table where an envelope with her materials and name tag awaited. She moved away from the conference table and noticed an elegant, light-haired young woman, who also had picked up the same conference package. Heidi smiled shyly at her and told her how much she admired her navy cashmere coat and her chocolate-brown briefcase. Together they studied the campus map, laughed at their mutual unfamiliarity with the grounds, and headed off to find the residences, eager to begin their professional lives.

Internarrative: Getting Clearer Vision

It is time for the voice of the mother to be heard in education.
—Noddings, 1989

The woman I needed to call my mother was silenced before I was born.
—Rich, 1974

The first time I noticed Moira, she was sitting in the front, right-hand desk as I faced the classroom. I handed out a science review quiz, carefully constructed the weekend before, to find out what my first class of Grade 9 Science students knew, coming fresh out of Grade 8. It was the first day of their classes in September and because it was also my first year of teaching (I was twenty-eight years old—"no neophyte" I thought), I was intent on setting the tone of serious learning for their last year of junior high school, before going on to the big high school where their futures would be determined. I wanted to contribute to their best preparation possible.

I briskly called the register, introduced myself, and handed out a four-page course outline that accounted for every week of class in the semester. It had been organized in accordance with the curriculum prescribed, and I was excited about what we could accomplish together. It struck me as important to find out, with this initial testing, what the students already knew so that I could compose one week's review relevant to them before we began the significant work of developing young scientific minds.

After they were done their quiz, I planned to hand out a "school-supplies gift" to them—a neat, black, hard-cover lab book for each individual student—and then take them into the real science lab for a short, "hands-on" experience. They would begin by doing a formal inventory of their equipment, practice some glass blowing and construction, and even on Day One, discover entry points into my beloved world of scientific inquiry. This was going to be a passionate, educational journey together.

But about five minutes into my white-lab-coated-high-heeled pacing up and down the rows, smiling to encourage any student who looked up, I heard something splash onto the floor. I whirled around ready to admonish the culprit who probably had smuggled in a coke, wasn't paying enough attention, and had spilled it on the classroom linoleum. That would teach him a lesson. But it came from the front right-hand desk, and the splashing sound came again.

The girl in that desk had both hands cupped over her mouth and was sitting as quietly as she could, vomiting into her hands, down over my beloved pristine white exam paper with the pale-blue, spirit-master duplicator ink, vomiting down her new white lace blouse, down her lovely new reversible plaid skirt, down her new white socks, down her new brown penny loafers, into a continuous series of waves that began to emanate from her feet under her desk. She was still trying to stem the volcanic, emetic pressure with her hands and so began to have trouble breathing. I converted my fear at her imminent aspirating and snapped at the boy behind her who was yelling, "GROSS!" I ordered him to get a box of paper towels from the bathroom, told another student to go to the office to send somebody down to take over the class, and yet another to find the caretaker with a mop and bucket. While I grabbed several lab towels and handed them to the wretched girl, I told the class to turn over their papers, take a five-minute recess outside and be back on time, sitting in their desks, "working or else."

"Let's go to the sink at the back of the room, dear. It'll be all right. Let's get you cleaned up and see if we can get your mother on the phone and get you home to lie down. Let me help you get cleaned up here. I have a clean pair of sweats I use for running in the morning. I will get the counsellor to show you where the showers are and then you can change and wait in the office or the nurse's room. Why didn't you just get up and go to the bathroom, dear?"

Tears continued to stream down her face as we wiped and washed and rinsed and as I talked seriously to my own gag reflex. The vomiting stopped but she still had not said a word. I remembered fleetingly that she had raised her hand but not her eyes, not her voice, when I had called her name from the register.

"What is your name, dear? This is a tough morning for you, but this will all be forgotten in a few days. Don't worry about what other people think, dear, everybody on the planet has thrown up at some time or other."

Her head, and especially her eyes, remained lowered. Not yet had we made eye contact and I knew her shame was extreme. She stood absolutely limp and passive as she allowed me to clean her up, wash her face, wipe her eyes, which continued to stream, and like a preschool child, even wipe her nose. Her sense of shame and necessity vied for my decision making about what to do. The class would be returning any minute, although no doubt one of them had been elected to watch the door and give the sign for the rest to come back in if I appeared in the hall looking for them.

I knelt down, took her hand, and asked, "Please tell me your name."

This time I had the sense to shut up and wait in silence for the answer. It took over a minute, and then she whispered, "Moira."

"Moira. Moira, I have been talking non-stop and telling you what I think you should do. What do you need to do?" and again I waited. No answer. "I am going to get another teacher to finish this class, Moira, and see if we can't get you what you need. Okay?" She nodded, eyes still down.

I called Harv, the six-foot-four, gentle-giant principal, and said I needed to look after a very upset student and could he take my Grade 9 Science class, who would need rounding up from the doorways where they smoked and "hung out."

"Yeah, of course, one of your students already warned me. Be there in two. Do what you have to and come back when you are ready."

Moira curled into herself and followed closely behind me to the nurse's quarters where there was a shower. I ran the water to a full warm temperature and then said, "I will be back in three minutes with some sweats and then we will see what to do. Do you still feel sick?" She shook her head no. I handed her two towels to set on the bench and closed the door.

After a few minutes I knocked on the door and asked if she was ready to come out. She whispered, "Yes." I gently pushed open the door; she sat, wearing my sweats, huddled in the corner on the bench by the shower stall.

"What happened back in the classroom, Moira, and what do I need to know from you so that it doesn't happen again? It's too hard on you. Do you have the flu, dear? Please try to talk to me."

"No-no . . . not the flu, I just . . . hate . . . tests. And, and . . . c-can't do them. I am . . . just . . . p-placed, placed in . . . Grade 9 here. I was r-really sick when I was a little g-girl. I am seventeen now, and I just can't . . . d-do . . . t-t-tests. I can't do them. You are s-so nice and I wanted to write this t-test and I told myself to just write. M-maybe this year could be a fresh s-start, like you said in your welcome, and maybe anybody c-can learn and maybe you could help me g-get it right this time and then maybe my mother won't think I'm so d-dumb all the time and maybe the kids won't t-tease me and maybe it won't matter that I limp from bad knee surgery from the boy kicking me last year and then and then. I-I-I . . . c-couldn't, I couldn't . . . couldn't . . . see the l-letters and couldn't remember . . . couldn't remember and . . . you walked up and down and up and down and I knew you'd b-be coming to look at my paper . . . and I wouldn't have anything written (sobbing) and then you'd be mad . . . (sobbing) and would order me out of the class and then I would have to b-be at home, at home with my mother all year again."

"So first thing, Moira, you don't want me to call your mother about this, right?"

"Oh no, Miss Fowler, oh no. I AM seventeen. Please don't call her, please don't." And for the first time since I saw her, she looked at me. There will never be fully accurate words for what I saw there: hopeless hope, tender fear, seedlings of possibilities, with deep knowledge that disappointment always is the ending to any story, but maybe, just this once . . .?

"Moira, second thing. I am not going to ask you to leave! You are my student and I want you here with me and the class this year. Second, we have lots of work to do together. And third thing, Moira—whenever you need to go to the bathroom or be sick or get a drink of water, please don't ask permission. That is a basic need; just get up and go. You never need permission from me to go to the bathroom. And if you need help you must learn to say so."

"But Miss Fowler, I don't know where the bathroom is in this school."

. . .

That year Moira was diagnosed as dyslexic, with some cognitive "holes" because of suffering a bout of meningitis in her second year, and she got glasses. We also devised an oral testing for all her exams, because all science tests were multiple choice in those days, and "surprise, surprise," the "b's" and "d's" were wrong about half of the time. Her grades were in between the 30 and 40 percent range on exams until we began the oral examining. Her grades then jumped to percentages in the high 50s and 60s, and if the questions were asked in declarative sentences, asking for short answers, her scores often fell into the 70 percent range. For her particular difficulties, the oral conversational assessment indicated a fairly good knowledge of all materials studied in class. This made a critical difference in a school year's final report and certainly a critical difference in Moira's educational life.

I taught at the same school for four years and taught Moira both English and science at the Grade 10 and 11 levels. My colleagues ribbed me about how badly she would do without me, but she learned to ask for what she needed. Sometimes she changed teachers at the beginning of September, but she got 52 percent on her biology 30 provincial diploma exam and 51 percent on her English diploma exam and graduated with high school matriculation at the age of twenty.

We kept in touch for sixteen years. Just six years ago at our yearly lunch, she confided that her mother had been sexually abusing her for years and still was. Recently, she had seen a television program where somebody was describing what had happened to her and how she felt about that, and Moira wondered what she could do about that herself and did I think she could manage living on her own away from her mother?

We found some help, and she has been in an apartment on her own and working with an optician grinding lenses and making eyeglasses. She told me she believes her job is really important because unless people have clear vision they cannot fully live. Indeed!

For the last 19 years of my teaching, in both secondary and post-secondary classes, the first day of any course is the one where I tell the location of the bathroom and the fire escape, and I explain how to get help in an emergency. It is all said with high humour, of course, but the information is there. I do not pace up and down rows, and most of the time we do not have the desks in rows in our classes. I try to explain what my vision is for the class, and I ask them for theirs. And the first day of any course, I never, never, give tests, just in case there is a Moira.

Chapter 9: Seventh Orbital—Aesthetics and Mindfulness in Research and Teaching

"We need . . . to know more about teachers' lives."

–Goodson, 1991, p. 138

"It is no chance matter we are discussing, but how one should live."

–Plato, *The Republic*

Startled by what I discover, uncover in the narratives, see in the narrative mirror, I return to breathing and Being. Deaths and losses, joys and love have woven themselves into my autobiography since I began this narrative research journey into difficulty, and began writing this book. Daily I sit in Vipassana meditation, with an attitude of compassionate attentiveness and ethical concern for all beings in the world including myself. I also work to be able to understand more about existential anxieties and changes of being. In research and teaching I also encounter those difficulties, which are my responsibility to understand, manage, and transform so that I can contribute in generative ways. I have noticed the difficulties of others and how they are often so like mine. In complicated conversations with friends, colleagues, students we think and talk deeply about what has changed after all the narratives are told about difficulty. What can change is nothing less than the experience of the nature of being. As Buddhists teach, three characteristics of existence are impermanence and change (*Anicca*), unsatisfactoriness and vulnerability (*Dukkha*), and being without inherent self (*Annata*). I concentrate on mindfulness of those characteristics and work at fostering the ability to be present, without judgment, in attentiveness to what is called for.

Now after all the narratives I notice the breath again. I attend to and gently name experiences, then let go and return to being, to the present moment. I notice much more these days in the phenomenology of being. And then again I return to breathing and meditation. Resting in being, I am capable of mindful attentiveness and attunement in a poetics of teaching.

I come to research and teaching in more skilful ways as narrator and artist, as one deeply engaged in poetics and philosophy. I can simply "let learning," especially in difficulty. Everything trembles, especially possibility. I want to leave computing, copying, (re)cording, (pre)diction, and instead, pay mindful attention to revelation rather than rubric, rupture rather than rote, rapture rather than mortal ramparts. With a narrative literacy I read poetics into being and refresh my engagement in teaching.

Poetics, according to Aristotle, has its strength in *mimesis*, in how life and nature are given the density of the real in art, drama, and literature. Narratives of teaching are both comedic and tragic, with high emotion and drama in their own harmonies and rhythms (language and breathing). Plots arise out of the action of the (teaching) story itself toward fresh, new images of teaching never before created. Aristotle spoke of comedy, where people are shown to be worse than they really are, and tragedy, which sees people as being greater than they are and invokes our pity and fear, effecting a releasing or catharsis. The same is true of narratives of the teaching self in difficulty, which can also teach us to move beyond fear, pity, and disgust to notice the poetics, aesthetics, and freedom in Being in teaching. The detritus can be released and the essence of teaching and learning emerge in beautiful complicated conversations.

Lure of the Aesthetic

Something in us does seem to want a more-ness in life: more meaning, more mattering, more beauty, more truth, more justice, more love. I work toward a more aesthetic existence in teaching and research to open both realms of common and private reality in education, openings (in)vented directly through my intense work on the narratives I wrote. Classical questions of poetics and philosophy about beauty, truth, freedom, and meaning appear and insinuate themselves into my attention. I consider more about how and why I am teaching[1] after all the other orbitals of narrative research and teaching have engaged me. I return again and again to that perpetual question: Who is the Self that Teaches?

Beauty in Teaching

Sometimes lately, on any ordinary weekday morning, I have been surprised by what beautiful work education can be. At its best, teaching and learning form one of the most beautiful complicated conversations in life. Teacher and student, student and teacher re/cognize each other and the world. Curriculum is in the continual motion and method of *currere* (see William F. Pinar's work). Redefining my thinking and being offers up a greater freedom and truth in teaching. I have changed my way of being and my way of understanding of self and teaching. Education makes for some of the best and most hopeful work on the planet, as we reflectively witness engagements of ourselves and our students, in the process of reconstituting life narratives toward more aesthetic, artful existence. As Dewey (1931) reminds us:

> Art throws off the covers that hide the expressiveness of experienced things: it quickens us from the slackness of routine and enables us to forget ourselves in the delight of experiencing the world about us in its varied qualities and forms. It intercepts every shade of expressiveness found in objects and orders them in a new experience of life.
>
> –p. 104

In the realm of poetics, in conjunction with hermeneutics and phenomenology of pedagogy in teacherly texts, my work stretches ahead, in advance of my being there. Moments of quiet understanding, gentle exhalations of "Ah, so that is what teaching might be," have begun to give me pause and courage to continue. Those moments of clarity are rare, but they are enough for this resilient and concerned teacher to keep focused on what is continually being revealed in the acts of teaching and learning (so inextricably fused). I see clearly that difficulty is natural and important for both student and teacher. Difficulty invites me still, in pursuit of my research through artistic narratives about difficulty, toward the poetics of being Teacher.

Researching Truths in Teaching

Narrative research is qualitatively autobiographical and phenomenological in nature and this is always revealed in the stories we choose to speak, read, write, or invent. This is not trivial or narcissistic research. *Teacher* can be conceptualized as curriculum worker, as scientist, but also as artist and philosopher who studies truths without judgement. As Pinar (1981) writes:

> Qualitative research is politically progressive, as it is epistemologically sophisticated, because it understands that a basic meaning of human life is movement, conflict, resolution, each thesis and anti-thesis opposing each other in ways that give birth to a new order of understanding and life. The task is not to control this movement, nor is it merely to portray it. It is to contribute to it, acting as midwives in the labor which is human history coming to form. This contribution can be made in work with ourselves, as well as work with others. It is work that cultivates the specificity of ourselves, the particularity of self and situation. Autobiographical method is one strategy by which this work can be conducted. In another sense autobiographical work, because it focuses

upon the self and its history, slows down movement, makes it stay, so it becomes more visible, its detail discernible. It is like a blow-up in a photographic sense. A character in Virginia Woolf's *The Years* seeks to see the same: "There must be another life, here and now, she repeated. This is too short, too broken. We know nothing, even about ourselves. We're only just beginning, she thought, to understand, here and there. She held her hand hallowed: she felt that she wanted to enclose the present and future, until it shone, whole, bright, deep with understanding."

–p. 173

These narratives I laboured over do indeed provide scaffolding to slow down life/movement, to make visible what is often hidden, and contribute to meaning developed around understanding of teachers' lives and the selves who dwell in such difficult places. Narrative scaffolding provides temporary (temporal) containment for research that engages others to begin constructing personal poetics, teaching, relationship, understanding, and meaning in the middle of difficulty in their own lives.

Aesthetic Government of the Inner Teaching Self

I am beginning to understand deeply here and there and have caught glimmerings of several fresh aesthetic self-governing images of a teaching life that could shine "whole, bright, deep with understanding" within our teaching community. Along with that understanding come aesthetic frames that arise out of the research. That knowing becomes the masonry for self-government, one of the essential qualities needed for an ethical teaching self.

One frame of self-government is in the wholesome desire for being the best teacher possible in every teaching action. Most teachers I know are indeed their best human selves in a classroom, modeling what it is to be an ethical, reflective, and present human being, living toward all that is best in human life.

A second frame of self-government is the place to hermeneutically notice the "given-ness" and original difficulties of teaching and then consciously re-story being without interfering with students or taking their openings for learning away from them.

A third frame in self-governing narrative research in education may be the place of openings provided by the researcher as a place to rebuild praxis or deconstruct/reconstruct scaffolding as a ground on which to stand in teaching at the edge of the mortal abyss and still know the possibility of joy, love, and meaning. We become able to have a practice of freedom in teaching and to conduct liberatory practices in research. As bell hooks (1994) invites, we can teach to transgress an unacceptable status quo by calling into question in a pedagogic space what is wrong or what needs our attention. Narratives offer one powerful pedagogic space to study together what is called for in right action and wholesome living.

A fourth frame of inner government returns us to full breathing in teaching and reminds us of the rhythm and harmony of (in)spiration and (ex)piration, recycling breath in language, embodying understanding and interpretation in a quantum quintessence of reflectivity. I struggle toward that kind of being, resist *distraction*, and choose to dwell mindfully in my present Being and Time.

Difficult Curricula: Toward Participating in "Complicated Conversations"

In coming to a terminus with this book, I want to return to an examination of my own epistemological and ontological narrative. Autobiographical narrative reveals underpinnings and persistent themes that become intentional research, which, in turn, provides a way to talk about difficulty at the site of the (professional) self. In early childhood days struggling toward understanding of myself, my experiences, and my world, I learned a vast range of plot lines, but not until I participated in the difficult curriculum of narrative research did I study patterns, connections, historical detail, cultural niches, and social relations of people's real and possible lives, mine among them (Kerby, 1991; Polkinghorne, 1988).

At sixteen years of age I began my first of four summers working as recreational therapist at a provincial institution for people with severe mental and physical disabilities. I gained a new understanding of the miracle of Whitman's "body electric" and the horrific alternatives. There, where more than a hundred Dickensian "Smikes" dwelled, I learned my hardest lessons of difficulty in the human condition. I learned how to find the smallest window of opening for relational connection with damaged bodies and souls. I discovered the importance of learning and using names of the people with whom I work. I learned to begin in the middle of things and work generatively in impossible situations. I learned the uselessness of expecting that what I planned to teach or say or do would actually happen. I learned that the focus of teaching work is to pay alert attention to the living curriculum as described by philosophers and reformers (such as A. N. Whitehead and John Dewey), to notice even at the edge of the abyss (Caputo, 1987) what really is going on, and to question what the original difficulty might be in order to understand what is being called for in the moment.

In Loco Parentis

Throughout my adolescence I also baby-sat on a daily basis for my sister and two brothers, who are a more than a decade younger than I. Those surrogate mothering years taught me about total care, human development from birth, and naive-but-wise points of view of children. I do not have children of my own; however, as teacher in the contractual, practical, and ethical position of *in loco parentis*, I often reach back to those early experiences. Those kind of physical and emotional needs must be met for people of all ages before cognitive requirements of literacy can be attended to.

Resisting Coming to Teaching

As chapter 1 revealed, I held many jobs and took many different roads on my journey toward teaching. I worked in a bookstore. I worked "grave-yard shift" as a mail sorter for Canada Post. I waitressed in an exclusive Muskoka hotel in Ontario. I taught people how to drive cars. I had my own house-painting business, calling myself "The Paintress." All of these were part- or full-time jobs. At the same time, at university, I was actively studying English, Canadian, and American literature, children's literature, Jacobean drama, linguistics, Latin, French, and German, concomitantly with organic and inorganic chemistry, zoology, microbiology, genetics, physics, immunology, physiology, and physical education. After obtaining a Bachelor of Science degree in biology, I studied and did radiation genetics research on resistant strains of bacteria and super-antibiotics for a year. All of these separate lives, deep with multiple narratives of self and other, are enfolded beneath the narratives I bring to my teaching work and to this book.

Being Thrown into Education

In 1976 I applied to medical school and was selected from eighteen hundred applicants for one of three hundred interviews. The interview was a disaster. First I was asked by my Sikh male interviewer why I was divorced, then told I was quite old (twenty-five!), and finally told that I did not have the absolute top grade-point average. He did not recommend that white-female-I be accepted into the program. I felt the taste of discrimination and of profound failure as long-term dreams of being a physician crashed down around me. Devastated by the experience, I went into education reluctantly to get a job. Unwittingly, that man was one of Fate's turning points and taught me lessons that have served me well as a teacher. Experience of failure and potential for discrimination are two places in myself, and others, where I have learned to be mindful. Becoming a teacher catapulted me into learning more about myself, my assumptions, my commitments, my direction, my very existence. It became important to me to be conscious of what I was bringing to the classroom, which was useful because it drew my attention to the need also to be present in teaching, a lifelong enterprise of both self-understanding and self-forgetting.

Classroom Teaching

After studying secondary biology and English methods, educational foundations, philosophy, education history, comparative education, moral education, and counselling, I graduated with a Bachelor of Education and took a teaching post at a new high school in a small rural town forty-minutes' drive from home. I began to invest my whole being into educational work, while continuing to write fiction and poetry in my leisure time. In teaching I began to see myself, my being in the world, in a very different light than I had before in the world of empirical science.

In 1982 after four years of teaching biology, chemistry, physics, and English to students in grades 9 to 12, I was called by a local community college and asked if I would like to teach communications, composition, film and novel, Canadian literature, women's literature, children's literature, and humanities courses. Having learned my secondary work well, I was interested in teaching at the post-secondary level. The timing was right for me to keep growing and learning, and for the next eight years, on a yearly contractual basis, I taught subjects in the humanities to students in law enforcement, nursing, child care work, early childhood education, media, library science, and general arts and sciences. During the last four years at the college, while working full-time, I completed a master's degree in English Education, a thesis[2]—far too enjoyable—about what published writers who also teach writing have to say to teachers of composition.

Needing a change with new horizons and irritated with seemingly infinite sessional work, I started a fresh commitment in a continuing contract with an urban public school board. The first year there I began as if a neophyte teacher, at the bottom of the ladder, given all non-academic students in new-to-me courses. That twelfth year of my teaching, both the students and I learned a great deal. Out of 134 students, I lost 3 students: one to a move out-of-province, one to the working world of prostitution, and one to suicide by hanging. I was told the program was an enormous success, and my principal wrote my praises to the board for the "highest retention rate" in the district. Even though I needed to accept no blame—we worked productively to-gether—I kept thinking of the two lost students. Whatever they had learned, it was not enough for them to be able to save themselves.

The second year at that urban high school, I became an English department head of sixteen teachers, and the third year I was promoted to curriculum coordinator for the whole school with its teaching staff of eighty and student population of two thousand. My work with difficult *kids at risk* was balanced by my work with the top academic students. I began Advanced Placement and Staying in School programs with a core of teachers committed to generative changes within the larger faculty. We experimented with alternatives in timeta-bles, examinations, and course requirements. Mature students were allowed to accelerate through courses as long as they did all the work and passed their tests. We arranged half-day schooling time-tables (with Saturday morning seminars) for those students who needed to work, pay rent, and look after their own children. Our success rate was high, and we were encouraged to talk at professional development days about our goals, methods, and good results. Difficulties began to be glossed over in the rhetoric we fashioned in the reports and presentations we were encouraged to submit as the school basked in its ameliorating work. I was in the classroom less and less. The "stories" I was being asked to tell teachers and administrators seemed like metaconstructions of common reality, which took me away from truths of teaching for aggran-dizement of school and teacher performance, forgetting the individual hearts and minds of the students in my educational care. With my experience of increased political stakes, sloppy research, and Elmer Gantry-esque lectures to others to teach the use of our "models," disillusionment began to set in, and whether I was in my own classroom or someone else's, Sisyphean teaching days began to tumble down on my head, knocking me into the abyss. I began to *fall*.

Especially when I am in difficulty I turn to narratives of Other. While fal-ling, on weekends and holidays I continued to read the winners of the Booker, Whitbread, Pulitzer, Nobel, and Governors-General prizes for literature and continued to write fiction. The combination is always humbling: being im-mersed in all the best writing in the world and then attempting one's own narrative work. When I could not write, I kept myself to the discipline of at least a page of prose each day, even if it was raging *freewriting* (Fowler, 1989; Elbow 1973, 1981; Goldberg, 1994). Little did I know that I was apprenticing in rigorous work for my doctorate: Difficulty in teaching began to be an obsession.

When I left the public secondary, I and my classes looked to be very successful: I had the highest student attendance rate, a higher-than-usual class average for most teachers—in spite of my non-academic classes—and Canadian Achievement Test scores that looked wonderful and meant very little in terms of what work students actually did. I was exhausted by the sheer will, energy, and hours required just to keep me and my students from drowning, while being required to put on a happy face. Perhaps I have always been too idealistic, but I developed a profound disgust with the way the system worked, scooping in tax dollars, politicking, and merely containing, rather than doing meaningful work with the youth of our nation, day after day after day, as pretenses of civility were sand-papered away by inner psychologies and needs that were neither recognized nor confronted. The possibility of meaningful existence, truth, ethics, and beauty trickled away from my work and life. My modern structural concept of self caused me to experience a life-threatening, fissured slippage between my outer, successful, public educator role and my inner, distressed, private mortal human being. The inconsistencies and paradoxes began to tear at my (teaching) self. From a privately broken, angry, quitting teacher (clinging to the limp parchment from my provincial government and school board in 1992 that publicly declared my excellence in teaching) I came out the other side of five years of intensive, qualitative doctoral research on all aspects of my being with full respect for the remarkable work that real teachers, I among them, are called to do.

Opening Difficulty in Being the Mentor Teacher

In 1992 I escaped from forty years of dwelling on the Canadian prairies and fourteen years of rural and urban secondary and post-secondary classroom teaching and moved to a beautiful Gulf Island in British Columbia with the intention of writing full-time on the novels and plays I had in progress. In my fiction writing I encountered my self and my unknowing. Needing to learn more about intentional being, I began doctoral work in curriculum studies at the University of Victoria, taking courses, and writing fictional narratives about difficulty in teaching. Thus began my work as mentor teacher.

Also in 1992 I began sessional teaching of English language arts methods and curriculum courses to student teachers, as well as being a teaching assistant and faculty supervisor of student teachers. Being responsible for supervision of students in their practicum placements especially pressed my nose against the perpetual dark glass of difficulty in education.[3] Difficulty in teaching becomes foregrounded in the internship process of novice teachers as they explicitly struggle with control of themselves, their materials, plans and activities, assessment and evaluation, and of course, their students. As witness and helper in development of teaching practice, I literally observed difficulty (and continue to encounter it in each practicum round) in the practices of other teachers—both in apprentices and in their classroom mentors. Memories and confrontations with my own practice always ensue.

Being a mentor teacher, a faculty supervisor in my case, opens questions of difficulty about assessment and evaluation as well. Especially being in a position of "judgment" about whether or not student teachers are "capable" and show evidence of attitudes, knowledge, skills, and professional conduct to indicate their readiness for becoming fully engaged teachers (responsible in contractual, academic, psychological, practical, and ethical ways) I felt the call to examine my own practices, theories, and work. While assessment and evaluation are not the domain of this study, they do reveal themselves as persistent loci of difficulty and are embedded narratively in the work I do.

Because of my long, deep relationship with narrative—a long history of writing and reading, with a rich interior life as a result of those two human endeavours—it was natural to make sense of teaching through writing and narrative research. Stories began to tumble out of my pen before I was aware of what was happening and what might lie beneath the surface of those storied texts. To discover what I think, know, and understand about difficulty in teaching, I began at the beginning again, thrown back to first experiences and naive, inchoate writings. I needed to "language" myself into truthful meaning.

A Perpetual Hermeneut

It is always a difficulty to speak certain truths,[4] but for me the difficulty became too great not to speak. Precisely because of the way my life was for so many years, I am an hermeneuticist who looks for subtext, assumes there are things hidden behind what is visible, does not trust labels as accurate or descriptive, wants to return to the original difficulty of things, and desires multiple, textual interpretations as essential methods for getting at truths and meaning that shift and move continually. This hermeneutic orientation affects the teaching work I do, demanding that I bring a sharp presence of (com)passionate attention. Perhaps the Bible is right about the relationship between truth and freedom.

Part of authentic narrative research is constituting an earned new freedom arising from the exploration about truths of teaching, especially those difficult to confront and know. Old confining professional and personal stories can be set down. Theorizing and interpreting meaning from narratives of difficulty and self has proven to be healing (hooks, 1994), generative, and useful in its implications for educational and relational practices. New more generative identities and being can emerge.

Displays of Difficulty: Uncomfortable Data in the Research of Narratives
Years ago I intuitively began to write narratives about difficulty in teaching as an ethical way to make sense of educational work, to examine perplexing places of my own pedagogical actions (Greene, 1973, 1987; Grumet, 1988; Pinar, 1994; Pinar et al., 1995), to deal with the hundred tiny griefs in a school day, and to explore my own life (Giroux, 1983) in order to understand better what I bring to that which lies beneath the prescribed curricula I teach. The topic of difficulty reveals itself as the consistent integral theme in existential being and in teaching work. Questions always arise about the nature of difficulty and how it might be understood, opened up, reframed with different perspectives, and used in productive, educative, relational contexts. No doubt I will continue to work autobiographically and narratively to (re)search and explore other better possibilities for dwelling in engagements with students and learning (Middleton, 1993).

In pursuit of exploring and understanding my topic of difficulty, I unravel many of my silences (two of them maintained for over forty years) and learn to speak (however awkwardly) about questions of difficulty and truth that reveal themselves. I continue to learn the important lessons they have to teach me. I continue to write narratively as I research difficulty.

After the Narratives

While researching inductively through multiple writings, readings, and interpretations of my narratives grounded in life experiences, seven relational orbitals seemed to emerge through narrative exploration of difficulty around the teaching self. With these seven orbitals—naive storying, psychological de/reconstruction, psychotherapeutic ethics, narrative craft, hermeneutic enterprise, curriculum and pedagogy, and aesthetics and mindfulness in teaching—I continue to uncover and discover persistent questions and openings. Difficulties are revealed, calling for work with the self and with others. Possibilities emerge for creative play with difficulty. Throughout the text I have included references about the influence of writers and researchers whose projects and ideas resonate with the work I am doing.

In my present role as education professor working with undergraduate and graduate students and teachers and administrators in the field, I have an increasing hopefulness, compassion, and humility because I can see and know the durable strength of teachers' matter/energy field-of-self that engages with students. Daily, successful teachers, students, and educational leaders reconstitute themselves and answer again and again with their lives (Casey, 1993). I hope readers find something of substance and encouragement here that provokes and invites other thoughts, stories, conversations, (re)search—perhaps even provokes other teaching, as we each move toward continuous reconstitution as *teacher*.

The poet Hirshfield (1997) says: "I know that hope is the hardest love we carry" (p. 39). This book is one (research) story, among many, of an enduring narrative, hermeneutic reconstitution of the relational field of difficulty in self, theory, and practice in teaching. Although the narratives in my own voice are about difficulty, they are also about hope, love, and meaning.

We seem to spend so much of our lives as human *doings* rather than human beings. We struggle, at odds with mortal time ticking away our non-renewable life minutes, hoping for something other than what is. What often continues to provide an existential anchor and source of meaning arises out of the narratives we live. While many seem to dwell in future shock in a harsh, warring, degenerating planet, I want to think that hope (for ourselves, for others, for the educational enterprise) is possible through creating a new literacy of narrative, which in turn fosters a literacy of metaphor, hermeneutics, and relationship.

If we think of narrative literacy as an authentic mode of meaning-making, as ways to come to know the world and participate in the world more fully, then narrative texts, metaphoric thinking, hermeneutic practices, and relational education can be included in the research work of educators and practitioners who work with narrative.

Unless I develop narrative literacy, I lose my own life plot with its sudden heuristic and soul-chilling discoveries of memory, perception and imagination. Unless I have narrative literacy, I cannot find my way to hopeful daily being in a larger sense. But there is a narrative gene in most of us. As I find my narratives, I consider their fit and meaning among others. I am encouraged by Hirshfield's poem "Da Capo" (1997) where she reminds me as her reader:

You may do this, I tell you, it is permitted
Begin again the story of your life.

–p. 19

And so I return to my own narrative literacy, a shifting site for my research on the (teaching) self. And narrative truths lead to reconceptualizing metaphors; we need new storied metaphors to think well. In the first paragraph of her novel *Unless* (2002) Shields writes:

> But happiness is not what I thought. Happiness is the lucky pane of glass you carry in your head. It takes all your cunning just to hang on to it, and once it's smashed you have to move into a different sort of life.

–p. 1

Happiness in teaching is continually smashed, and we continue to move into new lives, using narrative and metaphor to bear life. Unless I play with a metaphoric literacy to make radical connections across disciplines and lived life, I cannot imagine a more inclusive way in which real conversations could happen about why we are here and what we are doing.

Shields (2002) gives me another pane through which to see and think about narrative metaphors:

> We don't make metaphors in order to distract ourselves. Metaphors hold their own power over us ... . They're as real as the peony bushes we observe when we're children, lying flat on the grass and looking straight up to the undersides of leaves and petals and marvelling: Oh, this is secret territory, we think, an inverted world grown-ups can't see. But in fact, everyone knows about this palpable world; it stands for nothing but the world itself.

–p. 61

Everyone knows about metaphor. As I was cleaning my metaphoric windows one recent spring, someone once dear to me called my own literacy and research practices into serious question. Although appalling, unexpected, wounding, and difficult as it was, that challenge served the purpose of a necessary smashing of a particular glass of happiness. It cracked open some key metaphoric and relational education assumptions that forced me to re/search my teaching work. That smashing IS having the effect of moving me into a different sort of life. To do that requires a thoughtful attention to complicated conversation about the curriculum difficulty in the (teaching) self.

We languaged and languaging creatures have a historical fondness for narrative nouns and verbs. Witness all the liturgical, historical, and literary texts, revealing a near-genetic fondness for characters and plot. But I feel a certain slant of fatigue that nouns and verbs have too much to do with power and its uses, abuses, and intricacies. Bare subjects and predicates seem somehow too Neanderthal for these times. Complex, conditional narratives seem a richer source of knowing in the social sciences than they used to be.

Startled and moved by reading narratives through these seven orbitals of research thinking, I appreciate that *now* is the time we have. Perhaps this book may constitute hopeful beginnings of new narrative literacies to find, express, and hear meaning. And metaphors in this narrative research inevitably lead me to hermeneutics, with its care for meaning and message as a literacy committed to essential questions of interpretation and original difficulty: How we are reading, writing, speaking sub/text and inter/text? How do I mean? How do you? Why do we? How do we go on amid difficulty with ethical good will, humour, generative real work, and intelligent compassion?

I recognize the ontological mantle of my research cynicism as a defense mechanism against failing discourses and dwindling meaning in a complicated and brutal world. I will myself to ask: What do I need to learn, want to know, like to understand so that life and living would be better in this community of mortals (Caputo, 1987)? What might that imply for a working life in education? How do I stay in the *mysterical* and ethical play of research into difficulty in teaching?

I used to believe I had control over my narrative literacy skills, could write when looking for meaning—pedagogic, professional, literary, or personal. I have loved (perfect past tense) to play with and in language, as a central happiness amid all else. But that glass of happiness in language has been smashed. I must move into a different sort of life and reach back toward questions of relationship. Unless I/we attend to relational literacy, with its call to read the world, one's self, others, and the spaces between, what hope can prevail against diaspora? Unless we attend to the relational matrices of our lives, the language that "grows in the middle" (Aoki, 1993), we may die or be killed. I do not want to live in such a world, so I need to consider what narratives are conduits for best selves in (educational) relationship.

What we do not yet know about self and other, through lack of narrative connection, can be a fatal absence of a certain kind of literacy, a "radical incompetence at being human" (Le Guin, 1989, p. 43). Shields (2002) speaks of formative difficulties of ignorance that threaten the development of narrative relational literacy:

Most of what I remember from the early years is my own appalling ignorance. A partial view of the world was handed to me . . . and the rest I had to pretend to know. Like all children, I was obliged to stagger from one faulty recognition to the next, always about to stumble into shame. It isn't what we know but what we don't know that does us in. Blushing and fumbling, shuffling and stuttering—these are surface expressions of a deeper pain. The shame of ignorance is killing. [The] questions, more like miracles in their phenomenological shapes, gathered around me and formed the oxygen I breathed and what they whispered to me was: You will very possibly be killed because of your ignorance. It could happen at any moment.

–pp. 142–143

As a teacher educator, I am in the business of anti-ignorance curriculum, but it is still so humbling to look at epistemological roots of unknowing. The hope is in the formation of trust, empathy, narrative connection, and reflexivity, elements of friendship described by Donawa (1999) that constitute the best of relational literacy. It is in relation we learn and become ourselves. Our academic communities could do with more such friendships, and those can begin in conversations, conferences, and shared reading of one another's texts, such as this one.

Unless I engage in the curriculum of "complicated conversations" about narrative research, especially needed in a mature life in teaching, I do not believe that we can move forward—autobiographically, politically, culturally. Unless my students reflect on their teaching lives, I suspect that they cannot really move forward either. If we communicate narratively, metaphorically, hermeneutically, and relationally, we can enlarge the boundaries of discourse and understanding.

Hirshfield's (1997) poem "Three Times My Life Has Opened" offers hope. She writes: "There is a door. It opens. Then it is closed. But a slip of light stays, like a scrap of unreadable paper left on the floor" (p. 108). Hope returns: I believe thoughtful narrative research like I suggest and complicated conversations about professional knowledge and practice can move unreadable scraps of narrative, relational being into new understanding. Let me invite others to contribute narratively and autobiographically to the curriculum of "sounds of silence breaking" (Miller, 2005).

Let us not crumble. Let us tell our narratives, write our stories, talk freely of many things. Let us find the subjunctive minerals in narrative, metaphor, hermeneutics, and relationship. Let us consider: Unless we explore essential narratives together in complicated conversations, how can we remain human and humane in a community of scholars dwelling in the difficult world?

Narrative research continues to offer particular truths in our deep understanding about the difficulty of being human and what it is we still need to learn and practice together in an environment of *educaritas*.

> It is the task of the writer to become that permeable and transparent: to become . . . a person on whom nothing is lost. What is put into the care of such a person will be well tended. Such a person can be trusted to tell the stories she is given to tell, and to tell them with the compassion that comes when the self's deepest interest is not in the self, but in turning outward and into awareness.
>
> Hirshfield, 1997, p. 223

I turn outward. I write. I think. I teach. I witness difficulty in the relational field of my teaching self. I am aware. I honour the fullness of Being.

Again, I begin narrative research in education and the practice of teaching.

Namaste, Teacher.

Internarrative: The Small Brown Duck

[This manuscript] is made up of scraps of nothing, which put together, made the trimming and furnished the sweetness for what might otherwise have been a drab life sucked away without a crunch. . . . It was these tiny things that, collectively, taught me how to live.
–Emily Carr in her introduction to *Hundreds and Thousands: The Journals of Emily Carr*, 1966

That's what metaphors do: teach one how to live.

–Wylie, 1995, p. 217

On the way to the market and post office we were sidetracked by a half-dozen common Mallard ducks that belonged to one of our neighbours up the road. From their mossy pond half a kilometre away, they had strayed down the main island asphalt highway, crossed over the yellow line, and waddled down our lane—"away without leave." Worrying that they would not find their way home without misadventure, I got out of my car and walked behind them with a closed umbrella serving as a staff to herd them back home.

I clucked and scolded and talked to them in their endearing home-trundling. I noticed that if I waved the umbrella left, they unfailingly swerved to the right. Waving the umbrella and moving to their right behind them, they contrarily veered left. To and fro we proceeded back up the highway in the relative safety of the ditch as ferry-bound logging trucks lumbered by, overusing "jake" brakes on the steep incline to maintain control at the expense of noise pollution. The ducks seemed oblivious to our potential oblivion.

One of the smaller female ducks, brown and white, could not quite keep up with her contango of feathered friends. Each time the denizen of ducks all went over a log or little obstacle, she would tumble forward onto her chest and neck and then bravely get up again, struggling to keep up with everybody else. Over and over, she fell and hurried and fell and hurried. But each time she fell a little further behind.

The difficulty of keeping up, as she was expected to, increased with time and distance. As the gap between her and the others increased she began to glance skyward, in vague remembrance of eagles. She paid more attention to what was left and right of her, listening for what might be behind, hurrying an extra step in her pace as she took in my presence and perhaps imagined ghosts past of big black dogs.

I watched one of the younger ducks hurrying at the front, who seemed uncertain about the way to their destination. She kept glancing back as if she noticed the difficulty the small brown duck had with keeping up. The young one slowed her pace as though to wait. The older one seemed to notice the young one waiting and was able to hurry a little more. It was almost as though they encouraged each other. The elder duck seemed to know the way and the young duck seemed to have energy enough for both of them. They made a successful journey, and we all arrived safely back at the farmyard. I like to imagine that they lived out the rest of their lives in relative peace, knowing that each was valued.

Notes

Chapter One

1 Such narratives are also the stuff of teaching and learning.

2 Throughout writing I struggle neologistically with crossovers of multiple word meanings, the insufficiency of language, the need to attend to nuance and subtext, the power of punctuation, and the creative call for linguistic invention, not to annoy the reader, but to make visible the perpetual difficulty of language and thought. I believe in the genetics of language, the sex of the text, in its potential for infinite powers of recombination to produce new, young texts that grow up, mature, and may (if not killed) become wise texts.

3 Kerby (1991) better explains: "Narratives are a primary embodiment of our understanding of the world, of experience, and ultimately of ourselves" (p. 3).

4 Pinar's "Method of *Currere,*" written in 1975, is one of those readings that shifts meaning each time I read it and continues to influence me. Actually doing the kind of work he advocates requires a confrontation with all of one's minotaurs in labyrinths of ever-revealing consciousness, soul, and being. It is not for the faint of heart and requires lionhearted courage. Researcher's caveat: Don't do this at home alone! You will certainly need wise mentors, a rich community of scholars both in text and in person, and perhaps thoroughgoing psychotherapy while on such research journeys. Nonetheless, I think it is a worthy curriculum journey for every teacher.

5 For example, Anna Freud, Alice Miller, and, more recently, Deborah Britzman.

6 Robert Musil wrote two books (*Man Without Qualities* and *Young Torless*) that to my mind explore the causes, terrible dangers, and fascist consequences of a vacuous, undeveloped, unexamined, amoral existence.

7 This concern has arisen in a number of collegial encounters. Two recent and notable examples: Janet Miller referred to the too many "cheerful" stories of teaching that abound in the literature (in conversation, April 2000 in Baton Rouge), and Jean Clandinin has also expressed concern to me about stories of teaching passing as educational research (in conversation at an oral defense at the University of Lethbridge in summer of 2000).

Chapter Two

1 For example, *The Creative Process*, first edited by Brewster Ghiselin in 1952.

2 John Irving's (1989) novel, A *Prayer for Owen Meany*, is for me an incredible study of the way everything in our lives works together and is evident at every moment if we pay attention to it. As a teacher, this is one of my own deep learning responsibilities: to understand how things work together in the *me* when I am in the classroom.

3 Translates as "shitty weather."

4 This brings to mind Mikhail Bahktin's (1986) important work around *dialogics* (regarding texts as many-voiced and intertextually rich, with shifting dynamics—between and among—

how the writer and reader responsively use text) and *intertextuality*, regarding our understanding of the relationships between texts and our seeing intertextuality as a starting place for understanding education as the development of communicative (relational) competence. (See also Beach, Green, Kamil, & Shanahan, 1992, pp. 181-210.)

5   Ricoeur (1981, p. 39) wrote that the world of the text may explode the world of the author.

6   Wounded by the spear of my own pen, and needing to be free, I attempt to restore truthful relics about teaching to their rightful places, but move out of the (educational) "wasteland" toward self-redemption. T. S. Eliot's poem by that name comes to mind and sends my authorial self off in other directions—but back to the task at hand, are you with me?

Chapter Four

1   To use Vygotsky's *(1978)* sense of *internalization* and of *zones of proximal development* (chapters 1 through 4) and throughout his work from 1987.

2   Madeleine Grumet (1988) talks about transference in *Bitter Milk*, and is also referred to in Pinar et al. (1995, p. 378). Transference is a psychotherapeutic term referring to "the reproduction of past emotional patterns in present relationships [and] denotes the displacement of original, often traumatic feelings that are transferred from those first associated with them [to another]". (p. 378). More of this in the psychotherapeutic ethics section.

3   Not to push a rather structural, literal (littoral?) metaphor too far, my Piscean nature reveals itself here in its attraction to things marine, watery, and albedo-esque. (See Jung's alchemical imagery in the *nigredo, albedo,* and *rubedo* realms in his *The Little Book of Dreams*.)

Chapter Five

1   In an assignment, a recent student of mine included a quote of Kierkegaard's that I have been unable to locate: "On wild trees, the flowers are fragrant; on cultivated trees, the fruit."

2   See, for example, Jane Rule's novels, short stories, essays, as well as documentary films about her life and work. See also the 1997 National Film Board 24-minute video "School's Out" in which gay and lesbian students speak about their experiences of growing up and being at school.

3   The story of Psyche—recall that the common nouns, *life* and *soul,* are often given as synonyms for psyche—and the danger of naming the lover is a story in need of rewriting so that we don't have to wander forever in search of the "lost" portion of our selves we expect to have completed by another. Why should we not name our selves, our knowledge, our loves? To continue to refuse self-knowledge, we remain at risk as humans, as learners, as teachers driven in eternal search of what is missing, rather than engagements with what is present. (Psyche's relationship with Venus, the cruel goddess of beauty and love, is a story to pursue elsewhere.)

4   Criminal stalking is another matter entirely, but also a difficulty in teaching.

5   Yes, even here, as matter shifts to energy, where perhaps inner light can be revealed.

Chapter Six

1   For example, Chamberlain (1990), Chambers (1984), Champigny (1972), Chatman (1978), Culler (1982), Genette (1979, 1980, 1988), Kerby (1991), Polkinghorne (1988), Ricoeur (1981, 1986), Scholes & Kellogg (1966), Spence (1982, 1986)—to name only a very few time-honoured scholars of narrative.

2   In the hermeneutic section ahead, Heidegger says a good deal about teacher as this kind of learner. As an English teacher perhaps it is possible to teach reading and writing without being a reader and writer, but the quality of the teaching work I call for in myself requires that I "know and am able to do" that which I teach. To teach writing well, I must write. To teach reading well, I must learn, understand, and practice reading. My own master's thesis constitutes a long argument for teaching from the inside of knowing and being, so that I am a learner alongside my students, as one who has been at learning longer and at more depth than they have. (I am less sure of this as time goes by.) To teach teachers, I must learn teaching. This is perhaps one of the fundamental differences between teacher and a student's helping peer and answers how as teacher I am more than mortal peer, not socially or politically, but in terms of self-knowledge.

3   Genette (1979, p. 34) writes at length about *muthos* and *dianoia*.

4   In the form of teaching narrative, for example.

5   It seems to me that this is precisely the process involved in moving the "particularity" of a story toward the "universal," making it available for "appropriation" to worthy readers.

6   Which leads me to wonder if teachers themselves hold the pen, what worlds will be signified, what possibilities for new ways of being (in school) might be read? And how can teachers grasp the pen and come to writing in order to write themselves?

7   Did Cixous and Caputo read each other's writing?

8   Is it a cold hermeneutic shudder?

9   I grew up with the danger and protection of not telling certain stories, however true, and envied the Fool in Shakespeare's *Lear* because he was the only one allowed to tell the "truth" to the king.

10   I am suspicious when someone says an exact number in such cases.

11   Horace said, "Let a manuscript be kept nine years; once out, it can't be stopped." It is now nearly time!

12   I chose not to include the work of Donald Murray, Donald Graves, Linda Flower, and those people who worked on questions of the composing process, because much of that work is included in my unpublished master's thesis (1989) *Gifts from the Tribe*.

13   Perhaps this is the deep apprenticeship of a writer. I think of the word *author* as "au Thor," struck to the quantum core of myself with textual narrative bolts of lighting, altering my balance in the field-of-self.

Internarrative: The Abysmal Performance of Miss Tofelize

1   Cumulative, confidential education history records of each child, held in school offices.

Chapter Seven

1   Phonological, syntactic, semantic, pragmatic

2   I am also interested in theology and jurisprudence, but those influences will not be explored here in detail; rather I will focus on the philosophical contexts of influence.

3   Hermes = *Her* and the plural *me*, which invites playful thinking about signifier, signified, and the distance and space of a writer with respect to her own text and the Dopplerian echoes that might be heard!

4   The question "what is an author?" is taken up in fascinating ways in Foucault's (Rabinow, 1984) essay of the same name.

5   Those first professional teachers ostensibly dealing in wisdom, rhetoric, and persuasion, who affirmed things as they were and stood for law and order, became caricatures for contempt as their "genuine knowledge" was called into question and found lacking—probably because of their ultimate goal of winning a debate rather than engaging in questions and answers of truth.

6   I had a wonderful German teacher at the undergraduate level, a Quaker woman who was a 12th-century German literature scholar. She introduced me to chamber music and the *Beyond War* peace movement, which have a very important place in my life. Several years after I studied with her, she had a massive cerebral hemorrhage and lost her ability to speak or understand English. I went often to read to her. After reading, at her insistence, English novels by Jane Austen that her hands still knew but not her comprehension, we switched to German literature, and I had to read and communicate with her entirely in German. The ways we are required to learn our subjects can be astonishing. She also spoke with me at length about Heidegger.

7   This concept is explored more fully in the section about Caputo's influence on me.

8   This strikes me as one of the most poignant and true descriptions of teacher burnout I have encountered.

9   What *is* underneath, hidden, in teaching?

10   This is an essential characteristic of all teaching and learning: knowing in part and needing to remember contextual place and relation among the disciplines, subjects, syllabi, and experiences lived in the classroom.

11   As though objectivity were truly possible.

12   This is useful information for my methods of working with narrative descriptions of everyday teaching.

13   Is this an intellectual (and false) equivalent to the search for the perfect mate in fairy tales?

14   *Unheimlich* is defined as "weird, uncanny, sinister," but also as "tremendous, terrific"; *heim* is translated as "home"; *heimlich* is translated as "secret, stealthy, furtive" (Langensheidt's pocket dictionary).

15   With Kierkegaard's concern for (re)constituting the self in order to "make Progress" in one's lifetime, how else to do that except deeply facing up to the original difficulty and truth of one's own mortal existence?

16   Sartre's famous novel *La Nausee* and Cixous's *Angst* retrace themselves in my memory here.

17   A phrase from the first line of W. B. Yeats' (1920) poem, "The Second Coming."

18   I disagree with Derrida that "messengers" ought to become obsolete—he lived in an artificial, privileged world where all are not dealt the same intellectual, social, financial, linguistic, and philosophical cards he got. Most do not decipher all messages as well as he assumes he does. But what of kids at risk, English as a Second Language students, poor students, "challenged" students, trying to decipher messages of their worlds alone? Can they not benefit from messengers, or perhaps teaching is obsolete?

19   Translated as "laying out" and "letting be."

20   Or fall, or are "thrown," I would add. At the very least it is a post-Kierkegaardian leap, without the intention of repetition or progress.

21   The ancient question of mothers—who told you life would be easy?—is deeply hermeneutic in its own right, projecting us right back into the *flux*.

22   Reference to Yeats' (1920) poem again.

Chapter Eight

1 Geologically, these are cavities in limestone into which a stream disappears. I am interested in the concept of this term as a possible phenomenon applied to the ethical, quantum infrastructure of teachers, if one can speak this way.

Chapter Nine

1 I did not and will not separately analyze my stories as critic because as Rilke says, "Works of art are of an infinite loneliness and with nothing to be so little appreciated as with criticism. Only love can grasp and hold and fairly judge them" (on the copyright page of every edition of *Brick: A Literary Journal*). As the writer of these difficult and incomplete and awkward stories I choose only to love them in their beginningness. Even for a research text, I do not wish to subject many of my stories to dissection—I leave that to the scholarly pathologists interested in the anatomy of narrative text.

2 My unpublished thesis (1989) *Gifts from the Tribe: The Writing and Teaching of Five Canadian Authors*, provides practical, important information for teaching writing. The authors, interviewed in the tradition of the *Paris Review* series, include Jane Rule, Rudy Wiebe, Bill Valgardson, Marsha Mildon, and Aritha van Herk.

3 Oblique reference to always only knowing in part: "through a glass darkly" (1 Cor. 13:12).

Bibliography

Anderson, L. (1997). The stories teachers tell and what they tell us. *Teaching and Teacher Education, 13*(1), 131–136.

Aoki, T. (Ed.). (n.d.). *Voices of teaching*. Monograph, Volume 1. Program for quality teaching. Vancouver, British Columbia, Canada: British Columbia's Teaching Federation.

———. (1981). *Inspiring curriculum and pedagogy: Talks to teachers*. Edmonton, Alberta, Canada: University of Alberta, Faculty of Education.

———. (1984). Towards a reconceptualization of curriculum implementation. In D. Hopkins & M. Wideen (Eds.), *Alternative perspectives on school improvement*. London, England: Falmer.

———. (Ed.). (1985). *Understanding curriculum as lived: Curriculum Canada VII*. Vancouver, British Columbia, Canada: University of British Columbia, Faculty of Education, Centre for the Study of Curriculum and Instruction.

———. (1986a). Interests, knowledge and evaluation: Alternative approaches to curriculum evaluation. *JCT*, 6 (4), 27–44.

———. (1986b). Teaching as in-dwelling between two curriculum worlds. *The B.C. Teacher,* April/May, 8–10.

———. (1990a, January/February). Inspiring the curriculum. *The ATA Magazine, 37*–42.

———. (1990b). Sonare and videre: Questioning the primacy of the eye in curriculum talk. In G. Willis & W. Schubert (Eds.), *Reflections from the heart of educational inquiry: Understanding curriculum and teaching through the arts* (pp. 182–189). Albany, NY: State University of New York Press.

———. (1992a). *Teachers narrating/narratives teaching*. Victoria, British Columbia, Canada: Ministry of Education and Ministry Responsible for Multiculturalism and Human Rights, Province of British Columbia.

———. (1992b). Layered understandings of teaching: The uncannily correct and the elusively true. In W. Pinar & W. Reynolds (Eds.), *Understanding curriculum as phenomenological and deconstructed text* (pp. 17–27). New York: Columbia Teachers College Press.

———. (1993). In the midst of the slippery theme-words: Toward designing multicultural curriculum. In T. Aoki & M. Shamasher (Eds.), *The call of teaching* (pp. 87–100). Vancouver, British Columbia, Canada: British Columbia's Teaching Federation.

Arac, J., Godzich, W., & Martin, W. (Eds.). (1983). *The Yale critics: Deconstruction in America*. Minneapolis: University of Minnesota Press. *Theory and history of literature*: Vol. 6 (Especially Part I: "Variations on Authority: Some Deconstructive Transformations of the New Criticism" and "The Domestication of Derrida" and Part III: "Joining the Text: From Heidegger to Derrida." The editors Geoffrey Hartman and Paul de Man "represent what we (as critics, scholars, humanists, teachers, and perhaps citizens) should be against."

Bachelard, G. (1964). *The poetics of space*. Boston: Beacon Press.

Bakhtin, M. (1986). *Speech genres and other late essays*. (C. Emerson & M. Holquist, Eds., V. W. McGee, Trans.). Austin: University of Texas Press. (Original work published 1979)

Bannerji, H., Carty, L., Dehli, K., Heald, S., & McKenna, K. (1991). *Unsettling relations: The university as a site of feminist struggles.* Toronto: Women's Press.

Barone, T. (1987). Educational platforms, teacher selection, and school reform: Issues emanating from a biographical case study. *Journal of Teacher Education, 38*(2), March-April, 12–17.

Barthes, R. (1986). *The rustle of language* (R. Howard, Trans.). New York: Hill & Wang.

Beach, A., Green, J., Kamil, M., & Shanahan, T. (1992). *Multidisciplinary perspectives on literacy research.* Urbana, IL: National Council of Teachers of English.

Beck, E. (1983). Self-disclosure and the commitment to social change. *Women's Studies International Forum, 6*(2), 159–164.

Belenky, M., Clinchy, B., Goldberger, N., & Tarule, J. (1986). *Women's ways of knowing: The development of self, voice, and mind.* New York: Basic Books.

Benet's Reader's Encyclopedia (3rd ed.). (1987). New York: Harper and Row.

Benstock, S. (Ed.). (1987). *Feminist issues in literary scholarship.* Bloomington: Indiana University Press.

Besner, N. (Ed.). (2003). *Carol Shields: The arts of a writing life.* Winnipeg, MAN: Prairie Fire Press.

Bettelheim, B. (1975). *The uses of enchantment: The meaning and importance of fairy tales.* New York: Knopf.

Bleicher, J. (1980). *Contemporary hermeneutics: Hermeneutics as method, philosophy, and critique.* London: Routledge & Kegan Paul.

Bloom, E. (1964). *The order of fiction: An introduction.* New York: Odyssey Press.

Boeckh, P. (1968). *On interpretation and criticism.* (J. Pritchard Norman, Trans. & Ed.). OK: University of Oklahoma Press.

Bogdan, R., & Biklen, S. (1992). *Qualitative research for education: An introduction to theory and methods.* Needham Heights, MA: Allyn & Bacon.

Britzman, D. (1991). *Practice makes practice: A critical study of learning to teach.* Albany, NY: State University of New York Press.

———. (1992). The terrible problem of knowing thyself: Toward a poststructural account of teacher identity. *Journal of Curriculum Theorizing, 9*(3), 23–46.

———. (1993). Slips that show and tell: Fashioning multiculture as a problem of representation. In C. McCarthy & W. Crichlow (Eds.), *Race, identity, and representation in education* (pp. 188–200). New York: Routledge.

Brodsky, G., & Day, S. (1989). *Canadian charter equality rights for women: One step forward or two steps back?* Ottawa: Canadian Advisory Council on the Status of Women.

Brodzki, B., & Schenck, C. (Eds.). (1988). *Life/lines: Theorizing women's autobiography.* Ithaca & London: Cornell University Press.

Brookes, A-L. (1992). *Feminist pedagogy: An autobiographical approach.* Halifax: Fernwood Publishing.

Brooks, P. (1985). *Reading for the plot: Design and intention in narrative.* New York: Vintage Books.

Broudy, H. (1982). What knowledge is of most worth? *Educational Leadership,* May, 574–578.

———. (1988). Aesthethics and the curriculum. In W. Pinar (Ed.), *Contemporary curriculum discourses* (pp. 332–342). Scottsdale, AZ: Gorsuch Scarisbrick.

Brown, L., & Gilligan, C. (1992). *Meeting at the crossroads: The landmark book about the turning points in girls' and women's lives.* New York: Ballantine Books.

Bruner, J. (1986). *Actual minds, possible worlds.* Cambridge, MA: Harvard University Press.

Bunch, C. (1987). *Passionate politics: Feminist theory in action.* New York: St. Martin's Press.

Bunch, C., & Pollack, S. (1983). *Learning our way: Essays in feminist education.* Trumansburg, NY: Crossing Press.

Butler, S., & Bentley, R. (1997). *Lifewriting: Learning through personal narrative.* Scarborough, ON: Pippin.

Campbell, J. (1988). *The power of myth*. New York: Anchor Books (Doubleday).

Caputo, J. D. (1978). *The mystical element in Heidegger's thought*. Athens, OH; Ohio University Press.

———. (1982). *Heidegger and Aquinas: An essay on overcoming metaphysics*. New York: Fordham University Press.

———. (1987). *Radical hermeneutics: Repetition, deconstruction, and the hermeneutic project*. Bloomington: Indiana University Press.

———. (2000). *More radical hermeneutics: On not knowing ourselves*. Bloomington: Indiana University Press.

Carr, D. (1985). Life and the narrator's art. In H. Silverman & D. Ihde (Eds.), *Hermeneutics and deconstruction*. Albany: State University of New York Press.

———. (1991). Ricoeur on narrative. In David Wood (Ed.), *On Paul Ricoeur: Narrative and interpretation*. London: Routledge.

Carr, E. (1966). *Hundreds and thousands: The journals of Emily Carr*.

Carroll, D. (1982). *The subject in question: The languages of theory and the strategies of fiction*. Chicago: University of Chicago Press.

Carter, K. (1993). The place of story in the study of teaching and teacher education. *Educational Researcher, 22*(1), 5–12, 18.

Casey, E. S. (1987). *Remembering: A phenomenological study*. Bloomington: Indiana University Press.

Casey, K. (1993). *I answer with my life: Life histories of women teachers working for social change*. New York: Routledge.

Chamberlain, D. (1990). *Narrative perspective in fiction*. Toronto: University of Toronto Press.

Chambers, C. (2004, Spring). Research Matters: Finding a Path With Heart. *Journal of Canadian Association of Curriculum Studies*, 1(3), 1-17.

Chambers, C. (2004, Spring). Antoinette Oberg: A Real Teacher … and An Organic but not so Public Intellectual. *Journal of Canadian Association of Curriculum Studies*, 1(3), 1-17.

Chambers, C. (2003, Fall). Things I carried with me…: A pilgrimage to Manitow Sakahikan (text plus 2 minutes streamed video). *Educational Insights*.
<http://www.csci.educ.ubc.ca/publication/insights/index.html

Cynthia Chambers. (2003). On Being a Disciple of Memoir. In Erika Hasebe-Ludt & Wanda Hurren (Eds.) *Curriculum Intertext*, pp. 103-109. New York, NY: Peter Lang.

Chambers, Cynthia. (2001). Confessions on learning the curriculum of love. *English Quarterly*, Vol. 33, Numbers 1 & 2., pp. 34-37.

Chambers, C. (1999). Chambers, C. (2004, Spring). Research Matters: Finding a Path With Heart. *Journal of Canadian Association of Curriculum Studies*, 1(3), 1-17.

Chambers, C. (1999). A Topography for Canadian Curriculum Theory. *Canadian Journal of Education*, 24(2), pp. 137-150).

Chambers, C. M. (1998). Composition and Composure, *Alberta English*, 36(2), 21-27.

Chambers, Cynthia (1998). On Taking My Own (Love) Medicine: Memory Work in Writing and Pedagogy. *Journal of Curriculum Theorizing*, Winter, 1998, pp. 14-20.

Chambers, R. (1984). *Story and situation: Narrative seduction and the power of fiction*. Minneapolis: University of Minnesota.

Champigny, R. (1972). *The ontology of narrative: An analysis*. The Hague: Mouton.

Chatman, S. (1978). *Story and discourse: Narrative structure in fiction and film*. Ithaca: Cornell University Press.

Cixous, H. (1976). The laugh of the Medusa. *Signs: Journal of Women in Culture and Society, 1*(4), 875–893.

Clandinin, J., & Connelly, M. (1987). Teachers' personal practical knowledge: What counts as "personal" is studies of the personal. *Journal of Curriculum Studies, 19*(6), 487–500.

————. (1990). Narrative, experience and the study of curriculum. *Cambridge Journal of Education, 20*(3), 241–254.

————. (1991). Narrative and story in practice and research. In D. Schon (Ed.), *The reflective turn: Case studies in and on educational practice* (pp. 258–281). New York: Teachers College Press.

————. (2000). *Narrative inquiry: Experience and story in qualitative research.* San Francisco: Jossey Bass.

Code, L. (1991). *What can she know? Feminist theory and the construction of knowledge.* Ithaca & London: Cornell University Press.

Coffey, A., & Atkinson, P. (1996). *Making sense of qualitative data: Complementary research strategies.* Thousand Oaks: Sage.

Cole, E. B. (1993). *Philosophy and feminist criticism.* New York: Paragon House.

Coles, R. (1989). *The call of stories: Teaching and the moral imagination.* Boston: Houghton Mifflin.

Connelly, M., & Clandinin, J. (1990). Stories of experience and narrative inquiry. *Educational Researcher, 19*(5), 2–14.

Crabtree, B., & Miller, W. (Eds.). (1992). *Doing qualitative research.* (Especially Chapter 5: A template approach to text analysis: Developing and using code-books, and Chapter 6: Grounded hermeneutic research.) Newbury Park, CA: Sage.

Culler, J. (1982). *On deconstruction.* Ithaca: Cornell University Press.

Danto, A. (1985). *Narration and knowledge.* New York: Columbia University Press.

Day, S. (1973). *A report on the status of women at the University of British Columbia.* Vancouver, BC: Talonbooks.

De Concini, B. (1990). *Narrative remembering.* Lantham, New York, London: University Press of America.

Dewey, J. (1897). My pedagogic creed. *The School Journal, 54*(3), 77–80.

————. (1931). *The way out of educational confusion.* Cambridge, MA: Harvard University Press.

————. (1959). *Dewey on education: Selections.* (M. Dworkin, Ed.). New York: Teachers College Press.

Dilliard, A. (1982). *Living by fiction.* New York: Harper and Row.

Dilthey, W. (1976). The development of hermeneutics. In H. P. Rickman (Ed., trans., & intro.), *Selected Writings.* Cambridge: Cambridge University Press.

Doerr, H. (1995). *Tiger in the snow: Stories and other inventions.* New York: Penguin.

Doll, W., Jr. (1993). *A post-modern perspective on curriculum.* New York: Teachers College Press.

Donawa, W. (1999). *A rebel band of friends: Understanding through women's narratives of friendship, identity, and moral agency.* Unpublished doctoral dissertation, University of Victoria, Victoria, British Columbia, Canada.

Droysen, J. (1897). *Outline of the principles of history.* (E. Andrews, Trans. & intro.). Boston: Ginn & Co. [8th ed. Munich: R. Oldenbourg, 1977]

Elbaz, F. (1981). The teacher's "practical knowledge": Report of a case study. *Curriculum Inquiry, 11*(1), 43–71.

Elbaz, F. & Elbaz, R. (1988). Curriculum and textuality. JCT, 8(2), 107–131.

Elbow, P. (1973). *Writing without teachers.* New York: Oxford University Press.

————. (1981). *Writing with power.* New York: Oxford University Press.

Ellsworth, E. (1989). Why doesn't this feel empowering? Working through the repressive myths of critical pedagogy. *Harvard Educational Review, 59*(3), 297–324.

Erikson, E. (1968). *Identity: Youth and crisis.* New York: Norton.

————. (1976). Reflections on Dr. Borg's life cycle. In E. Erikson (Ed.), *Adulthood.* New York: W. W. Norton.

Ermath, M. (1978). *Wilhelm Dilthey: The critique of historical reason.* Chicago: University of Chicago Press.

Evans, M. (1983). The teacher's tale: On teaching women's studies. *Women's Studies International Forum, 6*(3), 325–330.

Faludi, S. (1991). *Backlash: The undeclared war against American women.* New York: Crown Publishers.

Fenstermacher, G. (1997). On narrative. *Teaching and Teacher Education, 13*(1), 119–124.

Finson, S. (1985). *On the other side of silence: Patriarchy, consciousness, and silence—Some women's experience of theological education.* D. Min. thesis, Boston University, Boston, MA.

Forsas-Scott, H. (1991). *Textual liberation: European feminist writing in the twentieth century.* London & New York: Routledge.

Fowler, L. (1989). *Gifts from the tribe: The writing and teaching of five Canadian authors.* Unpublished Master of Education thesis, University of Alberta, Edmonton, AB.

Fox, F. (1993). Pirate: Self (fiction). *Feminist Studies, 19*(2), 31.

Frankl, V. (1963). *Man's search for meaning.* Boston: Beacon Press.

Freire, P. (1972). *Pedagogy of the oppressed.* Hammondsworth: Penguin.

Fullan, M. (1993). *The (new) meaning of educational change.* Toronto: Ontario Institute for Studies in Education (Teachers College Press).

Gadamer, H-G. (1975). *Truth and method: Outline for a Philosophical Hermeneutics.* New York: Crossroads.

———. (1984). The hermeneutics of suspicion. In G. Shapiri & A. Seed (Eds.), *Hermeneutics: Questions and interpretations.* Amherst, MA: University of Massachusetts Press.

Gadamer, H-G. (1986). *Philosophical apprenticeships.* New York: Crossroads.

Gaskell, J., & McLaren, A. (1991). *Women and education* (2nd ed.). Calgary, AB: Detselig Enterprises.

Genette, G. (1972). *Narrative discourse: An essay in method* (J. Lewin, Trans. & J. Culler foreward). Ithaca, NY: Cornell University Press.

———. (1988). *Narrative discourse revisited.* Ithaca, NY: Cornell University Press.

———. (1979, 1992). *The architexte: An introduction.* Oxford: University of California.

Ghiselin, B. (Ed.). (1952). *The creative process.* New York: Mentor Books.

Gilligan, C. (1982). *In a different voice: Psychological theory and women's development.* Cambridge, MA: Harvard University Press.

Gilligan, C., Lyons, N., & Hanmer, T. (Eds.). (1990). *Making connections: The relational worlds of adolescent girls at Emma Willard School.* Cambridge, MA: Harvard University Press.

Giroux, H. (1983). *Theory and resistance in education.* South Hadley, MA: Bergin & Garvey.

———. (1996). Radical pedagogy and the politics of the student voice. *Interchange, 17,* 48–69.

Giroux, H., Lankshear, C., McLaren, P., & Peters, M. (1996). *Counternarratives: Cultural studies and critical pedagogies in post-modern spaces.* New York & London: Routledge.

Glesne, C. (1999). *Becoming qualitative researchers: An introduction.* New York: Addison Wesley Longman.

Gluck, S. B., & Patai, D. (Eds.). (1991). *Women's worlds: The feminist practice of oral history.* New York: Routledge.

Goldberg, N. (1994). *Writing down the bones: Freeing the writer within.* Boston: Shambhala.

Goodson, I. (Ed.). (1991). *Teachers' lives and educational research.* In I. Goodson & R. Walker (Eds.), *Biography, identity, and schooling.* (137–149). London, England: Falmer.

Graham, R. (1993). Voice, archive, practice: The textual construction of professional identity. *Journal of Educational Thought, 27*(2), 186-193.

Greene, M. (1973). *Teacher as stranger.* Belmont, CA: Wadsworth.

———. (1987). Sense-making through story: An autobiographical inquiry. *Teaching Education, 1*(2).

Griffiths, M., & Whitford, M. (1988). *Feminist perspectives in philosophy*. Bloomington: Indiana University Press.

Grumet, M. (1981a). Autobiography and reconceptualization. In H. Giroux, A. N. Penna, & W. F. Pinar, (Eds.), *Curriculum and instruction*. Berkeley: McCutchan.

———. (1981b). Restitution and reconstruction of educational experience: An autobiographical method for curriculum theory. In M. Lawn & L. Barton (Eds.), *Rethinking curriculum studies: A radical approach*. New York: John Wiley.

———. (1988). *Bitter milk: Women and teaching*. Amherst: University of Massachusetts Press.

Habermas, J. (1993). *Interpretive social science vs. hermeneuticism*. In N. Haan, R. Bellah, P. Rabinow, & W. Sullivan (Eds.), *Social science as moral inquiry*. New York: Columbia University Press.

Hamilton, J. (1994). *The map of the world*. New York: Anchor Books (Doubleday).

Harding, S. (1991). *Whose science? Whose knowledge? Thinking from women's lives*. Ithaca, NY: Cornell University Press.

Hasebe-Ludt, E., & Hurren, W. (2001). *Curriculum intertext*: Place/language/pedagogy. New York: Peter Lang.

Havel, V. (1988). *Letters to Olga*. New York: Knopf.

———. *Open letters: Selected writings*, 1965–1990. New York: Knopf.

———. (1997). *The art of the impossible*. Toronto: Knopf.

Hayakawa, S. (1939). *Language in thought and action*. New York: Harcourt Brace Jovanovich.

Hayes, E. (1989). Insights from women's experiences for teaching and learning. *New Directions for Continuing Education, 43*(9).

Heidegger, M. (1962). *Being and time*. (J. Macquarrie & E. Robinson, Trans.). New York: Harper & Row. (Original work published 1927)

———. (1971). *Poetry, language, thought*. (A. Hofstadter, Trans.). New York: Harper Colophon Books.

Heilbrun, C. (1988). *Writing a woman's life*. New York: Ballantine.

Heshusius, L. (1992). Freeing ourselves from objectivity: Managing subjectivity or moving toward participatory knowledge? Paper presented at the Third Invitational Pedagogy Conference, Victoria, BC.

Hirsch, E. D. (1967). *Validity in interpretation*. New Haven: Yale University Press.

Hirshfield, J. (1997a). *Nine gates: Entering the mind of poetry*. New York: HarperPerennial.

———. (1997b). *Lives of the heart*. New York: HarperCollins.

———. (2001). *Given sugar, given salt*. New York: HarperCollins.

Hogsett, C. (1994). Women's ways of knowing Bloom's taxonomy. *Feminist Teacher, 7*(3), 27–32.

hooks, bell. (1994). *Teaching to transgress: Education as the practice of freedom*. New York, London: Routledge.

Howard, R. J. (1982). *Three faces of hermeneutics: An introduction to current theories of understanding*. Berkeley: University of California Press.

Hoy, P. C. (Ed.). (1990). *Women's voices: Visions and perspectives*. New York & Toronto: McGraw Hill.

Hunsberger, M. (1992). The time of texts. In W. F. Pinar & W. Reynolds, *Understanding curriculum as phenomenological and deconstructed text* . New York: Teachers College Press.

Hunt, D. (1990). Change: Comments on Deborah P. Britzman's review of *Beginning with ourselves*. In *Person, culture, and the initiations of change*. Toronto: John Wiley & Sons. (Ontario Institute for Studies in Education).

Irigaray, L. (1989). When our lips speak together (C. Burke, Trans.). *Signs, 6*(1), Autumn, 69–79.

Irving, J. (1989). *A prayer for Owen Meany*. New York: Ballantine Books.

Jacobus, M. (1979). The difference of view. In M. Jacobus (Ed.), *Women writing and writing about women* (pp. 10–21). New York: Barnes & Noble.

Jardine, D. (1992a). Reflections on education, hermeneutics and ambiguity: Hermeneutics as a restoring of life to its original difficulty. In W. Pinar & W. Reynolds (Eds.), *Understanding curriculum as phenomenological and deconstructed text.* New York: Teachers College Press.

———. (1992b). *Speaking with a boneless tongue.* Bragg Creek, AB: Makyo Press.

Jauss, H-R. (1982). *Aesthetic experience and literary hermeneutics.* Minneapolis: University of Minnesota Press. Theory and History of Literature, Vol. 3. (Especially A-5, Poiesis: the productive side of aesthetic experience [*construire et connaitre*]; A-6, Aesthesis: the receptive side of aesthetic experience [*voir plus de choses qu'on n'en sait*]; A-7 Catharsis: the communicative efficacy of aesthetic experience [*movere* et *conciliare*]; A-8, Aesthetic experience among the problems of everyday life: problems of delimitation).

Jensen, D. (Ed.). (1991). *Coming to writing and other essays: Hélène Cixous.* Cambridge: Harvard University Press.

Jung, C. G. (1971). *The portable Jung.* (J. Campbell, Ed.). New York: Penguin.

Kant, I. (1964). *Critique of pure reason* (N. K. Smith, Trans.). London: Macmillan.

Kerby, P. (1991). *Narrative and the self.* Bloomington: Indiana University Press.

Kirby, S., & McKenna, K. (1989). *Experience, research, social change: Methods from the margins.* Toronto: Garamond Press.

Kockelmans, J. J. (1986). *A companion to Martin Heidegger's "Being and Time."* Washington, DC: Centre for Advanced Research in Phenomenology & University Press of America.

Kohlberg, L. (1981). *The philosophy of moral development.* San Francisco: Harper & Row.

Krall, F. (1988). From the inside out: Personal history as educational research. *Educational Theory, 38*(4), Fall.

Krell, D. (1977). On the manifold meaning of *Aletheia*: Brentano, Aristotle, Heidegger. *Research in Phenomenology, 5*, 77–94.

Kristeva, J. (1986). From symbol to sign. In T. Moi (Ed.), *The Kristeva reader.* New York: Columbia University Press.

Kroetsch, R. (1995). *A likely story: The writing life.* Red Deer, AB: Red Deer College Press.

Lather, P. (1991). *Getting smart: Feminist methods.* New York: Routledge.

Laurence, M. (1964). *The stone angel.* Toronto: New Canadian Library, McClelland & Stewart.

———. (1976). *Heart of a stranger.* Toronto: McClelland & Stewart.

Lieblich, A., Tuval-Mashiach, R., & Zilber, T. (1998). *Narrative research: Reading, analysis, and interpretation.* Thousand Oaks, CA: Sage.

Le Guin, U. (1980). A quotation from *Critical Inquiry*, Autumn, 192.

———. (1989). *Dancing at the edge of the world: Thoughts on words, women, and places.* New York: Harper & Row.

Lionnet, F. (1989). *Autobiographical voices: Race, gender, self-portraiture.* Ithaca, London: Cornell University Press.

Longxi, Z. (1992). *The tao and the logos: Literary hermeneutics, east and west.* Durham, NC: Duke University Press.

Lortie, D. C. (1975). *School teacher: A sociological study.* Chicago: University of Chicago Press.

Luce-Kapler, R. (2000). When reading meets writing: Understanding short stories and poetry. In *Young adolescents meet literature: Intersections for learning.* M.C. Cortland & T. J. Gambell (Eds.) 178–200.

Madison, G. (1988). *The hermeneutics of postmodernity: Figures and themes.* Bloomington: Indiana University Press. Especially "Dialogue on metaphor," "Hermeneutics of (inter) subjectivity, or: The mind-body deconstructed," and "Ricoeur and the hermeneutics of the subject."

McCarthy, T. (1982). Rationality and relativism: Habermas' *overcoming* of hermeneutics. In J. Thompson & D. Held (Eds.), *Habermas: Critical debates.* Cambridge: MIT Press.

McClay, J. (

McEwan, H. (1997). The functions of narrative and research on teaching. *Teaching and Teacher Education, 13*(1), 85–92.

McEwan, H., & Egan, H. (Eds). (1996). *Narrative in teaching, learning, and research.* New York: Teachers College Press.

McQuillan, M. (Ed.). (2000). *The narrative reader.* London: Routledge.

Merleau-Ponty, M. (1978). *Phenomenology of perception* (C. Smith, Trans.). London: Routledge Classics.

Middleton, S. (1993). *Educating feminists: Life histories and pedagogy.* New York: Teachers College Press.

Miller, A. (1981). *Prisoners of childhood* (R. Ward, Trans.). New York: Basic Books. (Paperback title: *The drama of the gifted child.*)

———. (1983). *For your own good: Hidden cruelty in child-rearing and the roots of violence.* New York: Farrar Straus.

———. (1988a). *Banished knowledge.* Frankfurt: Suhrkamp.

———. (1988b). *The untouched key: Tracing childhood trauma in creativity and destructiveness.* New York: Doubleday (Anchor Books).

Miller, J. L. (2005). *Sounds of silence breaking: Women, autobiography, curriculum.* New York: Peter Lang.

Miller, J., & Seller, W. (1990). *Curriculum: Perspectives and practice.* Toronto: Copp Clark Pitman.

Miller, N. (1988). *Subject to change: Reading feminist writing.* New York: Columbia.

Mishler, E. G. (1986). *Research interviewing: Context and narrative.* Cambridge: Harvard University Press.

Mitchell, W. J. T. (Ed.). (1983). *On narrative.* Chicago: University of Chicago Press.

Mitrano, B. (1981). Feminism and curricular theory: Implications for teacher education. *Journal of Curricular Theorizing, 3*(2), 5–85.

Moffet, M. J., & Painter, C. (1974). *Revelations: Diaries of women.* New York: Random House.

Moustakis, C. (1990). *Heuristics.* Thousand Oaks, CA: Sage.

Mueller-Vollmer, K. (Ed.). (1985). *The hermeneutics reader: Texts of the German tradition from the Enlightenment to the present.* Oxford: Basil Blackwell.

Musil, R. (1964). *Young Torless.* New York: New American Library.

———. (1965). *Man without qualities.* New York: Capricorn Books.

Noddings, N. (1989). *Women and evil.* Berkeley: University of California Press.

Nussbaum, M. (1990). *Love's knowledge: Essays on philosophy and literature.* New York: Oxford University Press.

Oberg, A., & Artz, S. (1992). Teaching for reflection: Being reflective. In Munby, H. & Russell, T. (Eds.) *Teachers and teaching: From classroom to reflection.* Kingston, Ontario: Queens University Press, pp. 138–155.

Olsen, T. (1965). *Silences.* New York: Laurel.

Opie, A. (1992). Qualitative research, appropriation of the "other" and empowerment. *Feminist Review,* Spring (40).

Packer, M. (1985). *The hermeneutic circle.* Boston: Addison Wesley.

Packer, M., & Addison, R. (Eds.). (1990). *Entering the circle: Hermeneutic investigation in psychology.* Albany: State University of New York Press.

Palmer, R. E. (1969a). Thirty theses on interpretation: On the hermeneutical experience. In *Hermeneutics: Interpretation theory in Dilthey, Heidegger, and Gadamer* (chapter 14). Evanston, IL: Northwestern University Press.

———. (1969b). Toward reopening the question: What is interpretation? In *Hermeneutics. Interpretation theory in Dilthey, Heidegger, and Gadamer*. Evanston, IL: Northwestern University Press.

Piaget, J. (1971). *Genetic epistemology* (E. Duckworth, Trans.). New York: Norton.

Pinar, W. F. (1981). "Whole, bright, deep with understanding": Issues in autobiographical method and qualitative research. *Journal of Curriculum Studies, 13*(3), 173–188.

———. (1994). *Autobiography, politics, and sexuality: Essays in curriculum theory, 1972–1992*. New York: Peter Lang.

———. (2004). *What is curriculum theory?* Mahwah, NJ: Lawrence Erlbaum.

Pinar, W. F., & Reynolds, W. (1992). *Understanding curriculum as phenomenological and deconstructed text*. New York: Teachers College Press.

Pinar, W. F., Reynolds, W., Slattery, P., & Taubman, P. (1995). *Understanding curriculum*. New York: Peter Lang.

Plimpton, G. (Ed.). (1953-1988). *Writers at work: The Paris Review interviews* (Eight volumes). New York: Viking Penguin.

———. (Ed.) (1989). *Women writers at work: The Paris Review interviews*. New York & London: Viking Press.

Polanyi, M. (1958). *Personal knowledge: Towards a post-critical philosophy*. Chicago: University of Chicago Press.

———. (1975). *The tacit dimension*. Chicago: University of Chicago Press.

Polkinghorne, D. (1988). *Narrative knowing and the human sciences*. Albany: State University of New York Press.

Postman, N., & Weingartner, C. (1972). *Teaching as a subversive activity*. New York: Dell Publishing.

———. (1973). *The school book*. New York: Dell Publishing.

Rabinow, P. (Ed.). (1984). *The Foucault reader*. New York: Pantheon Books.

Rabinow, P., & Sullivan, W. (1979). The interpretive turn: Emergence of an approach. In P. Rabinow & W. Sullivan (Eds.), *Interpretive social science: A reader*. Berkeley: University of California Press.

Rich, A. (1974). *Secrets, lies, and silences*. New York: W. W. Norton.

———. (1975). The burning of paper instead of children. In *Adrienne Rich's poetry*. New York: W. W. Norton.

———. (1978). *The dream of a common language: Poems 1974–1977*. New York: W. W. Norton.

———. (1979). *On lies, secrets, and silence: Selected prose 1966–1978*. New York: W. W. Norton.

———. (1995). *Dark fields of the republic*. New York: W. W. Norton.

Ricoeur, P. (1981). Phenomenology and hermeneutics. In *Hermeneutics and the human sciences* (J. Thompson, Ed. & Trans.). Cambridge: Cambridge University Press.

———. (1986). *Time and narrative* (Vol. 2). Chicago: University of Chicago Press.

Rilke, R. (1985). *Love and other difficulties*. New York: W. W. Norton.

Rosenblatt, L. (1938). *Exploration of literature: The transactional theory of literary work*. New York: Appleton-Century.

———. (1978). *The reader, the text, the poem: The transactional theory of the literary work*. Carbondale: Southern Illinois University Press.

———. (1948). *Literature as exploration*. New York: Columbia University Press.

Rule, J. (1964). *Desert of the heart*. Tallahassee, FL: Naiad Press.

———. (1970). *This is not for you*. Tallahassee, FL: Naiad Press.

———. (1971). *Against the season*. Tallahassee, FL: Naiad Press.

———. (1975). *Theme for diverse instruments: Stories by Jane Rule*. Vancouver, BC: Talon Books.

———. (1980). *Contract with the world*. New York: Harcourt, Brace, Jovanovich.

———. (1982). *Outlander*. Tallahassee, FL: Naiad Press.

————. (1986). *A hot-eyed moderate.* Toronto: Lester & Orpen Dennys.

————. (1987). *Memory board.* Toronto: Macmillan.

————. (1989). *After the fire.* Tallahassee, FL: Naiad Press.

Russ, J. (1983). *How to suppress women's writing.* Austin: University of Texas Press.

Sartre, J–P. (1964). *Nausea.* New York: New Directions.

————. (1972). The artist and his conscience. In B. Lang & F. Williams (Eds.), *Marxism and art.* New York: David McKay.

Sarton, M. (1968). *Plant dreaming deep.* New York: W. W. Norton.

————. (1973). *Journal of a solitude.* New York: W.W. Norton.

Saussure, F. (1966). *Course in general linguistics.* [From 1916 lecture notes.] New York: McGraw-Hill.

Schlee, E. (1993). The subject is dead: Long live the female subject. *Feminist Issues,* Fall, 60-80.

Schleiermacher, F. (1978). The hermeneutics: Outline of the 1819 lectures. *New Literary History,* *X*(1), Autumn.

Scholes, R., & Kellogg, R. (1966). *The nature of narrative.* New York: Oxford University Press.

Schulman, A. (1979). Overcoming silences: Teaching writing for women. *Harvard Educational Review,* *49*(4), 527–533.

Sears, J. & Marshall, D. (Eds.). (1990). *Teaching and thinking about curriculum: Critical inquiries.* New York: Teachers College Press.

Serres, M. (1989). *Detachment.* Athens: Ohio University Press.

Serres, M., & Latour, B. (1995). *Conversations on science, culture, and time.* Ann Arbor: University of Michigan Press.

Shields, C. (1993). *The stone diaries.* Toronto: Vintage Books.

————. (2002). *Unless. A novel.* New York: HarperCollins.

Showalter, E. (1982). Feminist criticism in the wilderness. In E. Abel (Ed.), *Writing and sexual difference* (pp. 9–36). Chicago: University of Chicago Press.

————. (1990). Rethinking the seventies: Women writers and violence. In P.C. Hoy (Ed.), *Women's voices: Visions and perspectives.* New York & Toronto: McGraw–Hill.

Shrewsbury, C. (1987). What is feminist pedagogy? *Women's Studies Quarterly,* *15*(3, 4), 8–16.

Silverman, H. (Ed.). (1989). *Derrida and deconstruction.* London: Routledge. (Especially Chapter 9: Derrida, Heidegger, and the time of the line, pp. 154–168.)

Smith, D. (1987). *The everyday world as problematic: A feminist sociology.* Boston: Northeastern University Press.

————. (1990a). *Texts, facts, and femininity: Exploring the relations of ruling.* London: Routledge.

————. (1990b). *Texts, facts, and femininity: Exploring the relations of ruling.* London: Routledge.

Smith, D. G. (1991). The hermeneutic imagination and the pedagogic text. In E. Short (Ed.), *Forms of curriculum inquiry.* New York: SUNY.

Smith, F. (1986). *Insult to intelligence: The bureaucratic invasion of our classrooms.* New York: Arbor House.

Spence, D. (1982). *Narrative truth and historical truth: Meaning and interpretation in psychoanalysis.* New York: W. W. Norton.

————. (1986). Narrative smoothing and clinical wisdom. In T. R. Sarbin (Ed.), *Narrative psychology: The storied nature of human conduct* (pp. 211–232). New York: Praeger Special Studies.

Spender, D. (1982). Hitting a nerve: Women and education. *Women of ideas: And what men have done to them* (pp. 446–456). London: Pandora Press.

————. (1989). *The writing or the sex? Or why you don't have to read women's writing to know it's no good.* New York: Pergamon Press.

Stegner, W. (1971). *Angle of repose.* New York: Penguin.

Sternburg, J. (1980). *The writer on her work.* New York: W. W. Norton.

Sumara, D. (1996). *Private readings in public: Schooling the literary imagination.* New York: Peter Lang.

—————. (1998). Fictionalizing acts: Reading and the making of identity. *Theory into practice,* 37, (3)203–210.

—————. (xxxx). *Why reading still matters.*

Tappan, M., & Packer, M. (1991). *Narrative and storytelling: Implications for understanding moral development.* San Francisco: Jossey-Bass.

Tirrell, L. (1993). Definition and power: Toward authority without privilege. *Hypatia,* 8(4), 1–34.

Todd, J. (1988). *Feminist literary history: A defence.* Oxford, England: Polity Press with Basil Blackwell Ltd.

Todorov, T. (1977). *The poetics of prose.* Trans. Richard Howard. Ithaca, NY: Cornell University Press.

Twigg, A. (1988). *Strong voices: Conversations with 50 Canadian authors.* Madeira Park, BC: Harbour Publishing.

van Manen, M. (1990). *Researching lived experience: Human science for an action sensitive pedagogy.* London, ON: Althaus Press.

Vygotsky, L. (1962, 1934). *Thought and language* (E. Hanfamann & G. Vakar, Ed. & Trans.). New York & London, England: MIT Press & John Wiley & Sons.

Wagner, B. (1997). Lansdowne scholar lecture, July 1997, University of Victoria, BC, Canada.

Walcott, A. (1990). *Writing up qualitative research.* (Qualitative Research Methods Series #20). Newbury Park, CA; London; New Delhi: Sage.

Walker, A. (1982). *The color purple.* New York: Pocket.

Waring, M. (1988). *If women counted: A new feminist economics.* (G. Steinem, Introduction). San Francisco: HarperCollins.

White, H. (1981). The value of narrativity in the representation of reality. In W. Mitchell (Ed.), *On narrative.* Chicago: University of Chicago Press.

Whitehead. A. N. (1929, 1967). *The aims of education.* New York: Free Press. London, England: Macmillan.

Willis, G., & Schubert, W. (1991). *Reflections from the heart of educational inquiry: Understanding curriculum and teaching through the arts.* Albany, NY: SUNY.

Witherell, C., & Noddings, N. (1991). *Stories lives tell: Narrative and dialogue in education.* New York: Teachers College, Columbia University.

Wittgenstein, L. (1967). *Lectures and conversations on aesthetics, psychology, and religious belief.* Berkeley: University of California Press.

Wolcott, H. (1990). *Writing up qualitative research* (Vol. 20). Newbury Park: Sage.

Woolf, V. (1929, 1938). *A room of one's own and three guineas.* New York: Quality Paperback Book Club.

Wurman, R. S. (1989). *Information anxiety.* New York: Bantam Books.

Wylie. B-J. (1995). *Women's diaries: Reading between the lines.* Toronto: Key Porter.

Yeats, W. B. (1920). The second coming. In M. Abrams et al. (Eds.), *The Norton Anthology of English Literature* (Vol. 2, 3rd ed.). New York: W.W. Norton.

Zwicky, J. (1992). *Lyric philosophy.* Toronto: University of Toronto Press.

Author Index

Subject Index

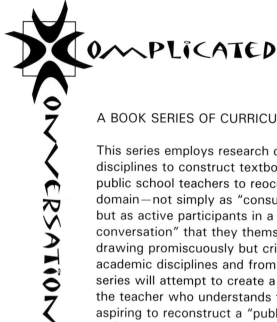

OMPLICATED

CONVERSATION

A BOOK SERIES OF CURRICULUM STUDIES

This series employs research completed in various disciplines to construct textbooks that will enable public school teachers to reoccupy a vacated public domain—not simply as "consumers" of knowledge, but as active participants in a "complicated conversation" that they themselves will lead. In drawing promiscuously but critically from various academic disciplines and from popular culture, this series will attempt to create a conceptual montage for the teacher who understands that positionality as aspiring to reconstruct a "public" space. *Complicated Conversation* works to resuscitate the progressive project—an educational project in which self-realization and democratization are inevitably intertwined; its task as the new century begins is nothing less than the intellectual formation of a public sphere in education.

The series editor is:

Dr. William F. Pinar
Department of Curriculum and Instruction
223 Peabody Hall
Louisiana State University
Baton Rouge, LA 70803-4728

To order other books in this series, please contact our Customer Service Department:

(800) 770-LANG (within the U.S.)
(212) 647-7706 (outside the U.S.)
(212) 647-7707 FAX

Or browse online by series:

www.peterlangusa.com